"*Woman Plus Woman* is a solid, beautiful book. . . . filled with sensitive analysis, historical perspectives. . . . a scathing and thoroughly logical examination of psychiatric mishmash and mythology about lesbians. . . . she prints questionnaire responses by women who have never before been interviewed about their lesbianism. This "silent majority" has no single voice or point of view — and their diversity is strong testimony against . . . attempts at pigeon-holing and stereotyping lesbians."

The Boston Globe

". . . very well writt . . . An ext mely intelligent Prelude coh rently outlines the author's intentions: to examine existing research on female homosexuality; to discuss the lives and times of some articulate lesbians . . . and to allow some present-day lesbians to bear witness through the vehicle of anonymous questionnaires. . . . [T]he author makes the eloquent point that sexual behavior is just one component of total life experience and that everyone has a "right to a private life of feeling."

Publishers Weekly

". . . directed . . . at the desire of lesbians for their own history. . . . It is instructive to follow Klaich's critical sense constantly at work . . . as she takes a contagious pleasure in trashing inaccuracy."

Ms. Magazine

"One of the best books on the subject — informative, non-didactic, written in precisely the right unhysterical tone to accomplish its goal. . . . a fine history of lesbians both in history and the medical movement (villains Krafft-Ebing, Freud . . .). . . . It is just too bad that this fine book is necessary in these supposedly enlightened times."

Kirkus

". . . I want to recommend Dolores Klaich's new book. . . . The book impressed me on two grounds: the sheer amount of new information on lesbian history — and especially on the fascinating circle that gathered around Natalie Barney in Paris — and also its tone — scrupulous, direct, gentle, and with a total absence of polemics or over-statement."

Martin Duberman;
The Partisan Review

". . . Examining reactions to female homosexuality from Sappho's time onward to Gay Pride demonstrations, Klaich proselytizes only for an end to bigotry. . . . Her historical research is impressively scholarly without being pedantic. . . . Klaich . . . acquaints us with . . . some anonymous living lesbians . . . [one of whom] speculates: 'It's one of the mysteries . . . Maybe we are one of Nature's ways of population control . . . Maybe society *needs* more than two sexes. . . . It's good to have a few mysteries.'. . . . [O]pen-minded readers of whatever sexual persuasion will find it valuable, illuminating and not the least sensational."

Jane Howard
Mademoiselle

DOLORES KLAICH

WOMAN PLUS WOMAN

Naiad Press, Inc.
1989

First Naiad Press Edition   1989
Printed in the United States of America

Cover design by Catherine Hopkins
Typeset by Sandi Stancil

The author and publisher wish to thank the following for permission to reprint certain excerpts:
    Basic Books, Inc., New York: for excerpts from *Collected Papers of Sigmund Freud*, edited by Ernest Jones, M.D., Vol. II; translation under the supervision of Joan Riviere; by arrangement with The Hogarth Press Ltd. and The Institute of Psycho-Analysis, London, copyright © 1959.
    Grove Press, New York: for excerpts from *Female Homosexuality*, by Frank S. Caprio, copyright © 1954 by Frank S. Caprio.
    International Journal of Psychoanalysis, London: for excerpt from "On Female Homosexuality," by Helene Deutsch, copyright © 1933 by Helene Deutsch.
    Normal Holmes Pearson: for excerpts from *Tribute to Freud*, by H. D., copyright © 1956 by Pantheon Books.
    University of California Press, Berkeley, California: for excerpts from *Sappho: A New Translation*, by Mary Barnard, copyright © 1958.
    Yale University Press, New Haven, Connecticut: for excerpts from *Bee Time Vine and Other Pieces*, by Gertrude Stein, copyright © 1953 by Alice B. Toklas.

Library of Congress Cataloging in Publication Data

    Klaich, Dolores.
    Woman plus woman.
    Reprint. Originally published: Woman + woman. New
York : Morrow, c1974.
    Bibliography: p.
    Includes index.
    1. Lesbianism.   I. Title
HQ75.5.K59 1989   306.7663   88-29141
ISBN 0-941483-28-2 (pbk.)

This book is dedicated to
ALLYN AMUNDSON

Acknowledgments

My thanks to Helen Brann and Jonathan Dolger for believing in this book and waiting so patiently for its delivery' to Gene Damon (Barbara Grier), former editor of *The Ladder*, for invaluable help with research, to Adrianne Blue, whose savvy editing helped bring mountains of research into some semblance of form; to Joseph McCrindle, for long-term kindnesses; to the New York Public Library for existing; and to the anonymous women who were kind enough and interested enough to answer questionnaires.

Contents

Introduction

The book you are about to read was written and published in the early 1970s.

The Elder Stateswoman's words that close the book are those of Elsa Gidlow, the poet and essayist, a fact I did not come to know until two years after the book's publication.

Here's the story of how we met.

In December 1976 I received a letter from Barbara Grier, publisher of Naiad Press, in which she enclosed a letter written to her by Elsa, who wrote: "Women have been asking me for a year or two if I had an article or chapter in a book embodying questionnaires to Lesbians — called, if I remember correctly, 'Woman to Woman' or something like that and the author, Dorothy Klaiches. My reply was always in the negative, as I had no recollection of ever having written anything for such a book."

Elsa went on to say that three of her friends in California, where she lived, told her that they felt one of the sections of the book could not have been contributed by anyone but her. They sent her a copy of the section.

"It certainly was from me," Elsa continued in her letter to Barbara. "And then I recollected, years ago, it seems, having gone against my usual practice of declining to take part in questionnaire projects by people I do not know, and replied to a questionnaire. Never heard anything more about it. And that was that. Forgotten."

I wrote to Elsa immediately, sending a copy of the book, thrilled to know that she was the Elder Stateswoman. Hers had been one of the anonymous questionnaires I cherished (I even stored it in the refrigerator with other bits of irreplaceable research). I often wished I knew who she was, somehow sensing that a talk with her would buoy me up during fallow periods of research and writing. In my letter to Elsa I asked if it would be all right to reveal her identity now that I knew it, explaining that after the book's publication many people had asked me about her.

"Yes," Elsa wrote back, "you may tell anyone who asks you who the Elder Stateswoman (!) is. Don't know, though, how I earned that designation."

Elsa liked *Woman Plus Woman;* called it wonderful things like civilized and beautiful; said she was entranced and delighted. I would use those exact words to describe Elsa's posthumously published autobiography, *Elsa, I Come With My Songs.* If you have not read this book, don't hesitate a moment more — you are greatly deprived.

In Elsa's first letter to me, she wrote: "I answered that questionnaire because I told myself, whatever sort of study this turned out to be, with all the nonsense and bias, maybe I had an obligation to my sisters to cut through with my own views. Provide an antidote. I hope that does not sound arrogant. I really am not."

I tell this story to pay tribute not only to Elsa, but to women like her who, in the bad old good old days, provided an antidote — women who did not censor their reality, women who did not surrender to custom, women who lived their lives in truth. There weren't all that many in Elsa's generation, nothing like today's rush of voices. Now, the floodgate is open, the silence is broken, and in great uppity numbers we are arrogantly delivering that message.

I'll close this introduction with something I wrote in 1983. It doesn't have a title. You might think of it as a claiming of essence.

*****

Jane Chambers, dead at forty-five of brain cancer.

The *New York Times* headline, February 17, 1983, read: "Jane Chambers Dead; Won Awards for Plays."

In the text of the obituary, the fact that much of Jane's playwriting had been concerned with lesbian issues was nowhere mentioned and the fact that she was survived by Beth Allen, her lover of fourteen years, was nowhere cited. Both of these fundamental truths about Jane had been edited out of the press release sent to the *Times*. For the record, Jane Chambers's essence never existed.

It was damp and cold that February day, a funeral day. Two hours east of New York City we approached the village of Southold, New York, a conservative Suffolk County settlement on Long Island's North Shore. This was farm country. Potato fields stretched, frozen, and vineyards, the grapevines looking fragile against the rough winter landscape, came into view. Traveling as we were toward a recognition of death, the vineyards, a new enterprise planted to save the farmland from developers, to make the land pay so as not to be destroyed, loomed symbolically.

I had tasted the fruit of the first of the vineyards at a wine-tasting benefit party held to raise monies for the library in the South Shore village of Bridgehampton. We, the East End Gay Organization for Human Rights, (EEGO), had donated to the library a specially bound edition of one of Jane's plays. It was given in memory of Linda Leibman, who had lived in Bridgehampton and had been active in local politics. Linda, a founder of EEGO, and one of my closest friends, died at the age of thirty-nine. She too had had cancer. Jane had come to the South Shore to Linda's funeral. Now I was going North to hers. Thirty-nine, forty-five. Such early deaths.

As we entered Southold, the church was unmistakable — tiny, plain, beautifully wooden white, a little lopsided with age — with a parking lot three times its size where already, early, cars were arriving. For the most part the cars were full of women. There were some men, some nuclear male-female families, but mostly women, carload after carload. Inside, I found close friends with whom to sit.

I had heard the news of Jane's death while in New York and had driven out from the city with a young woman, a stranger. She had been a recent acquaintance of Jane's; she had interviewed Jane and the cast of one of her plays for a radio show she hosts on a local New York station. The young woman had talked non-stop during our two-hour trip, her life story tumbling out in an amphetamine-like rush. It had been good, the way she had filled my silences. She was so alive at twenty-five. She was so openly lesbian: "Yes," she had said, "everyone at the radio station knows. I feel no need to hide. What do they think? I think they're curious."

We who were gathered in the church were mostly of a certain age. We had been through the closeted family wars: weddings where our lovers came disguised as best friends; graduations, bar mitzvahs, christenings, holidays. Funerals. Through the years these social verities had offered no honest place for most of us. At the best of times it had been awkward, at the worst, tragic. We had learned to play society's closeted game; we had endured and we had survived. So many of our friends had not. Excited, direct, my young passenger came with no such dissembling baggage.

Then, there were Lucille Field and Patsy Rogers at the piano, Lucille singing one of Patsy's songs. In the front pew sat Beth Allen, Jane's lover. Next to Beth was Jane's mother, Clarice, a deep Georgia woman with the accent of many of Jane's plays. Clear-eyed, erect, salt of the American earth, Clarice sat with her arm around Beth, a strong presence. Next to Clarice were a row of caretakers, the women friends who had seen Jane through her dying. In front of me sat Dolores Alexander and Jill Ward who, in the heady feminist '70s, had opened Mother Courage, the first women's movement restaurant in New York. Dolores had been one of the women who, in Betty Friedan's kitchen, had helped to establish the National Organization for Women. A few years later she had been purged from NOW for being lesbian, which she wasn't, at that time. To my left sat a friend, a psychiatrist, long a force in the American Psychiatric Association, and, in recent years, a spokesperson for that organization's Committee on Gay, Lesbian, and Bisexual Issues. Next to me sat Irene

Gould, a survivor of Nazi Germany, now an officer of the East End Gay Organization for Human Rights. Next to Irene sat Chuck Hitchcock, a professor at a local college, disowned by his family because he is gay. David Wilt, his lover of many years, was down front, a pallbearer. And on. Survivors, all of us.

Then, the faces I did not recognize — parishioners. Jane was a member of this Unitarian church. During the service, the parishioners would join in sharing spoken memories of her. Three of them would play, scratchily but movingly, a Bach violin concerto.

The minister rose, a young woman with an Afro-like hairdo. She spoke of parishioner Jane, she who had sung the hymns too loudly — slightly off-key. The Reverend Sara Campbell stressed the devotion and caring of Beth, whom she called Jane's life companion; she saluted the core of women who had helped Jane through her dying; she honored Jane's social consciousness work on behalf of women, blacks, lesbians, pausing after she said lesbians, the word causing a terrific silence in the church. In a church, at a funeral, in a conservative Suffolk County, New York small town. Granted, the church *was* Unitarian. Nonetheless, tears came. This was not a lesbians and gays-only memorial service held in some closeted environment which, until recently, had been the only way we could mourn honestly.

There were hymns, John Denver's "Country Roads," an eerily beautiful a cappella chant called "Simple Ceremonies" about a Native American woman who was a healer. Prayers, meditation. During the sharing of memories a young woman, an actress from one of Jane's plays, rose and said Jane had introduced her to her lover, who sat next to her and stood to read a poem she had written for Jane. Others rose — lesbians, gays, straights: mourners. Then, near the close, another actress, a close friend of Jane's, read Lil's goodbye speech from Jane's play *Last Summer at Bluefish Cove* — Lil, who was dying of cancer. Last came the ringing of the church bell, led by survivor Beth, followed by Clarice, and rung by all of us as we exited the church.

Later, at the small cemetery we stood stunned. It had been an extraordinarily moving service, a service of grace. In awe we said to one another: Ten years ago this never could have been. Jane's was an honest funeral. There had not been one hypocritical word or gesture. Good God, I thought, a real lesbian funeral, a funeral of a woman who was, among many things, lesbian, and so acknowledged. The normalcy of that.

Jane, knowing she was to die, had planned her exit. The honesty with which she had lived her lesbianism in her last productive years continued with her death. So many of us remembered the isolated dying and deaths of friends and lovers through the years — those years when most of us hid our loving, required to be dishonest for the sake of . . . of what, decorum? Good God! We thought of how those friends and lovers had been shipped off without us to family burial grounds for ritualistic burials and eulogies that had little to do with the essence of their lives, how we had endured the pain of that, suffered the humiliation, internalized our grief and mourning. The toll of that.

Jane Chambers, New York City playwright, daughter of the deep South, with her lover Beth Allen, had set down roots in a small town on the North Shore of eastern Long Island. There, she practiced her art, living a full, honest life, integrated into the community, nudging it when prejudices reared. As I threw my handful of dirt onto Jane's casket, words of Adrienne Rich, which I had read at my friend Linda's funeral the year before, came to mind: "When a woman tells the truth, she is creating the possibility for more truth around her."

*****

Now, let us return to the early 1970s, a time when the documenting of essence was, more often than not, just beyond the saying. The text you are about to read was published in 1974.

Dolores Klaich
Huntington, New York
September, 1988

Prelude

IF YOU turn to the frontispiece of this book, you will find reproduced there a small terra-cotta figure executed by an unknown Greek sculptor in about 200 B.C. The figure is titled: "Women Gossiping." I first saw the figure at the British Museum, when I was just beginning my researches for this book. I bought a postcard reproduction, which I eventually taped above my work desk. In the midst of the Museum's splendors, the work was a decidedly insignificant piece, something one was apt to pass by without a second thought. Once isolated on my study wall, however, the figure became quite significant, a small but perfect symbol of the incredible hypocrisy that, with rare historical exception, has always surrounded the phenomenon of lesbianism.

The women, obviously, are not gossiping. The visual sensuality of the piece—the closeness of the women's bodies, their tender looks, the one woman's bared breast—is striking. However, after trying and failing to find any written material about the figure I at times thought that perhaps, immersed in the subject as I was, I was overreacting. After all, British archeological experts or museum curators saw fit not to dub the

9

women lovers. For a while, bending over backward to be objective, I considered the possibility that the figure perhaps was meant to be one of consolation, the woman on the left consoling the other, perhaps on the event of some personal tragedy. I periodically considered removing the postcard from view. Then, about a year later, I found the figure reproduced in a copy of the lesbian publication *The Ladder*, accompanied by the words of art critic Sarah Whitworth. The work, she wrote, is "sensually lesbian in tone . . . [its title] has no foundation in visual criteria whatsoever. There is definitely a feeling of communication between the two women but their closed lips would indicate that the conversation itself was not primarily oral and thus far from an indulgence in gossip. But as it is assumed by many that women come together for the sole purpose of this petty diversion, the misnomer is at least not unexpected."[1] I left the postcard in view. And later, when I found that, as a matter of course, early British translators of a Sappho love poem rendered the woman with whom the poet had been in love as a man (it took almost 200 years for the pronoun to be straightened out), I framed the postcard and began thinking Conspiracy.

What one should be prepared to find in a close examination of historical attitudes toward lesbianism is indeed found, not only a tangled skein of hypocrisy and fantasy but, most in evidence, theory—a cartload of contradictory theories, each an attempt to offer a definitive explanation of the phenomenon and each, in some way, falling short of the mark. In contrast, the objective essentials stand out clearly and can be stated in a few sentences:

• Lesbianism exists and always has existed, among all peoples, in all parts of the world, at all historical times.

• Lesbianism is generally defined as pertaining to women whose *primary* sexual and emotional attractions are fulfilled not by men, which is considered the societal norm, but by women, which is not considered the societal norm.

• Historically, with rare exception, such attractions have been condemned. The beginning of official Western institutional condemnation can be traced to religious censure wherein lesbianism was declared a sin. After this, civil law in most Western countries, taking its text from ecclesiastic law, decided lesbianism was a crime. Later, the medical profession labeled it a congenital disease, and finally, in our day, certain segments of the American psychiatric community have pronounced it a mental illness.

• As a reaction to such condemnation, the vast majority of lesbians throughout history have hidden their lesbianism.

Although there are today some who consider lesbianism to be a sin and others who feel it is a crime, the prevailing *popular* attitude in this country, to judge from nationwide polls,* is that lesbianism is a psychological sickness, a mental illness— and this despite the fact that in the professional psychotherapeutic community there is considerable disagreement as to whether or not homosexuality is in fact a psychological illness. But putting aside for the moment the professional controversy, the prevailing public challenge to current popular opinion is embodied in the statements of certain lesbians and groups of lesbians who are loosely banded into what has come to be called the gay liberation movement. The movement's challenge: lesbianism is not a sickness.

---

* In the late sixties a Gallup poll showed that 93 percent of respondents regarded homosexuality as a sickness; a CBS television poll showed that 76 percent of respondents felt that homosexuality was a sickness; a Louis Harris survey showed that 63 percent of respondents believed that homosexuals were harmful to American life. In addition, a 1969-1973 study conducted by researchers from Indiana University's Institute for Sex Research showed that the attitudes toward homosexuality of the three thousand people interviewed were on the whole strongly negative. E.g., 86 percent of those interviewed objected to homosexual relations without love, 79 percent objected to homosexual relations with love, and 60 percent disapproved of the fact that there are now laws in nine U.S. states that do not forbid sex acts between persons of the same sex if they are done in privacy between consenting adults.

About five years ago, before the homosexual-rights movement in its current manifestation burst upon the public's
consciousness, information about lesbians and lesbianism
that reached the public did so, on the whole, through the
filter of psychological and sociological studies conducted
among lesbians who in some way were visible and available
for investigation. The women were psychiatric patients or
they were behind bars for criminal acts other than lesbianism,
usually for prostitution. To a lesser degree they were women
who were members of early lesbian social organizations or
women who led social lives that revolved around lesbian bars
in big cities. In other words, the women in these studies
were members of very small and very special segments of the
lesbian population as a whole. Now, no one knows how many
American women are lesbian. There exists no up-to-date national census of sexual behavior, much less one that totes up
emotional behavior. Modern-day establishment bodies put
the figure at some five million, and follow their guesses with
strings of qualifications. Homosexual-rights groups say ten
million—another guess. But what is known is that the vast
majority of whatever figure one chooses to believe are
women who do not declare their lesbianism publicly. To all
intents, these women are invisible, their lives and their attitudes toward their lives unknown. They are, in current par-
lance, "in the closet." These women—who are neither patients, criminals, prostitutes, barflies, nor joiners of sororial
clubs—did not figure in studies by the social scientists.

Since the advent of the gay rights movement, certain lesbian activists and groups of activists have come forth to strip
away the filter of the psychological and sociological establishment to offer their own information. The public has dealt
with this phenomenon in two ways. On the one hand, because the statements of the activists do not have seals of approval from those who today are considered experts—mainly
psychiatrists—certain segments of the public have dismissed

the statements of the activists. On the other hand, certain segments have formed the opinion that lesbians, *all* lesbians, finally have come out of hiding to speak for themselves. It is one of the contentions of this book that the polemics of the lesbian activists (who also form a very small and very special segment of the lesbian population as a whole) no more tell us anything definitive about *all* women who are lesbian than do the severely limited studies of the so-called experts.

Certain of today's activists (by no means all, but certain of the most vocal, and by vocal we mean that they have been discovered by the mass media, and thus the public), whose important efforts to attain basic rights have put them into the misguided position of stating that all lesbian relationships are sterling examples of bliss and the participants paragons of constructive living, are as guilty of shortsightedness as are certain of today's psychiatrists (some of them, by no means all, again the most vocal) who point and say sick, the whole damn bunch, sick.

Both points of view are based on the assumption that all women who are lesbian can be considered, described, and judged as one. Any attempt to dump five or ten million women into one definitive category makes a mockery of the concept of allowing human beings the right to stand tall or fall flat on the basis of their individual strengths or frailties. Contrary to popular belief, women who are lesbian form an extremely heterogeneous group in our society. How they handle what they do have in common—attractions to other women and societal condemnation of these attractions— varies enormously. Women who are lesbian tend to be thought of *only* in terms of their sex lives. So and so is lesbian. Oh. She sleeps with women. Right. Identity established —and condemned. Whatever else she may be about is beside the point. Unless she hides her sex life she is relegated to the lesbian ghetto, is granted only partial identity and in turn is condemned for that which she has been granted. Little wonder that the great majority of such women avoid the ghetto by choosing the closet, in essence not a free choice, only the lesser of the two psychically crippling evils available. It's a wonder that many *do* manage to overcome this debilitating situation—but never without some cost. Members of all ghettos are denied the breathing room necessary to claim openly their total identity, their full humanness. The same holds true for those in closets. As a small part of the effort to offer members of the' lesbian ghetto and the lesbian closet the possibility of claiming their full identity, this book proposes that wholesale condemnation of a human being based solely on an imposed ghetto identity is wholesale discrimination, an invasion and trampling of a person's private humanity, and as such should discontinue.

Historically, societies that have condemned the woman who is lesbian have dealt with her in several ways. At times they have tried to destroy her: by burning her at the stake, by hanging her, by guillotining her. At times they have tried to "cure" her: by asking her to remove from her life any type of eroticism, or by asking her to change her erotic orientation. If the end goal of such tactics has been to eliminate the phenomenon of women loving other women, clearly these tactics have not worked. It would seem that now that all things sexual are beginning to be talked of in a rational manner, with only vestiges of hysteria, it is time to confront the situation on a more realistic basis and to forgo the search for yet other tactics to suppress certain types of human loving.

The bias of this particular book should be abundantly clear by now. I do not believe that lesbianism is a sin, a crime, or a sickness. I do feel that lesbianism is a way of loving, a natural possibility, and as such, like the other possibilities, it can be a matter of joy, of mutual growth, of constructive human interaction. But also, like the other possibilities, it can be a matter of mutual stagnation, even destruction.

On this point I would agree with Simone de Beauvoir's reasoned analysis: "Like all human behavior, homosexuality leads to make-believe, disequilibrium, frustration, lies, or, on the contrary, it becomes the source of rewarding experiences, in accordance with its manner of expression in actual living—whether in bad faith, laziness, and falsity, or in lucidity, generosity, and freedom."[2]

It is with this analysis in mind that this book attempts to offer some background notes toward a social history of lesbianism, notes that are directed to the layman/woman, especially to those who automatically, with little actual knowledge, condemn. This book, in its examination of some past and present *attitudes* toward the phenomenon of lesbianism, was undertaken to ensure (in its own small way) that the present dialogue on the subject of homosexuality will continue. The book is not primarily an historical chronicle of lesbianism itself, for when a phenomenon's events seldom have been recorded and its participants for the most part have hidden the fact that they were participating, innumerable dead ends are encountered and enormous gaps cannot be filled. The notes have been gathered outside the context of any institutional discipline and also outside the context of the gay liberation movement that is challenging such disciplines. Historically, there have been other challenges to the sin/crime/sickness pronouncements, but in the main they merely form footnotes to what has become a monumental legacy of negativism. Whether the current gay liberation challenge will go the way of an historical footnote is yet to be seen; in the meantime the challenge stands, and in this book it will be considered as such.

In no way does this book claim to be definitive. It is in fact an argument against the many attempts to pin down the phenomenon of lesbianism in definitive terms. As the 1969 Final Report of the National Institute of Mental Health Task Force on Homosexuality states, "Homosexuality is not a unitary phenomenon, but rather represents a variety of phenomena which take in a wide spectrum of overt behaviors and psychological experiences. . . . Contrary to the frequently held notion that all homosexuals are alike, they are in fact very heterogeneous."[3]

Part I of this book outlines some of the sexual, medical, psychological, and purely scientific research that has been conducted in the field of female homosexuality—all of this material dealing with visible lesbians, those who in some way made themselves available for investigation. This part is bracketed by two interviews with women who, by choosing to hide their lesbianism, are members of the invisible majority. Their feelings about their lives would never be found in the written material of professionals such as that examined in Part I. Nor would their views be found in the statements of present-day gay liberation activists. Part II discusses the lives and times of some of the more articulate historical figures who chose not to be silent about their love lives, beginning with Sappho of Lesbos (who did not have to *choose* to live openly, since in her particular society condemnation of lesbianism did not exist), and examines a selective group of poetry and fiction written by some of these women. Part III allows some present-day lesbians to bear witness through the vehicle of anonymous questionnaires, discussing the social, legal, religious, economic, and purely personal problems with which such women must deal, and examines what gay liberationists and various social institutions are attempting to do to solve these problems.

Dolores Klaich
New York City, 1973

Part I

SEX AND PSYCHOLOGY

Like other men, scientists become deaf and blind to any argument or evidence that does not fit into the thought pattern which circumstances have led them to follow.

—RENÉ J. DUBOS

INTERVIEW 1

THE WOMAN interviewed here discovered her lesbianism some fifteen years ago, long before the advent of the current gay liberation movement. Her wish not to be identified "first and foremost by what I'm about sexually" has led her to live a life of selective anonymity. She agreed to talk only reluctantly, stressing that she speaks only for herself—"there are thousands of experiences." This interview, like the limited vehicles of the psychological case histories, the sociological studies, and the treatises of the lesbian activists, says nothing definitive about lesbians or lesbianism. The views expressed here are those of a woman whose sexual orientation is lesbian but whose sexual behavior is, as the National Institute of Mental Health Task Force on Homosexuality put it, "just one component in [her] total life experience."[1] She believes, to borrow the phrase but not the context from an essay by critic George Steiner, that she has a "right to a private life of feeling."[2] In both respects she represents, but does not speak for, the invisible majority of lesbians.

The woman is forty years old. She is a writer.

What is it you don't like about men?
Their smell.
———?
It's chemical—or something.
Just their smell?
No, of course not. I rather like some men. The ones with whom I can talk—the ones I can share talking with. You know, the ones who don't automatically slot women into a subordinate position without even knowing them.
Heterosexual men?
There are some.
Have you ever loved a man?
Sure. At least I thought I loved them at the time. In a way I guess I did. I didn't realize I was gay until I was twenty-six. I did live with a man once.
Married?
God, no. Even when I thought I was straight, marriage was something I knew was out of the question.
Why was that?
Because it's absurd. Freedom is important to me; I have my work. Sharing is important to me—equal sharing. There's no freedom in marriage, in the institution of marriage. The thought of marriage never crossed my mind. I don't know—well, an example. I had a drink about a year ago with an old friend, a writer, a male. When I met him for the drink he had been married a couple of years, and his wife—they were living way out in the country somewhere—his wife was getting bored and was shopping around for something to do. He was uneasy about it but allowed as how he'd set her up in a boutique in the nearby town if she wanted. I said fine, did she want it? He wasn't sure. Then he said, cross my heart, "The boutique's O.K., but *my* work is what's important, and if she wants to compose a symphony or something it wouldn't work. Marriage doesn't work that way." He couldn't have been more serious; it was rather pitiful. He wanted to set

her up in a boutique and he didn't even know if she'd like that. And this man is no dummy; and no young kid. He was in his mid-forties at the time, so was his wife. At their ages they had no illusions about the institution of marriage.

Surely there are marriages where the wife's work is important.

Oh, they're rare. And it's always a problem. But listen, marriage for me has never been of interest.

What about children?

I've never wanted children. Especially not when I found out I was pregnant—and, funny, it was then I *really* realized marriage was out of the question. The doctor asked me—after determining that I was indeed pregnant—he asked me if there was any possibility of marrying. I remember the question brought me up short. I had been living with the man for three years—*that* was marriage, if anything was. There I was sitting in a Park Avenue abortionist's office, all very neat and clean, a waiting room full of people with ordinary ailments, wanting an abortion, and the doctor asked if we could marry. When I answered no and he asked why, I was stuck. It was really the first time I realized that a solution to pregnancy could be marriage, not only abortion. The thought made me cringe. I've since thought about that and I suppose that what I was doing in that relationship was biding time—nicely, mind you, but biding time. I now know I've always been gay. Even then. And incidentally, that thing about feeling rosy and beautiful and full when pregnant is a lot of bullshit. I was nauseous, bloated, sick, miserable . . .

Was the abortion itself traumatic?

No, I didn't turn queer because of the rotten abortion. Things don't happen that way. But it was a mess—no anesthetic. And I hadn't been prepared for it. Here was this perfectly respectable old graying man with a normal practice; I naturally thought it would be a simple thing, no dirty back-alley stuff—it *is* a simple operation, you know. After, when I was resting, he took the cash—four hundred dollars—left me resting on a cot and returned half an hour later. No nurse present, nothing. Then the kindly old graying doctor gave me a slobbery kiss and I staggered out to a cab. Sounds frightfully melodramatic, but that's it.

And the man who had made you pregnant?

He was fine, couldn't have been more civilized, more gentle, under the circumstances. He paid for half the doctor's fee, incidentally. It was as much my fault as his.

Why did you break up?

Who knows exactly? Things end. We had a big sex thing. Actually, the relationship was based on sex. Now, I lived with this man for three years; we made it all the time; he was an interesting lover; bed was fine. Yet during the three years we were together I had one orgasm. One fucking orgasm in three years! Funny thing is, I didn't think much about it at the time, none of that worrying about being frigid or any of that. I did a lot of faking—this was the fifties—and I got a lot out of the sex anyway, at least I thought that was the way things were. I know better now. Any of the heterosexual affairs I've had have always first and foremost been into the sack immediately. Emotional rapport has never had anything to do with such affairs.

Never?

Never.

And it has with homosexual ones?

Always.

When did you realize you were gay?

Well, not overnight. I didn't even know homosexuality existed until I was twenty-three or so. You know, I guess I knew it existed all right, but somewhere out there, in books, in the lives of underground people. Not in my milieu—not with people I knew or cared about. And if it did, incidentally, they were hiding; I never knew about it. I myself realized I was gay during my first lesbian affair. Not before the affair,

but during it. I was twenty-six. The woman involved was a
close friend. We had known each other for five years. She
was straight at the time, too. Once, once we happened to
find ourselves in a place—one night we were talking late and
suddenly we both knew the next step was bed. Later on we
both admitted that a lot of chemistry was working, but we
also admitted that we had gone into the thing as an experiment, to see—we're both writers, God knows if that had anything to do with it, but it takes a lot of imagination to enter
such a thing. And I don't mean imagination for doing things
sexually, that comes naturally. But freedom and imagination
enough to suspend whatever cultural baggage we'd been
carting around for a lot of years and just swing with what
seemed right and good. It's quite impossible to describe that
aftermath of that first loving, an extraordinary thing, really.
Gentle, beautiful. Bells ringing, yes, all that, but something
more. I don't know—gentleness, kindness. This goddam extraordinary sense of peace and joy and—well, respect. It forced
me to face my sexuality—to really face being a woman.

Respect?

Respect. You know, no roles. No faking. Beautiful honesty, if you will. A capacity for that. Sharing—equally. None
of that little bit of holding back I had always experienced
with men. A great feeling of self, a merging, yet an independence. Two strong individuals merging for . . . for, well, for
growth. My loving is tied up closely with my work. That
first lesbian affair liberated me. All kinds of fuzzy pieces of
my life fell into place. We were together six years. It was
gloriously beneficial to both of us. Sounds corny, but we both
finished books that first year together.

Did you live together? Were there problems?

You mean problems because we were lesbians? We didn't
really go through any traumatic society-shunning things. Or
rarely. But you must understand that things like jobs and
families didn't come up. We were living abroad most of the

time, away from family; we were working at home, writing.
The nitty-gritty didn't come into it. Oh, sometimes. The
first time her family visited us—we were in the south of
France—her father knew what was going on, he was a prince.
Still is. Her mother either didn't know or didn't want to
know. I'd opt for the latter. Her mother and I have never
been friendly. The father still calls me; even tried to get me
into bed once in Paris. Crazy. Again, I wouldn't want to
speak for lesbians *per se*; how could I? There are thousands
of experiences. I happen to move in—well, liberal circles, if
you will. The occasional remark by some lonely drunk, or
for that matter my brother trying to be liberal—he isn't—and
putting his corporation foot into his corporation mouth.
Well, you can't live your life worrying over such vulgarities.

You seem to paint a rosy picture.

Life is not rosy. Lesbianism is!

*What I mean is—well, how, for example, did you cope
with the fact that you were breaking the law?*

You can't be serious. I hurt no one—least of all society.
Quite the opposite, really.

*Forgive me, but I wonder if perhaps your peaceful experi-
ence is helped by the fact that you're quite beautiful.*

Oh, for God's sake.

And independently wealthy.

Wealthy! No, I'm not at all wealthy. I have no inheritance, I don't even earn very much. I live simply. There's no
front to keep up. My profession means I could live in a cave
and go barefoot. There's no scene to be a part of.

*But you don't look like what a stereotyped lesbian is sup-
posed to look like. It seems to me a lot of censure—*

Oh, listen. Really. We look all different ways.

Of course, I know that. It's just—

O.K. I know what you're getting at. I pass. I pass beautifully. And if you pass, society—people—let you be. After you
reach a certain age relatives stop asking when you're going
to get married. You've established your identity as a career

woman. Hideous description, I know—*career* woman. Always reminds me of Joan Crawford in a severe suit in some forties movie. Nobody ever bothers about a man's identity—he's a man, that's all. Women have always had to establish their identity and until recently—well, actually still, society thinks the best identity to have is in relation to some man. Anything else is second best. I don't consciously try to hide my lesbianism, but I don't scream it, either. It really is only part of what I am. I don't cross-dress. I don't march in parades. That's another part of me. I'm not a joiner, never have been. I'd feel as out of place in a gay liberation parade as I would, say—oh, say, getting a pedicure.

You don't approve of the gay rights movement?

I do approve of it. Most aspects. But it's not my style. Artists have always been faced with the problem of activism—I write about hypocrisy; I try to do it through my writing. That may sound like a cop-out to some. But it's truth to me. Although I do understand perfectly the theory of change through revolution, only through revolution and not reform —however, it does come down to what is false for me and what is true.

There are those who say that closet lesbians—nonactivist lesbians—could do immense good for the movement. They call you elitists.

I accept the title. Pejorative as it is. I have a friend who's in the movement. Whatever *that* is, incidentally. Anyway, she's a spokeswoman. We have, of course, talked about this very thing. Her contention is: now or never, before the backlash. I respect her. I know her and I know this is a true thing for her.

I've found an awful lot of suspicion in the movement. Two things, just as examples: When I started researching I went to the then functioning New York chapter of the Daughters of Bilitis* and asked one of the then officers if I

---

* An early lesbian organization; see page 220 for details.

could perhaps use their library—they have a good one. She was standing at the door to the library in that new loft they had rented down on Prince Street, and when I asked she bristled. She then said it was private, for members only, slowly edging herself into the room. And then another time I sent a questionnaire to a fairly new women's literary magazine, thinking maybe someone on staff would want to answer, or someone would know someone to pass it on to. What happened was a strange blast in the magazine itself from one of the editors.

I think their suspicion is justified. You know, I never would have consented to this interview if I didn't know you. Surely you've read the dreadful stuff that manages to get into print—so much of it by men. That awful book *The Grapevine*.[3] Remember it? The author went to a few gay bars, talked to a few barflies, and came up with a "definitive" study. I for one related zero to that book.

What about gay bars? Do you go to them?

I have. Now only occasionally. Here in New York there's a very civilized place on the East Side. Nice fireplace in winter; an adult clientele. It's mixed, gay men and women. It's a comfortable place. I don't go cruising, if that's what you mean. Frankly, some of the bars scare me—tough women scare me. You know, some years ago, in my straight days, a bunch of us went to the Swing Rendezvous—ever hear of it? Down in the Village. Macdougal Street, I think. One of those streets. Anyway, here were all these youngish women dressed in drag, real drag I mean, no kidding around, all very spiffy. One of the men in our group said it was a call-in place—you know, women telephoning for service. I did notice some of the young women on the phone, which did ring constantly; then they would leave. There were a lot of raucous jokes at our heterosexual table. And I laughed right along with everyone else. I've often wondered how the man knew the inner workings of that bar.

Do you still laugh when someone makes a pejorative crack?

No. I don't. In fact, I make a point of saying something about the vulgarity of such remarks. But I do have some lesbian friends—actually it happens more often with gay men I know—who laugh themselves silly.

Do you have many male gay friends?

Yes, I do. They're long-time friends. Best friends, some of them.

What are they like?

Like? They're friends. Oh, I suppose if you analyzed it they're very much like me. They're not upset about their homosexuality. Their work is important to them—what else? I don't know, they're friends, that's all.

What about lovemaking?

What about it?

Well, would you mind talking about it?

Ask a question.

Do you use a dildo?

Christ!

You don't have to answer this.

It's not that. No, I don't use one. Never even saw one. Actually, I've always been curious myself to know how widespread the use is.

I've been trying to find out. But it's not easy. It seems to be one of those unanswerable questions.* Do you make love a lot?

What's a lot?

Well . . .

I have no idea how to answer that question. I've never averaged it out. It always seemed strange to me, those statistics that say such and such a population group makes love 3.2 times a week. What does that mean? Who keeps track?

---

* See pages 48–52 for some answers.

Well, then, how do you feel about the controversy over the vaginal versus the clitoral orgasm?

I personally feel these are misnomers. There are different orgasms but they differ only in intensity, not where they take place. Some are deep-seated convulsive experiences and others—well, less intense. It depends on mood and, well, tiredness, and perhaps a good deal has to do with health, what shape your body is in at the time. Actually, if you want to pinpoint the physical location of the orgasm I'd opt for the head.

Colette once wrote that orgasm is the proof of mutual trust.

Good for Colette.

Earlier we were talking about "passing." Could we come back to that for a moment?

Certainly.

How do you deal with the fact that you're living a lie?

It hurts. And I rationalize. But again I have to say that it's not that much of a problem with me. Friends know—those I work with, editors and so on, they know. I'm not close to my family, so that doesn't come into it. The occasion arises so seldom.

But it does arise?

Yes, occasionally. For instance, when I taught I had a small problem with some female students who became terribly attached—you know, calling up late at night, coming by, all that. Now, I knew that two of these young women, perhaps more, I'm not certain, would eventually discover their lesbianism. I was really torn as to how to handle the situations. When they brought the subject up I changed it. I wasn't worried about my job, but I was worried about the responsibility. They were, after all, partially in love with my work, with me as their teacher, and partially it seems with me, as a person, as someone they could relate to. But where is the dividing line among the young? On a human level I probably should have discussed the matter with them, reassuring them that they were not crazy, not freaks, perfectly all right. That perhaps some of them were simply going through a stage, that others would find it wasn't just a stage, but rather a life—a life with values. A perfectly fine life. Yet I didn't do any of this. It was one of my more cowardly periods, I suppose, but the responsibility—God. Had they been older and had they figured out other things about life it would have been different. Some of them were very troubled and they really had nowhere to turn.

When was this?

Some years ago. Let's see, seven or eight—yes, eight.

Would you act the same way today?

I wonder. Students have changed a lot, I think. I'm not at all sure about this, but it seems so. At any rate, the climate has changed. But I don't think I can answer that question, since I'm no longer teaching. However, it is a good question. You should ask it of someone who is teaching.

What about clothes? Do you always wear pants?

Yes, I do. Does it sound corny to say for comfort's sake? Have you ever seen a women's bowling team in some small town? You would swear you've run into the biggest den of bull dykes in town. But nothing of the sort. Wedding bands, kids hanging around drinking Cokes, hubbies in the other lanes, American flags on their bowling balls.

Can you automatically spot a woman who is lesbian?

Yes and no. I've made some real blunders. Especially a few years ago. You know, the women's movement has latched onto that old eyeball-to-eyeball look—funny—you know, really looking deep into a person. I met such a woman once. She came up to me after a lecture. We had dinner a couple of nights later. And, my God, what an experience. She was terribly attractive, terribly bright, and I was convinced that she was lesbian. Nothing of the sort. She wasn't averse to going to bed, mind you, but she presented a whole analysis of man-as-the-enemy, we've-got-to-relate-to-each-other stuff. It was really a cold, calculating thing that I'm afraid I had to explain to her would never stand up in bed. You either are or you aren't. So much is just basic chemistry. Then there was the time, the first time, I was in Paris, all those women running around with pinkie rings. A gold mine, I thought. Hilarious. I didn't realize then that Frenchwomen of all ages, heterosexual ones, have a habit of wearing pinkie rings.

Have you ever had an affair with a woman who had never had a lesbian affair?

My first. But we were both novices.

Have you ever wanted to seduce a heterosexual woman?

God, no. Firmly constituted heterosexual women don't interest me.

What are your feelings about heterosexual women?

They're missing a lot of joy. Seriously, if they're content with their sexuality—I can't imagine how they could be, but of course they'd say the same about someone like me—if they're content, fine. I have two very close friends who are heterosexual; I love them. I guess it comes down to . . . well, if a woman is at ease with her sexuality it's perfectly natural for her to accept lesbianism—in others. But save me from the heterosexual woman who is not at peace with her own sexuality. Not only will she be scared to death of lesbians, she'll probably despise them. And I think you'll find that she also despises a lot of other things. I couldn't agree less with the theory that all women are lesbians—despite Jill Johnston.* Although I do think she probably means it in a political sense. You know, how the Danes said, "We are all Jews" during the war. Meaning, of course, we are all op-

---

* Jill Johnston, a writer and a lesbian, is this country's most vocal proselytizer of lesbianism. For her views see Jill Johnston, *Lesbian Nation* (New York: Simon and Schuster, 1973), and her weekly column in New York City's *The Village Voice*.

pressed. Incidentally, I really love Jill Johnston. She's crazy, bold, sometimes brilliant, more often not, but that doesn't matter, sometimes incredible. I'm sure I'd have nothing to say to her if we ever met, but what a marvelous, bold crazie.

What about bisexual women?

There's no such thing.

There are those who would differ with you.

Of course. But if you're talking about just screwing, right, there are such. But I really believe there is always a preference for one or the other.

Since you realized you were lesbian, have you had heterosexual affairs?

I've had a few one-night stands. At various lonely times of my life. Once with a homosexual man; we were friends. None of it meant anything at all. Except maybe a passing human warmth. All very human—you know, a few drinks, a quiet night, even a fireplace once in Vermont. I really do prefer women.

You presently live with another woman.

Yes.

What kind of relationship is it?

Strange question.

What I mean is, does it by any chance fall into a butch–femme thing, or a mother–child, or a teacher–pupil?

No. I remember that from your questionnaire. The butch–femme thing, for instance, is nonsense.

You don't believe such exists?

Oh, it exists all right. You do see it—mostly among women my age and older. And I hear the bars are full of it. I don't think younger women are into this sort of arrangement, though.

And you're not?

No. I never have been. My affairs have been with women very much like me. I don't know—two independent souls who like to share things. There simply has to be a growth factor. I've found that my affairs have ended— Actually, I talk as if there have been a great many. There haven't.

How many?

Well, serious living together, you mean? Only two, including the present one. The others were short-term. And they ended when we realized there was nothing left to learn from each other—we were growing in different directions and didn't want to continue side by side.

Did they end amiably?

Mostly.

To get back to your present relationship. What's it like? I mean daily life.

It's just like anybody's life. We get up, we have breakfast, we work, we keep house, we go out, we see friends, we entertain, we travel, we have spats, we make love, we laugh, what can I tell you? I love her. I respect her independence of thought. I'm excited by her professional blossoming. I'm enriched by her trust of me, by her vulnerability. I trust her with *my* vulnerabilities. I like her devil-may-care days, the passion with which she detests housework, her ironic turn of mind, her seriousness, her enormous capacity for affection, her playfulness, her uncompromising individuality.

Have you heard about gay marriage ceremonies that some churches offer?

I've read about them, yes. It's an absurd idea. You can't reconcile a rebellious life—and lesbianism is that, you know —by adopting one of society's most nonrebellious institutions. Ridiculous. Not only the marriage bit, but religious approval! Incredible, when you come to think that the church has always been enemy number one to homosexuals. Talk about embracing your oppressor!

Let's talk about rebellion for a moment. Do you consider yourself an outcast?

Very definitely so. And I rather like it. The way American society is structured today is all that I believe in least. Such hypocrisy! Living abroad you forget, you mellow. It only hits you when you return. No, thank you. This business of basing values on money—for instance, you're an artist? How successful are you? Meaning, do you sell? Do you make a lot of money? What absurdity. As you know, I live in France a lot. Not that France isn't becoming, some say has become, very American; I don't agree. For instance, in the little town I live in there's the woman who runs the bakery. Very plain, ordinary woman. No formal education, I mean. Her family were bakers, her husband's family were bakers, she's a baker. Right? What do we talk about when I come to buy bread? Poetry! Balzac! We share the same passion for Balzac. There really is a respect for artists in Europe. It's what you do, it's your métier, it's like baking bread. The financial success you have with your work is never, but never, a question.

I quite agree. But I was asking if you felt an outcast in America because of your lesbianism, not because of your work.

Oh. Sorry. Strange. I missed your question. Which, of course, probably means that I don't—that is, I feel more of an outcast as a writer, which in turn means that I probably think of myself as a lesbian only secondly. Does that make sense? Wait a minute. Maybe it would be clearer this way. I belong to a minority group—several, in fact. I'm a dissenting writer, I'm a lesbian, I'm an agnostic—this is silly. I'm a lot of things. A lot of things society does not approve of. It's society that thinks I'm an outcast. How's that?

Then you don't think that lesbianism is abnormal? Only that society thinks so?

Oh, but I *do*. In the sense that it's not an average thing—in the sense that it's not part of the dominant majority. But of course this is not to say that the dominant majority is right. Far from it.

What about abnormal in the sense of unnatural, not in tune with nature?

Something that has existed in all times, all places, all species, is an element of nature. There's no getting around that. From an evolutionary and a physiological viewpoint, it's natural. This essential fact only gets clouded by whether or not society accepts such behavior. Society is not nature.

You then would say you are perfectly content living a lesbian life?

Yes. Women are important to my survival. I love women. There really is little more beautiful to me than a strong, independent, thinking woman. But, incidentally, this doesn't mean that I like all lesbian women. God forbid. I've met some dreadful such women and they really are not my sisters.

Do you think that hormones explain homosexuality?

Nothing *explains* homosexuality. Of course, I've tried to figure it all out. But I'm left with confusion. I once firmly believed that my very cold unloving mother had a lot to do with it. But then my lover has an intensely loving mother. The theories are really just that, you know—theories. It *would* be a relief to establish something, once and for all. And the hormone theory would do as well as any other. All this controversy makes me climb the walls. I read in some newsmagazine where some doctors are now fooling around with the urine of homosexuals.* You pee and he lets you know if you're queer. Incredible! It's not a particularly nice experience to constantly read about oneself like some germ under a microscope.

Have you ever consulted a psychiatrist about your lesbianism?

I've been to a psychiatrist once—not about lesbianism. We had eight or nine sessions only. It was pretty ridiculous.

Would you talk about it?

Well, my first lover convinced me to go. She was going; she had a worry that the orgasm she was experiencing was not

---

* For a scientific explanation of this phenomenon, see page 106.

a vaginal one! This was before Masters and Johnson. The man was a Freudian, brand-new in his profession, and downright nervous. I eventually asked him what his view on homosexuality was, explaining that I was not there to change my sexual orientation but merely to search out some things that were troubling me. No reply, of course. I realized almost immediately that I thought of this man as young, unworldly, someone whose personal experience was so far removed from my own. In short, I didn't trust his capacity to encompass my lesbianism as only one aspect of my life. I remember leaving one session, going down in the elevator, and thinking that if I got off on another floor and went into the office of another psychiatrist, perhaps a Jungian, things would take a different direction. And how was it possible to judge which direction things should go in? I decided to direct my own life. My own particular experience with a psychiatrist has more to do with finding the right professional than with lesbianism *per se*. I have a friend who is a psychologist—he's gay, and he has some gay patients. This kind of therapy, if one feels one needs therapy at all, seems to me worthwhile. You know, about fifteen years or so ago most psychiatrists—a terribly bourgeois bunch, by the way—were in the business of turning homosexuals into heterosexuals. I have numerous friends who have spent lifetimes on the couch. I remember somewhere around that time I was seeing a young man, a lovely person. At first there were never any sexual innuendos—I was straight, but I thought, great, a friend, a male friend. It wasn't so easy to have them, you know. But later on I began to feel seriously about him. One night at my door I simply wanted him to kiss me good night. He started to come near me, but then obviously couldn't. He panicked, broke out in a sweat. Then he just took my hand as usual and fled. I later learned that he was in therapy—he was homosexual, and his shrink had urged him to try to go straight, to date girls! It was really terrible. Poor guy, he really tried. And it didn't course—the man was gay. I've lost touch with him over the years, but ever since I realized I was gay I've thought of him, what kind of unnecessary suffering he must have gone through.

I take it, then, that you don't accept the "sickness" theory.

Absolutely not. There are sick lesbians, of course, just as there are sick anybodies. It's not the sexual expression that makes one sick.

What are your feelings about a transsexual operation?

Idiotic. Besides, I've heard they don't work for women—is that right?

Some parts of it do. Not a functioning penis, though.

God.

You don't approve.

Frankly, I think it's horrendous. Maiming of one's body, I think, is—well, what kind of desperation would lead to this? Desperation should be seen to, of course. I really can't comment on this intelligently. I don't know the intricacies of such things. It's so far removed from my personal comprehension.

Are there any myths about lesbianism you'd especially like to see destroyed?

Oh, I don't know. But I do wonder, do people still think we're lesbian because we couldn't catch a man? The better-than-nothing theory? I would, I suppose, really like it said once and for all that we love women by choice. By preference. And perhaps that that loving is simply a part of an overall value system we work by. No, that's not it exactly. I guess—well, in a way, at least in my case, it's partly a rejection of what society thinks women should be, a basic rejection of the traditional female role, that of the nondoer, that of the passive receptacle who is acted upon and who doesn't do the acting. I simply cannot comprehend going through life in such a manner, like a sleepwalker—no, like someone hypnotized.

Anything else?

I wonder if people still believe that we're all desperately unhappy. I often think of some women I know languishing out in suburbia drinking themselves into a stupor, lonely, frustrated. Some of us may be unhappy, certainly I have been at times, but not because I'm gay. Because I'm human. Nobody, not even lesbians, has a monopoly on loneliness.

I wonder—since you seem so open about your lesbianism, why do you want to remain anonymous in this interview?

I have no desire to be identified first and foremost by what I'm about sexually. And that's what I think would happen. Interviews are strange things, any interview, and one that concerns only someone's sex life is read, I really think, it's read voyeuristically. I know *I* read them that way. Everyone wants to know what everyone else does in bed—actually, in the end a tedious preoccupation. Also, since I'm somewhat known—what I mean is there are people who read my books, I'd hate for them, or others, to read my work always bearing in mind my private sex life. I *don't* consider that a compliment. Nor is it in the least worthwhile—such reading, I mean. There's also another reason, perhaps at the moment the most important. The woman I'm living with—her family doesn't know about her lesbianism, and since she's very close to her family, and I know her family, it would be cruel if they were to put two and two together from this interview if they happened to see it. This is no way to treat a family you're close to. It has to be done—if it's done at all—face to face. But really, I just don't want unknown people leering at our life, which is private and quiet. People we come into contact with socially are one thing; unknowns are another. Maybe I'll change my mind someday. Maybe I'll write an autobiography someday. Who knows? But not now.

CHAPTER ONE

Lesbian Sex: Reality and Myth

ON A FRIDAY afternoon in 1924, in Paris, Ezra Pound took his friend the poet and physician William Carlos Williams to visit Natalie Clifford Barney's celebrated salon at 20 rue Jacob. Barney, an American expatriate who lived and wrote in Paris for the better part of seventy years, was one of the city's more extraordinary salon-keepers, a woman who was utterly frank about her various lesbian liaisons; as her epitaph she once suggested: "She was the friend of men and lover of women, which for people full of ardor and drive is better than the other way around."[1] Inevitably, Barney drew to her salon a number of women who were lesbian. Williams has recorded the time Pound took him to call:

> [Barney] was extremely gracious and no fool to be sure, far less so than Ezra under the circumstances. She could tell a pickle from a clam any day in the week. I admired her and her lovely garden, well kept, her laughing doves, her Japanese servants. There were officers wearing red buttons in their lapels there and women of all descriptions. Out of the corner of my eye I saw a small clique of them sneaking off together

into a side room while casting surreptitious glances about them, hoping their exit had not been unnoticed. I went out and stood up to take a good piss.

The story is told of some member of the Chamber of Deputies, a big, red-faced guy who had turned up there after a routine social acceptance. To his annoyance, as he stood lonely in the center of the dance floor, he saw women about him, dancing gaily together on all sides. Thereupon he undid his pants buttons, took out his tool and, shaking it right and left, yelled out in a rage, "Have you never seen one of these?"[2]

The anecdote, apocryphal or no, nicely sums up the fact that people generally think of women who are lesbian only in terms of their sex lives. This being the case, we discuss at some length the matter of sex between women.

In baring his genitalia, the frustrated Frenchman at Barney's salon was asking the classic question, But what do lesbians do in bed? Meaning, of course, How, since one important piece of lovemaking equipment is missing, can they do anything at all? It seems odd that a discussion of lesbian sex should invariably center around the one thing with which it has nothing to do: a male appendage, the penis. Odd, but understandable. In today's climate of sexual openness and experimentation, it is easy to forget that until fairly recently sex as a sensual, emotional, or simply pleasurable experience was, except in operas and novels, frowned upon. In real life, sex was something one did solely to reproduce the species. It was a wife's "duty" in marriage, something for which she steeled herself; it was a husband's responsibility. Since reproduction required a penis, it seemed to follow that sex also needed one.

Medical researchers of the late nineteenth century, who were the first to attempt to put the matter of human sexuality on a scientific footing, propagated this view. One of them, Richard von Krafft-Ebing, wrote: "every expression of [the sexual instinct] that does not correspond with the purpose of nature—i.e., propagation—must be regarded as perverse."[3] Neither the scientific community of the time nor the public at large openly questioned this given. What went on in the privacy of their bedrooms was another matter. In the early years of *this* century when Sigmund Freud began to formulate his sex theories, he endangered his professional reputation with statements today considered mild: "If . . . you make the function of reproduction the kernel of sexuality, you run the risk of excluding from it a whole host of things like masturbation, or even kissing, which are not directed towards reproduction."[4] Halfway through the century, Alfred C. Kinsey, in his reports on the sexual behavior of American men and women, also risked his professional reputation by presenting endless statistics that attested to the fact that human sexual activity is not and never has been limited to the aim of reproduction. He wrote:

> Biologists and psychologists who have accepted the doctrine that the only natural function of sex is reproduction, have simply ignored the existence of sexual activity which is not reproductive. They have assumed that heterosexual responses are a part of an animal's innate "instinctive" equipment, and that all other types of sexual activity represent "perversions" of the "normal" instincts. Such interpretations are, however, mystical.[5]

Freud's early work was greeted with open hostility in Viennese medical circles. Krafft-Ebing, at the time the most respected neurologist in town, ticked off Freud's early papers by declaring them scientific fairy tales. The greater part of the public simply assumed Freud was mad. During the years Kinsey was conducting his researches in this country his more conservative colleagues at Indiana University attempted to get him dropped from the faculty. He was also roundly attacked by Indiana state legislators, presumably speaking for their constituents. When the Kinsey Reports were published, in 1948 and 1953, the attacks, from all corners of the country, especially from psychiatrists and religionists, multiplied, eventually pressuring the Rockefeller Foundation, which had bankrolled Kinsey's research, to withdraw its support.[6]

Krafft-Ebing's early theories have faded into historical curios, Freud's early troubles into historical footnotes. The attacks on Kinsey took place only twenty-five years ago. Since then, sex research in this country has moved incredibly fast, and although there are still institutions and private individuals who consider such work somehow immoral, attitudes, to say the very least, are changing. Today, few people still think of sex solely as a baby-making process. The widespread use of birth-control methods and the recent liberalization of abortion laws have emphasized this particular turnabout in attitude. Popular sex manuals and sex-cum-psychology books, invariably best sellers, seldom speak of reproduction; even sex as a serious expression of love is merely touched upon. These books all advocate the same canon: experimentation. One is urged to look upon sex as robust pleasure, or just plain satisfying, like a good meal. Take it in stride, anything goes. The penis, the organ of procreation, has by no means become irrelevant, but now it officially, or at least semiofficially, can be kissed, licked, sucked, swallowed, inserted in female places other than a vagina, and generally cavort, things it has always done, of course, but never with sanction. Everyone is urged to experiment, it's O.K., it's freedom, it's healthy—everyone, that is, except homosexuals.

Of all of Kinsey's conclusions, those concerning homosexuality caused the biggest furor. The Kinsey team of researchers not only concluded that homosexuality was widely practiced, but stated that from a biological viewpoint it was not an abnormal practice. One psychoanalyst of the time, Edmund Bergler, who was quite vocal about his belief that homosexuality was a "pernicious disease" that needed curing, was appalled by Kinsey's statistics. He wrote a long critique of the first report in which he said that if Kinsey's figures were correct then homosexuality "is *the predominant national disease*, overshadowing in numbers cancer, tuberculosis, heart failure, infantile paralysis . . ." This worried him to the point where he was moved to state that "Kinsey's erroneous psychological conclusions pertaining to homosexuality will be politically and propagandistically used against the United States abroad, stigmatizing the nation as a whole in a whisper campaign . . ."[7] In a country at the time concerned with Reds in the movie industry and fast approaching the day when Senator Joseph McCarthy would rail against Reds and Queers in government, thus linking in the public's mind Communism and homosexuality, Bergler's statement, that of an influential and publicly vocal psychoanalyst, did not fall on unreceptive ears. And Bergler's attack was by no means an isolated one.

Although attitudes toward heterosexual sex have changed a good deal since the Kinsey Reports, things on the homosexual sex scene haven't really changed much at all. Despite the controversy that exists in the American psychotherapeutic community as to whether or not homosexuality is a psychological sickness, most of the public considers homosexuality to be a sickness, something that should not be sanctioned.

Nowhere in recent popular literature has this been brought home more strongly than in the phenomenally best-selling *Everything You Always Wanted to Know About Sex* of a few years ago. The book's author, David Reuben, a psychiatrist, emphasizes that sex no longer means just reproductive sex, but he emphatically stresses that it still means hetero sex. In the book, he gives the go-ahead to heterosexual experimentation.[8] When speaking about lesbianism, which he does in his chapter on prostitution, Reuben censures, and he does so very much in keeping with our times—not with outraged morality but with schoolboy flippancy. He asks: "What do female homosexuals do with each other?" He answers: "Like their male counterparts, lesbians are handicapped by having only half the pieces in the anatomical jigsaw puzzle. Just as one penis plus one penis equals nothing, one vagina plus another vagina still equals zero."[9]

The statement is in the tradition of that uttered by the frustrated Frenchman at Natalie Barney's salon who whipped out his penis and flapped it at the assembled lesbians, calling out, "Have you never seen one of these?" Many heterosexual men (and women) sympathize with this man's feelings, but very few men actually resort to baring their genitalia in public (although one of this country's supposedly more sophisticated writers, when backed into a corner at a women's liberation discussion, offered to "put my modest little Jewish dick on the table for you to spit on it").[10] It is, of course, highly understandable that a man considers a penis essential to lovemaking. Since he gets so much immediate pleasure from this organ, and since at times his female partner reinforces this pleasure, it's natural for him to think that any other kind of pleasure is only second best—just as it's natural for lesbians to disagree.

Lesbian lovemaking, contrary to what Reuben thinks, does not equal zero. It equals, among other things, orgasm. And orgasm, even in his thinking, is a rather basic aspect of any kind of lovemaking.

The female orgasm has been written of so extensively recently that only an outline is needed here. First of all, until the twentieth century, female orgasm was not formally acknowledged as existing. As will be noted in the next chapter, Krafft-Ebing and other nineteenth-century medical men felt that women did not have orgasms—"good breeding" controlled their sexual response. Women did not expect to have orgasms, and when they didn't come, which for the most part they didn't, well, that was life. Women who did have orgasms did not talk about them, just as they never talked about anything else sexual. Freud knew very well that women did have orgasms. In fact, he postulated that they had two varieties of them: clitoral (which he considered immature) and vaginal (which he considered grown-up). As a result, women could acknowledge their sexual response, but they had to worry about its adultness.

Then in the mid-1960s, the physiologists said that there was no such thing as vaginal orgasm. They based their conclusion on the anatomical fact that the walls of the vagina had few nerve endings, too few to trigger orgasm. Masters and Johnson are generally credited with this discovery—the publicity of a few years ago was overwhelming. It is little known that Kinsey, who said that the vaginal orgasm was "a biologic impossibility,"[11] and others had come to that conclusion some years earlier.

For a while, after the debunking of "the myth of the vaginal orgasm,"[12] women could relax and enjoy that which they were always capable of enjoying. But, as with many things sexual, there has come about a small orgasm backlash. It is argued by some that because the spasms of female orgasm are sometimes intense and prolonged and sometimes mild and short, the former take place in the vagina and the latter in the clitoris. Physiologists tell us that all of the spasms take place in the vagina, actually in the lower third of it, but they point out that they are triggered in any number of ways that have nothing to do with the vagina itself; they may even stem from a rich fantasy during which no part of the physical body is involved.

In addition to the reams of material written about the clitoral-versus-vaginal orgasm, there has been a proliferation of material written about the fact that usually women not only are slower to achieve orgasm than are men, but are also less likely to come at all. Male lovers who are concerned that their partners get as much enjoyment out of the sex act as possible have been counseled to take care, to slow down, to manipulate, to play the female body like a musical instrument (as endless tracts have advised), and also to consider the emotional factors—not to just plunge ahead and pump away. In short, men are cautioned to become acquainted with the nuances of the female body.

Many sex researchers have claimed that lesbians seem to have an easier time reaching orgasm than do heterosexual women. Some have pointed out that a woman is more apt to understand, from a gut level, the anatomy, the physiologic responses and the psychology of another woman than is a man, whose understanding must be learned. Lesbians, of course, agree. But theirs can be considered a biased viewpoint. One reads of certain French kings who preferred their mistresses to be "broken in" by other females, as, allegedly, the new mistresses quickly became more responsive and skilled in the arts of lovemaking. This practice was carried into the late nineteenth century by at least one other Frenchman, the Duc de Morny, a well-known sensualist and womanizer. The French writer Colette reports that Morny felt that a woman who had experienced penis-less love brought to the heterosexual love act an added dimension: "since diamond polishes diamond, a woman refines a woman, leaving her softened, more pliable."[13] The Duc de Morny was the father of the Marquise de Belboeuf, the woman with whom Colette lived for five years during her music-hall days. Kinsey's statistics showed a higher frequency of orgasm in the contacts of homosexual women than in the contacts of heterosexual women, which led him to state, among other things, that "heterosexual relationships could become more satisfactory if they more often utilized the sort of knowledge which most homosexual females have of female sexual anatomy and female psychology."[14]

What is this knowledge? Basically—and here I paraphrase

the physiologists—it is the knowledge that women prefer considerable generalized body stimulation. It is the knowledge that fingertips, mouth and tongue, *external* female genitalia, and unfettered imagination are fine instruments with which to produce sexual arousal. It is the knowledge that breasts, ears, the inner surfaces of thighs, the throat, the palms of the hand, the armpits, the soles of the feet, the buttocks, and so on are splendidly responsive areas of the body. It is the knowledge that the clitoris, the inner surfaces of the labia minora, the extension of these inner lips into the vestibule of the vagina, and the anus are the locations of the greatest concentration of nerve endings, nerve endings that respond readily to fingertips, mouth, teeth, tongue, breast, or another set of external female genitalia. It is the knowledge that the vagina, whether full of fingers *or* full of a penis, feels good when it is full, but better still in combination with arousal of other areas where the nerve endings are more concentrated. In addition to things touched, it is the knowledge that things seen, heard, smelled and tasted serve to heighten arousal. In other words, it is the knowledge that direct and immediate vaginal penetration is not what brings about female orgasm. As Simone de Beauvoir has written, "Between women love is contemplative; caresses are intended less to gain possession of the other than gradually to re-create the self through her; separateness is abolished, there is no struggle, no victory, no defeat; in exact reciprocity each is at once subject and object, sovereign and slave; duality becomes mutuality."[15]

In clinical terms, lesbians engage in simple kissing, deep kissing, generalized body caresses, manual and oral stimulation of the breast, of the genitalia, and of the anus. They also engage in tribadism (from the Greek "to rub"; genital areas brought together). Cunnilingus—oral–genital sex—can be performed by both partners at the same time (what is euphemistically called "69"), or it can be alternated. The individual techniques are as common or as rare as are the individual sexualities of the participating women.

It is not being suggested that male lovers cannot learn and have not learned, in some cases, what lesbian lovers know. In fact, it was suggested by the supposedly sophisticated writer quoted earlier in regard to his member that "any man who is a really superb lover can be about ninety percent as good to a woman as a lesbian. Just give me the things that a lesbian does, and he's got all the other stuff . . ."[16] True—but it might be considered that the equivalent of the male's "other stuff"—presumably a penis inside a vagina—is a soft breast pressuring a breast, and/or a clitoris brushing a clitoris. There is also the argument that the ninety percent the writer talks of is not at all the same as a lesbian's ninety percent—it feels different, it smells different, it tastes different. It cannot be equated. But comparisons of this sort are adolescent, a descent to an "Anything you can do . . ." posturing. Thinking of this sort completely ignores the participation of the psyche in matters sexual. Even Masters and Johnson, who so rigidly limited their observations to the anatomy and physiology of human sexual response, cautioned:

> It is well to restate from time to time the necessity for maintaining a concept of total involvement when any facet of human sexuality is to be considered. . . . Female orgasm, whether it is attained within the context of an interpersonal relationship (either heterosexual or homosexual) or by means of any combination of erotically stimulative activity and/or fantasy, remains a potpourri of psychophysiologic conditions and social influence.[17]

Or, as Colette once put it, less clinically, "these pleasures . . . which are lightly called physical."[18]

Clearly, female orgasm can be achieved without the participation of a penis. The female orgasm that is produced during a sex act between two women is *physiologically* no

different from one produced between a woman and a man.
That many people still cannot conceive of lesbian sex is a
holdover from the days when sex was thought of only in
terms of reproduction. A male orgasm is essential to reproduction; a female orgasm is not. This, in no little way, helps
to explain the incredible fact that until only recently even
the orgasm of the heterosexual woman was never given much
thought; with sex thought of as a matter of reproduction, female orgasm, which had nothing to do with reproduction, became merely a joy, something which the puritanical ideal
acknowledges, if at all, only uneasily. It was much more comfortable to simply ignore the fact of its existence.

This discussion of lesbian sex has not been presented to
argue that one way of making love is better than another—
except in the opinions of those involved—and it is also not
meant to say that a sex act between two women is guaranteed to be successful; there are unimaginative homosexual
lovers, as there are unimaginative heterosexual lovers. It is
presented to point out that when people like David Reuben
ask, "What do female homosexuals do with each other?" the
answer that they do nothing much, that they are handicapped because they are missing part of the jigsaw puzzle,
simply is not true.

Some readers are probably thinking, All right, but what
about dildoes, penis substitutes? Good question. Are they
used in lesbian relationships? Yes, sometimes, by some lesbians. Are they commonly used? No one really knows. Because this matter is rarely discussed (even though much wondered about), we consider it here in some detail.

In the late nineteenth century, Krafft-Ebing wrote: "the
desire to adopt the active role towards the beloved person of
the same sex seems to invite the use of the priapus."[19] But of
his seventeen lesbian case histories reported in *Psychopathia
Sexualis* only one of the women used a dildo; he was theorizing without clinical data. In our own day Kinsey found that

in his histories "vaginal penetrations with objects which had served as substitutes for the male penis had been quite rare."[20] But many have accused Kinsey's interviewed women of lying. For example, Edmund Bergler, the psychoanalyst worried about a "whisper campaign," dismissed Kinsey's conclusions that women were capable of multiple orgasms as "fantastic tales" which the female volunteers fabricated.[21] Twelve years later Masters and Johnson, in observing women volunteers actually having multiple orgasms and not just talking about them, affirmed Kinsey's conclusion. Bergler, however, had been spared the embarrassment of retraction: he died before the publication of *Human Sexual Response.*

Of the lesbians I interviewed, both in person and through anonymous questionnaires, some admitted the use of a dildo. Most answered that they themselves did not use them nor did anyone they knew intimately ever suggest the use of one. Others did not speak of their personal experiences but made general data-less statements about how widespread the use is. The answers of these particular lesbians prove nothing, of course, except that lesbian sex practices vary widely according to who is involved. Here are some of the responses that went beyond yes and no replies:

"I have never seen a dildo, but believe most lesbians probably use fingers, which are warm, soft, part of the human lover."

"I now have one—but I had never heard of their existence even among the depraved Nashville crowd I mentioned earlier, the ones I talked with much and widely, and drew my one-night stands from."

"I think they're an invention of male novelists—especially the 18th and 19th century pornographers."

"I feel that only those women with hangups about their sexual identity and desire to be as much a 'man' as possible use them consistently."

"I think it's very rare and uncommon, though I've done it."

"I think men are the ones who commonly suppose this—they can't conceive of how a woman can have sexual satisfaction without a penis, or at least a penis substitute. Being involved, I don't think it's all that ordinary."

"I used to use a handle of a hairbrush to masturbate. I don't know if that qualifies as a dildo. But since I turned gay I've never even thought of using one myself or having my lover use one on me. Who needs it?"

"Maybe heterosexual women use them. I don't."

"I have not used, nor do I know anyone, nor do I know anyone who knows anyone who uses a dildo. I have thought about using one—maybe all the others just aren't talking."

One attractive middle-aged lesbian, a journalist, who moves in sophisticated circles and has had numerous affairs, commented in a woman's magazine:

The lesbians who talk freely about using [dildoes] are invariably supersophisticated . . . Others are offended by them. . . . My own opinion is that a strong romantic lesbian attachment doesn't need any aid beyond imagination, energy, and the will to please. But, being the curious type, I have had experiences with dildoes and found them very kicky and amusing. I don't believe my reaction to these artificial sex aids differs much from that of most heterosexual men and women who use vibrators, penis extenders, or French ticklers; these devices can be fun sometimes, but are hardly essential to sexual enjoyment.[22]

Pornographic fiction is full of dildoes. Psychologists Phyllis and Eberhard Kronhausen systematically examined a body of worldwide ancient and modern pornographic literature written in the last five hundred years, and reported their findings in their book *Erotic Fantasies*. They separated literature that dealt with erotic realism—say, for instance, Lawrence Durrell's *Alexandria Quartet*—from hard-core stuff, fiction that depends on sex fantasies for its subject matter. It is the latter, deliberate pornography, that they examined. They found tons of lesbian scenes in such books—"written by and for men. Consequently they do not reflect the true feelings of female homosexuals, nor are they descriptive of lesbian attitudes or sexual practices." The Kronhausens theorize that the frequency of the use of dildoes in such fiction might be explained by the fact that the heterosexual male author or reader "projects himself through fantasy into the lesbian situation, seeing himself as one of the lesbian participants." He cannot appear penis-less, so one of the lesbians is "transformed into a male or, at least, into a phallic female."

The Kronhausens feel that the male authors of such books express "a typically male fantasy, projected onto a lesbian situation" when they have their lesbian heroines expressing the wish for a penis. "In real life, few women with homosexual preferences wish to have a penis (any more than most homosexual men would want to have a vagina). Implicit in this fantasy is the male overvaluation of the male organ, an emphasis which one encounters at every turn . . ." They also point out: "As one might expect, male homosexual fantasies in literature are much rarer than lesbian ones . . . Few heterosexual men ever have conscious male homosexual fantasies, since this would be too threatening to their self-esteem . . ."[23]

In real life, there is no way of knowing how extensive the use of dildoes is in lesbian relationships. Sex shops that sell such items don't keep records. And even if they did, dildoes are known to be used by heterosexual women and homosexual men for masturbation purposes. A dildo sold does not necessarily mean a dildo used between women. In the end, whether or not a lesbian uses a dildo depends on her individ-

ual psyche; it does not depend on the fact that a penis substitute is essential to lesbian lovemaking. It is probably safe
to say that lesbians use dildoes less frequently than men like
to think and more frequently than they themselves care to
admit publicly—the latter statement, in terms of sex aids of
any kind, being applicable to all humans, homosexual, heterosexual, or anywhere in between.

A great many laymen/women consider lesbian sex "unnatural," mistakenly assuming that in all species of life there
exists a sexual instinct, a natural drive, that propels the female of the species to the male and vice versa. There does
exist, way down on the evolutionary scale, sexual instinct of
this sort, as in the case of certain insects who are drawn together by special emitted odors. However, as one ascends the
evolutionary scale no such exclusively heterosexual instinct
exists.

One has only to spend some time on a farm, or walk the
streets of any city, to see that household animals, males and
females, often display homosexual behavior. For a scientific
statement, here is a noted researcher, Frank A. Beach:
"Every animal breeder knows that under certain conditions
female cattle, horses, swine, sheep, dogs and cats will mount
other females and go through the male's mating pattern.
. . . [The] masculine, or homosexual pattern is not unnatural; instead it constitutes a normal element in the sexual
repertoires of these species."[24] Kinsey and his team of researchers once shot four thousand feet of film on the sexual
behavior of cattle, sheep, hogs and rabbits at the Oregon
State Agricultural College farm. When they showed the film
to an eminent sex researcher not working on their particular
project he commented, "Every judge in the country who has
to deal with sex offenders should see this film. It might teach
him something about what the word 'unnatural' means."[25]
Beach states his opinion very succinctly: "People who say

that homosexual activities are biologically abnormal and unnatural are wrong."[26]

On the primate level, numerous studies of apes and monkeys have concluded that the sexual urge itself in these primates is instinctive, unlearned, but *not* the channeling of that urge into an exclusive heterosexual pattern. Harry and Margaret Harlow, at the University of Wisconsin, have conducted several much quoted studies on monkeys. The studies have various ramifications, but of concern here is the fact that when they brought a group of monkeys who had been raised in isolation into contact with other monkeys, the animals expressed sexual appetite but didn't know what to do with it. Most settled for solitary masturbation; in one study two females went off together. Some males wanted to thrust and they did so, on the backs of other monkeys or into their sides. They had no innate knowledge of where the pieces of the jigsaw puzzle went. No females became pregnant. Harlow commented that the animals "exhibited almost every kind of behavior except one—heterosexual behavior, which was conspicuous by its absence."[27] From their observations the Harlows offered the theory that monkeys have no innate heterosexual drive, that in monkeys adult heterosexual behavior is learned, usually by the young watching the behavior of their elders.

The step from monkeys to humans is and is not a large one. The argument that monkeys are not humans is acknowledged by all those who study animal behavior. However, most researchers admit that their end goal is to extend their findings to human application. As Beach has written: "the established facts of human evolution make it difficult to believe that behavior which appears with great regularity in all or nearly all mammals and particularly in all primates is completely aberrant in our own species."[28]

Actually, one has only to observe the erotic responses of children, as did Freud, to see that the human sex drive is by no means innately and exclusively heterosexual. Infants, as Freud postulated, are polymorphously perverse, capable of responding sexually to any number of objects, including members of their own sex. And these responses, Freud wrote, meet little resistance, "since the mental dams against sexual excesses—shame, disgust and morality—have either not yet been constructed at all or are only in course of construction, according to the age of the child."[29] Children, in Freud's view, must be educated to sexual taboos; their "purity" is learned; there are no "natural" taboos.

Clearly, when people say lesbian sex is unnatural, they are ignoring biological evidence and are saying that it is immoral —quite another question. Biologically, lesbian sex is a natural possibility, it resides in nature. To trace the origin of the attitude that says that this natural possibility is acted upon only by women who are off kilter psychologically, and thus is a "sick" possibility, we must return to the nineteenth century and examine the first attempts by pre-Freud medical men to put the subject of lesbianism on a scientific footing.

CHAPTER TWO

Pre-Freud Medical Groping

UNTIL THE mid- and late-nineteenth century, lesbianism was ignored by Western medical investigators; it was looked upon as a vice, and in some parts of the world as a crime—had been for centuries. The women who made up the phenomenon were labeled sinners or criminals or both, and as such they had been left in the hands of God and the courts. Now, with the researches of men like Richard von Krafft-Ebing, lesbianism began to be looked upon (by the medical profession) not as a vice, not as a crime, but as a disease, and primarily a congenital disease. This was revolutionary thinking for most of the nineteenth-century public who continued to adhere to the sin-and/or-crime pronouncement. But in broad historical terms it was at this time that lesbians began to pass out of the hands of God and the courts and into the hands of the medical men—where they remain, in one study or another, to this day.

Krafft-Ebing, in his major work, *Psychopathia Sexualis*, first published in Germany in 1882, attempted to round up, describe, and categorize every possible human sexual activity that deviated from basic unadorned male-female coitus. The book contains over two hundred medical case his-

tories, seventeen of them about lesbians. To find the lesbians
it is necessary to wade amongst necrophiliacs, lust murderers,
rapists, child molesters, zooerasts, flagellants, hair despoilers,
frotteurs, those who practice cannibalism, those who suffer
from coprolagnia, and those who favor sexual intercourse
with a hen—among other beings. Krafft-Ebing had long
served as psychiatric consultant to the courts of Germany
and Austria, and he wrote *Psychopathia Sexualis* "to record
the various psychopathological manifestations of sexual life
in man and to reduce them to their lawful conditions."[1]
Thus he provided a medico-forensic guidebook that could be
consulted by legal professionals who dealt with illegal sexual
acts. The book was meant for professionals, but the European public, eager for printed sex information, gobbled up
copies as fast as the many revisions and translations appeared. It is said that virtually every literate European household of the time possessed a copy, usually hidden away under
lock and key in the patriarch's library. When the book was
published in the United States, in 1886, its sale was limited
to members of the medical and legal professions. Copies did,
of course, reach ordinary readers. The complicated technical
terms and the fact that the juicy parts—the actual sex go-
ings-on—were written in Latin did not act as a deterrent. Although there were other men writing in the field, e.g. West-
phal, Moll and Hirschfeld in Germany, and Lombroso in
Italy, it was through the widespread reading of Krafft-Ebing's
work that the public got its first inside "scientific" look at
lesbianism, a subject about which they knew virtually nothing. For this reason, we examine Krafft-Ebing's research into
lesbianism in some detail.

    To understand how Krafft-Ebing came to his conclusions
about lesbianism it is necessary to understand his attitude toward women and his attitude toward sex, attitudes that were
shared by the pre-Freud medical investigators of the day.

    Krafft-Ebing on women: "Woman . . . if physically and

mentally normal, and properly educated, has but little sensual desire . . . She remains passive. Her sexual organization demands it, and the dictates of good breeding come to her aid." In addition: "The ultimate aim, the ideal, of woman, even when she is dragged in the mire of vice, ever is and will be marriage."

Krafft-Ebing on sex: "In sexual love the real object of the instinct [is] propagation of the species." He elaborates: "During the time of the maturation of physiological processes in the reproductive glands, desires arise in the consciousness of the individual, which have for their purpose the perpetuation of the species (sexual instinct)."

From his definitions of women it followed that lesbians, who first of all didn't just lie there (who were in his thinking oversexed), and who secondly did not consider marriage the be-all and end-all of existence, clearly were not "real" women. And from his definition of what sex is all about, lesbians, whose lovemaking did not have baby-making as a goal, clearly did not possess a "real" sexual instinct. Yet such women did fall in love, and did make love, as his cases showed him. But this he considered sex of another color, sex that had nothing to do with procreation, rather sex for the "lust" of it, a type of sex which Krafft-Ebing recognized as existing but for which he raised his prose to full Victorian condemnation: "Man puts himself at once on a level with the beast if he seeks to gratify lust alone, but he elevates his superior position when by curbing the animal desire, he combines with the sexual functions ideas of morality, of the sublime, and the beautiful."

Further: "Life is a never-ceasing duel between the animal instinct and morality. Only will power and a strong character can emancipate man from the meanness of his corrupt nature, and teach him how to enjoy the pure pleasures of love and pluck the noble fruits of earthly existence." Further still: "Love unbridled is a volcano that burns down and lays waste all around it; it is an abyss that devours all—honor, substance and health."

Love unbridled was anything that deviated from a man and a woman in a marriage bed employing a penis and a vagina (man on top, woman under, both plucking away at the noble fruits of earthly existence) with the sole aim of uniting sperm and ovum. Thus, lesbian love was very definitely unbridled love, and lesbians clearly did not fit into the "correct" sexual scheme of things.

Who, then, were such women? In an attempt to find out, Krafft-Ebing and his contemporaries, all of them pre-Freud, little interested in the psyche, concentrated on externals. They examined in great detail the physical bodies of their lesbian patients. By reading all of the case histories in *Psychopathia Sexualis*—some of which are from Krafft-Ebing's own files, others from the files of his contemporaries, others culled from court records and previously printed medical literature—it is seen that the circumferences of the heads of the patients examined varied from between fifty to fifty-three centimeters, no bigger and no smaller than the heads of heterosexual women. Feet were either small, large, or medium-sized. Pelvises were found to be generally feminine (not narrow) in structure. Mammae were not necessarily large, not necessarily small, and as for evidence of beard, there was none. Clitorises, like breasts, varied from small to large, thus calling into question the much believed myth that lesbians possessed extra-large clitorises, the better to penetrate their partners, a myth that made sense when one thought only in terms of a penis inside a vagina. In addition, a lesbian's mons veneris was found to be ordinarily hairy, except in one case where it was found to be exceedingly hairy. As for voice, to round out the investigation of primary and secondary sex characteristics, Krafft-Ebing quotes a study by a Dr. Flatau, who, "in examining the larynx of twenty-three homosexual women, found in several of them a decidedly masculine formation," a fact Krafft-Ebing considered "remarkable."

Perhaps the "several" deep voices and perhaps the one hairy bush did add up to something, but on the whole it was concluded that lesbians did not differ physically from heterosexual women: "the genitals are normally developed, the sexual glands perform their functions properly and the sexual type is completely differentiated." In other words, lesbians possessed all the necessary apparati that assigned them to the female of the species.

Perhaps, then, something was to be learned from the external *actions* of such women. Although Krafft-Ebing stated that one could not tell from her external actions whether or not a woman "suffered" from lesbianism, he mentioned a string of things for which one should be on the lookout. A dislike of attending balls is suspicious (one patient even went so far as to prefer intellectual talk to dancing). Smoking and drinking to excess is a telltale trait, and the disdain of sweetmeats and perfumes is listed as characteristic. Interest in "the sciences" rather than art, along with "painful reflections" about being denied college, points the finger.

Further: "*Uranism** may nearly always be suspected in females wearing their hair short, or who dress in the fashion of men, or pursue the sports and pastimes of their male acquaintances; also in opera singers and actresses who appear in male attire on the stage by preference." And: "Suspicion may always be turned toward homosexuality when one reads in the advertisement columns of the daily papers: 'Wanted, by a lady, a lady friend and companion.' " And not to be neglected is this, which he quotes from a French book, Cof-

---

* A term for homosexuality that originated with the German lawyer Carl Heinrich Ulrichs, who, in the 1860s, protested his country's harsh laws against homosexuality. Ulrichs thought of homosexuality as a congenital phenomenon in which in a woman "a male soul is trapped in a female body," and in a man the opposite. In Ulrich's terminology, a homosexual was an *Urning*.

fignon's *La Corruption à Paris*: "This vice [lesbianism] is, of late, quite the fashion, partly owing to novels on the subject, and partly as a result of excessive work on [pedal] sewing machines . . ."

His investigations completed, Krafft-Ebing turned to definition and theorizing. He coined the term "antipathic sexuality" to define homosexuality and described the phenomenon as "the total absence of sexual feeling toward the opposite sex. The physical and psychical properties of persons of the same sex alone exercise an aphrodisiac effect and awaken a desire for sexual union." And he concluded that since lesbians had normal sex glands and normal primary and secondary physical sex characteristics, their condition was a "cerebral anomaly," and since he believed that these "anomalies are chiefly the signs of an inherited diseased condition of the central nervous system," such women suffered from a "functional sign of degeneration."

In other words, lesbians were born queer; it was in their genes, which were degenerate. No outside influences worked on such women; their tendency developed spontaneously from an inbuilt predisposition.

However, because he had come across women who started out in life with heterosexual tendencies but later adopted homosexual practices, he added to his theory the hypothesis that lesbianism could be an acquired phenomenon. But even if it was acquired he felt that some congenital predisposition had to be present. Some "injurious influence" awakened the dormant tendency, something like excessive masturbation, impotence of husbands, fear of pregnancy, exposure to all-female boarding schools, prisons, and, in the case of prostitutes, a basic disgust of men; even, one assumes, proximity to pedal sewing machines. Of all these "injurious influences," masturbation, he concluded, was the greatest evil:

Nothing is so prone to contaminate—under certain circumstances, even to exhaust—the source of all noble and ideal sentiments, which arise of themselves from a normally developing sexual instinct, as the practice of masturbation in early years. It despoils the unfolding bud of perfume and beauty, and leaves behind only the coarse, animal desire for sexual satisfaction. If an individual, thus depraved, reaches the age of maturity, there is wanting in him that aesthetic, ideal, pure and free impulse which draws the opposite sexes together. The glow of sensual sensibility wanes, and the inclination toward the opposite sex is weakened.

Masturbators were, in Krafft-Ebing's scientific pronouncement, "sinners."

Throughout most of his career Krafft-Ebing thought that congenital lesbianism was pathological, a loathsome disease that had to be exorcised. Toward the end of his life he began to lean toward the English sexologist Havelock Ellis's theory that congenital lesbianism was not necessarily pathological, that the phenomenon, like the phenomenon of color blindness, was simply a biological failure that could be lived with.

But before Krafft-Ebing reached this stage he attempted to "cure" a number of women. His treatment consisted of four steps: stop them from masturbating; cure them of neurasthenia; encourage heterosexual feelings; encourage self-control. He thought that hypnotic suggestion could aid those women who had acquired their lesbianism. We don't have the hypnotic suggestions he gave to women, but those that he gave to men give an idea of what was involved. Mr. von X, Case No. 170, was put into an hypnotic trance by Krafft-Ebing and ordered to repeat the following: "(1) I abhor onanism, because it makes me weak and miserable. (2) I no longer have inclination toward men; for love for men is against religion, nature and law. (3) I feel an inclination toward woman; for woman is lovely and desirable, and created for man." Krafft-Ebing reports that some days after the fourth such sitting Mr. von X "sought the address of a brothel."

Although Krafft-Ebing used hypnotic therapy, ultimately he concluded that it really didn't have much true value. Lesbianism, being congenital, meant that a change to heterosexuality was impossible. The only "cure" was to give up sex, any kind of sex, to strive for the ideal of chastity, to become, as he reports one of his patients did, "a decent, sexually at least, neutral person." This patient was a twenty-six-year-old Viennese woman, Mrs. von T., Case History No. 160 in *Psychopathia Sexualis*.

Mrs. von T.'s husband brought her to Krafft-Ebing for consultation because a few weeks previous she had managed to bring an elegant dinner party to a standstill by falling upon the neck of another woman guest, covering her profusely with kisses and caressing her like a lover. Mrs. von T. had told her husband of her lesbianism before their marriage, but he had brushed it aside, telling her that married life would take care of all that. The dinner-party episode—a shocker, all agreed—took place only a few months after their wedding.

In Krafft-Ebing's words, Mrs. von T.

> was highly cultured and intellectual, felt her false position painfully, but rather on account of her family than her own self. She looked upon it all as fate, over which she had no control. She bewailed it and declared herself ready to do anything to rid herself of this perversion and become a true wife and good mother, for she would take good care that her child were brought up in the right way. She would do everything to reconcile her husband and perform her marital duties, but she could not bear his moustache . . .

> At twenty "she had sensual love affairs with girls by the scores. . . . She gave preference to unmarried women of high standing endowed with mental gifts, of voluptuous, Diana-like figure, but of modest and retiring disposition . . ."

At twenty-three "she furnished an apartment away from home, where she engaged in regular orgies *cum digito et lingua,** sometimes for hours . . ."

A year before her marriage, in a period of melancholia, she contemplated suicide and wrote a farewell letter to one of her lovers:

> The reading of French novels and lascivious companions taught me all the tricks of perverse erotics, and the latent impulse became a conscious perversity. Nature has made a mistake in the choice of my sexuality and I must do a lifelong penance for it, for the moral power to suffer the unavoidable with dignity is lost. Irresistibly I have been drawn into the maelstrom of passion and shall be swallowed up by it.

However, in the end Mrs. von T. rejected suicide and chose marriage. Then the dinner-party episode. Krafft-Ebing writes that after a few sessions "I sent her to an hydropathic establishment, where an experienced colleague succeeded in a few months to free this patient by means of hydro- and suggestive treatment, from her homosexual affliction. She became a decent, sexually at least, neutral person. The relatives with whom she lived afterward for a considerable time found her behavior absolutely correct."

Another of Krafft-Ebing's patients, a Miss X, was a celebrated beauty, "a born Aspasia," Case History No. 158. He tells us that at the age of seventeen Miss X met a charming young man at a spa and spent a pleasant day in his company. But "the next evening at twilight [Miss X] happened to witness the revolting scene of this charming young man right opposite from her window in the shrubbery of the gardens" doing something nasty in Latin. "Miss X was horrified, almost annihilated, and felt it difficult to recover her mental balance. For a long time she lost her sleep and appetite, and

---

* With the finger and the tongue.

from that time she saw in man only the embodiment of coarse vulgarity."

Two years after this experience Miss X met a young woman in a park. After much hesitation and several meetings they finally went to the woman's boudoir. Krafft-Ebing quotes his patient:

> One day she led me to her divan, and whilst she was seated I knelt down at her feet. She fastened her timid eyes upon me, stroked away the hair from my forehead, and said, "Ah! If I only could love you once really! May I?" I consented, and whilst we thus sat together, gazing into each other's eyes, we drifted into that current which allows of no retreat. . . . She was enchantingly beautiful. All I wished was to possess the power of the artist to immortalize that form upon the canvas. To me it was a novel experience. I was intoxicated. We abandoned ourselves to each other without restriction, drunk with the ravages of sensual feminine pleasure. I do not believe that man can ever grasp the exuberance of such piquant tenderness; man is not sufficiently refined; he is much too coarse. . . . Our wild orgy lasted until I sank down exhausted, powerless, unnerved. I fell asleep on her bed. Suddenly I awoke, with an unspeakable thrill, hitherto unknown to me, running through my whole being. She was upon me—*cunnilingus perficiens**— the highest pleasure for her, *tandem mihi non licebat altrum quam osculos dare ad mammae*,† which caused her to quiver convulsively.

Krafft-Ebing doesn't record what happened to Miss X. Perhaps she too went on to live a "correct" life as a neuter.

We discuss Krafft-Ebing's theories about lesbianism in some detail not because they are of scientific value today but because his book, *Psychopathia Sexualis*, is still read today; periodically any number of quick-sale paperback editions ap-

---

* Carrying out cunnilingus.

† All the while not allowing me to do anything except kiss her breasts.

pear, and publishers tend to tout the book as containing the
real stuff, the definitive treatise on abnormal sexuality, lesbianism included. So many of his extrascientific comments,
for instance his pronouncement that one should be suspicious of women who wear their hair short or of those who
are interested in what he called masculine pastimes, are still
believed. For his time, a time when matters sexual were relegated to a category called "nasty" and as such were seldom
discussed, he was a brave man indeed even to consider investigation in this field. However, he was by no means an objective observer. He was a very proper, highly respected establishment doctor who couched his findings in a nonobjective,
moralistic prose. He introduced his cases with such adjectives
as "revolting," "disgusting," "horrible," "shameful," "mon-
strous." In effect he said, Here is what exists, isn't it awful?
He excused himself for writing about such things by saying
that "the perverse sexual acts . . . are of the greatest importance clinically, socially, and forensically; and, therefore, they must here receive careful consideration; all aesthetic and moral disgust must be overcome."

There has always been an air of sensationalism about
Krafft-Ebing, and it is true that some of his cases do shock,
even today. Edward M. Brecher, in his book *The Sex Researchers*, quotes what Krafft-Ebing himself considered his
most horrible case, a case of a lust murder. The murderer is
talking of his female victim: "I opened her breast and with
a knife cut through the fleshy parts of the body. Then I arranged the body as a butcher does beef, and hacked it with
an axe into pieces of a size to fit the hole which I had dug up
in the mountain for burying it. I may say that while opening
the body I was so greedy that I trembled, and could have cut
out a piece and eaten it." Brecher comments:

> Having thus stretched his readers' terror, disgust, and con-
> tempt to their utmost, Krafft-Ebing went on to review in

much the same tone the cases of the fetishists attracted to
white kid gloves or high-heeled shoes, the cases of masochists
who liked women to tread on them, and the cases of homosexuals attracted to partners of their own sex. From our
horror at the details of lust murder it is but a step to horror at
all sexual variations . . .[2]

The point is well taken. One section of case histories of
lesbianism in *Psychopathia Sexualis* is followed by case histories of necrophilia and violation of children, all three topics
arranged under the heading "Unnatural Abuses." Groupings
of this sort ignore the fact that there are *degrees* of nonaverage sexual behavior. It would appear that Mrs. von T.'s neck
nuzzling and Miss X's "piquant tenderness"—even if thought
of as "unnatural abuses"—are far removed from, for example,
the force employed in the violation of a child.

Another point to be made about all lesbian medical case
histories is that they represent the study of only a tiny minority of women who are lesbians, those women who fall into
special categories. The women studied are either in psychiatric treatment or confined in mental hospitals or in prison,
or they make their livings as prostitutes. The great majority
of lesbians fall into none of these categories; case histories
about *these* women are practically nonexistent, yet by association they are considered in the same light as those who
fall into special categories. Take, for example, the case of a
lesbian who murders her female lover (such cases are numerous in medical roundups). A lesbian who murders her lover
has nothing to do with a lesbian who is not a murderer. If
anything, one has information about murderers, not about
lesbians. Yet there exists in the minds of many people the
feeling that lesbian love often leads to "crimes of passion."
The horror felt at the life-destroying act of lesbian murder
extends to the act of lesbian loving. No such connection is
ever made in the consideration of a heterosexual murder. No

one has ever suggested that a wife who kills her husband has anything to do with a wife who does no such thing. Crimes of passion are no more a homosexual specialty than they are a heterosexual one.

The pioneering sex research of the pre-Freud medical men took a long time to filter into the public's consciousness. Most people were satisfied to continue to think of lesbians as sinners and/or criminals; to recognize the newer, supposedly scientific theory that said lesbianism was a congenital phenomenon—the result, as Ulrichs had it, of a masculine soul heaving in a female bosom—was a step the public had difficulty in taking. To think of lesbians as possessors of degenerate genes, over which they had no control, was, among other things, to give those individuals the escape of martyrdom. Many lesbians themselves, long suffering under the sinner/criminal stigma, welcomed the congenital theory. Forty-six years after Krafft-Ebing's pronouncement, Radclyffe Hall, in her once notorious novel *The Well of Loneliness*, had her lesbian heroine plead, I was born this way, I can't help myself, don't dismiss me, "I'm some awful mistake—God's mistake."[3] Later in this book it will be seen how the public and the courts rejected Ms. Hall's "scientific" plea, continuing to align themselves on the side of the righteous against the "sinners."

CHAPTER THREE

Freud and a Poet / Patient

A DECADE after Krafft-Ebing's attempts to offer a physiological explanation of lesbianism there began to appear in certain medical circles a shift in emphasis to a psychological explanation. It is Sigmund Freud, of course, who is the best
known of the pioneers in this phase of theorizing. Unlike
Krafft-Ebing, however, Freud was not in the business of for-
mulating a rigid set of definitive statements on the matter.

Freud couched in tentative language his researches into
lesbianism. For example, he believed that lesbianism was not
necessarily a neurotic illness. Nor did he believe that it *necessarily* could be "cured." Of one of his patients, an eighteen-
year-old young woman, he wrote: "the girl was not in any
way ill—she did not suffer from anything in herself, nor did
she complain of her condition. . . . [The] task to be carried
out did not consist in resolving a neurotic conflict but in con-
verting one variety of genital organization of sexuality into
the other." This task, "the removal of genital inversion or
homosexuality," today called a "cure," Freud thought

never an easy matter. On the contrary, I have found success possible only under specially favorable circumstances. . . . One must remember that normal sexuality also depends upon a restriction in the choice of object; in general, to undertake to convert a fully developed homosexual into a heterosexual is not much more promising than to do the reverse, only that for good practical reasons the latter is never attempted.[1]

As will be noted in the next chapter, the school of psychoanalysis in this country which today categorically pronounces lesbianism a mental illness, and a curable mental illness, does not take, as is commonly supposed, its text directly from Freud.

Nor did Freud spend much of his time trying to determine whether lesbianism was congenital or acquired; this he thought a "fruitless" question: "we see in practice a continual mingling and blending of what in theory we should try to separate into a pair of opposites—namely, inherited and acquired factors."[2] Nor did he categorically lump lesbians into the broad area Krafft-Ebing had labeled "perversions." Although Freud did consider lesbianism to be a sexual practice that "deviates from the usual one," he felt that there were *degrees* of nonaverage sexual behavior; homosexuals, he wrote, "do at least seek to achieve very much the same ends with the objects of their desires as normal people do with theirs. But after them comes a long series of abnormal types, in whom the sexual activities become increasingly further removed from anything which appears attractive to a reasonable being."[3]

What Freud was primarily interested in discovering were the "psychical mechanisms" that resulted in a woman choosing as sexual partner another woman. This he attempted through the formulation of a general theory of female sexuality, a theory that lately has been under fire from a number of professional and laywomen quarters. Freud's theory of fe-

male sexuality, like the matter of female orgasm, has been
written of so extensively recently that only an outline, pertinent to lesbianism, is needed here. The theory begins with
the supposition that a female's libido at birth is composed of
both heterosexual and homosexual possibilities—i.e., a female
child starts out in life bisexual. In the process of her growing
up several stages of sexual development must be gone
through before one of the possibilities triumphs, becomes
overt, and the other is sublimated.

During very early childhood, Freud postulated, a girl's eroticism is focused on her mother, and her sexual activity is
centered on her clitoris. This phase he called the phallic or
pre-Oedipus situation. It is during this period that a girl dis-
covers that she does not possess a penis—to Freud, the most
traumatic experience the female of the species ever experiences, a discovery, the feeling of castration, that is the turning point in her life. To resolve the castration complex,
Freud felt that à girl child must transfer her libidinal attachment from her mother to her father and her erotic sensitivity
from her clitoris to her vagina. In rejecting her mother and
turning to her father she enters what Freud called the feminine Oedipus situation, a phase of passive sexuality. She does
so because of a wish to obtain a penis, something her mother
cannot give her and only her father can. If in turn she sub-
limates this wish for a penis into a wish for a child (a symbolic penis), the path is paved for eventual possible development of adult heterosexual behavior—for in later years the
girl may replace her father with another male figure who will
give her, in a nonincestuous situation, that symbolic penis,
a baby. If, however, the girl's attachment to her father has
been unusually strong, instead of projecting her need for a
baby/penis onto other men she may project the fear of incest onto them, and thus reject all men. In this instance the
girl is said to be fixated at an "immature" level of sexuality,
stuck with a feminine Oedipus complex. From here the way

is open (although not inevitably so) for a possible slide into adult homosexuality. That's one way, according to Freud, of becoming a lesbian.

Another way is for a girl never to enter the Oedipus phase at all. In this case, the girl child refuses to reject her first love object, her mother, and clings to active sexuality, clitoral masturbation, instead of entering the passive sexual phase. In so doing she thinks, unconsciously, that she already has a penis, so why go through the machinations of trying to get one from Father? In later years, this girl may project her erotic feelings for her mother onto other women, and in so doing she too is said to be fixated at an "immature" level of sexuality, stuck with not an Oedipus complex but a masculinity complex. Here too the path is open to possible adult homosexual behavior.

To further complicate matters, Freud theorized that a girl may work through all these various stages of sexual development, but there exists the possibility that she may, at some later date, experience a revival of the pre-Oedipus situation or the Oedipus situation itself, and thus *regress* to an "immature" level of sexual behavior.[4]

Lesbianism, then, in Freud's thinking, may result from an overdose of penis envy wherein a woman denies she does not possess this organ and lives her life within the framework of a masculinity complex; or lesbianism may center on a woman's unconscious fear of father–daughter incest which she projects into a fear of all men and thus lives her life within the framework of a feminine Oedipus complex.

Exactly why certain females remain fixated at or regress to these "immature" levels of sexuality, while others surmount the psychological hurdles, Freud did not know. Environmental situations, say for instance a father who actually attempts to seduce his daughter, Freud rejected; some of his patients who went through this did not become homosexual. Later in his career, in 1920, he said that *perhaps* the determining factor would turn out to be constitutional, that the strength of the homosexual element in the original bisexual makeup would turn out to have been greater than the heterosexual element, thus tipping the balance. He wrote: "It is not for psychoanalysis to solve the problem of homosexuality. It must rest content with disclosing the psychical mechanisms that resulted in determination of the object-choice, and with tracing the paths leading from them to the instinctual basis of the disposition. There its work ends, and it leaves the rest to biological research . . ."[5]

As mentioned, Freud did not hold out much hope for "cure" via psychoanalysis. A major stumbling block, in his view, was the inability of a homosexual woman to go through the transference stage with a male analyst, the step so necessary to a successful analysis. He elaborated on this problem in the 1920 case history of the eighteen-year-old young woman.

The young woman, beautiful and clever and of good family, consented to treatment to assuage the fury of her father when he learned of her homosexual leanings. The father, who regarded his daughter either "as vicious, as degenerate, or as mentally afflicted," wanted her cured. Freud told the father that "in actual numbers the successes achieved by psychoanalytic treatment of the various forms of homosexuality, which, to be sure, are manifold, are not very striking." But the father was determined, and if the analysis did fail he "had in reserve his strongest countermeasure—a speedy marriage." Freud was not very sympathetic to this father; he wrote: "By a healthy child [parents] mean one who never places [them] in difficulties, but only gives them pleasure."[6]

As for the young woman, she had no wish to be "cured"; she could not conceive of any other way of being in love; she was pained only at the grief she was causing her parents. She frankly told Freud that she intended to marry someday, "but only in order to escape from her father's tyranny and to follow her true inclinations undisturbed." There's no way of really telling, but various professional studies and other informal writings claim that a good many lesbians (and male homosexuals) married, at least before World War I, to hide their real inclinations. We have as well-known examples Edith Lees, Havelock Ellis's wife, Siri von Essen, Strindberg's wife, and Vita Sackville-West, Harold Nicolson's wife; they are only the very tip of the iceberg.

Freud concluded that his patient, in childhood, had gone through the feminine Oedipus complex "in a way that was not at all remarkable." However, when she was sixteen, she experienced a revival of the Oedipus complex, unconsciously wishing to have a child, a male one, by her father. At this point her mother became pregnant and the girl, bitter with resentment, "turned away from her father, and from men altogether." She turned to her mother as love object. "Since there was little to be done with the real mother, there arose from the conversion of feeling described the search for a mother substitute to whom [the girl] could become passionately attached." Freud emphasized that this patient's manner of coping with the situation was peculiarly her own: "We do not . . . mean to maintain that every girl who experiences a disappointment of this kind, of the longing for love that springs from the Oedipus attitude during puberty, will necessarily on that account fall a victim to homosexuality." In addition to this problem, Freud concluded that his patient had suffered from childhood from a strongly marked masculinity complex:

A spirited girl, always ready to fight, she was not at all prepared to be second to her slightly older brother; after inspecting his genital organs she had developed a pronounced envy of the penis, and the thoughts derived from this envy still continued to fill her mind. She was in fact a feminist; she felt it to be unjust that girls should not enjoy the same freedom as boys, and rebelled against the lot of woman in general.

The analysis went along smoothly enough in the beginning, almost without resistance, "the patient participating actively with her intellect, though absolutely tranquil emotionally. Once when I expounded to her a specially important part of the theory, one touching her nearly, she replied in an inimitable tone, 'How very interesting,' as though she were a *grande dame* being taken over a museum and glancing through her lorgnon at objects to which she was completely indifferent." However, buried under this attitude Freud said he found a well of resistance: the young woman's determination to remain homosexual to wound her father in revenge for the wound he had inflicted on her by giving her mother and not her a child. With this attitude, Freud found that further analytic sessions were useless; the only thing the patient was transferring to her analyst was "the deep antipathy to men which had dominated her ever since the disappointment she had suffered from her father. Bitterness against men is as a rule easy to gratify upon the analyst; it need not evoke any violent emotional manifestations, it simply expresses itself in rendering futile all his endeavors." Freud broke off the analysis and advised the patient and her father that "if it was thought worthwhile to continue the therapeutic efforts, it should be done by a woman." As with so many medical case histories of lesbians, we have no follow-up information about this Viennese eighteen-year-old. She very well may have married to satisfy her family's and society's expectations, in order to satisfy her own undisturbed. Or she may have been one of the few of the time to step out of what was expected and to gird herself for an independent life, perhaps frequently commenting, as the years passed, "How very interesting."

Freud was understandably frustrated by the resistance met in this patient, but, as his discipline dictated, he remained fairly unemotional about the situation. He wrote up the case in 1920, when he was still at the height of his intellectual delvings. Fourteen years later, when faced with what he considered another case of resistance by an intelligent woman, he was not so coolly detached. We have Freud's extraordinary response to this situation from the patient herself, the American poet H.D. (Hilda Doolittle):

> I did not know what enraged him suddenly. I veered round off the couch, my feet on the floor. I do not know exactly what I had said . . . I veer round, uncanonically seated stark upright with my feet on the floor. The Professor himself is uncanonical enough; he is beating with his hand, with his fist, on the headpiece of the old-fashioned horsehair sofa that had heard more secrets than the confession-box of any popular Roman Catholic father-confessor in his heyday. . . . *Consciously,* I was not aware of having said anything that might account for the Professor's outburst. And even as I veered round, facing him, my mind was detached enough to wonder if this was some idea of *his* for speeding up the analytic content or redirecting the flow of associated images. The Professor said, "The trouble is—I am an old man—*you do not think it worth your while to love me.*"[7]

These words of H.D.'s are taken from her exquisite and unusual book *Tribute to Freud,* an account of her analytic sessions with Professor Freud.

H.D. was forty-seven in 1933 when she first came to Vienna to see Freud. Freud was seventy-seven. She, an established poet of rare gift, had come to a point in her life when she wanted to "dig down and dig out, root out my personal weeds, strengthen my purpose, reaffirm my beliefs, canalize my energies." Freud had welcomed her; her preoccupation with Greek myth in her poems found a willing reader in Freud; he himself had a large and priceless collection of Greek figurines arranged in a semicircle on his desk in his study. He considered H.D. more of a "seeker," a stu-

dent, than a patient. He even tentatively suggested that she
would be one to carry forth his work after his death, although
he sternly warned her that she should never attempt to de-
fend him when she heard abusive remarks about his work.
He said that such a defense would only "drive the hatred or
the fear or the prejudice in deeper . . . If the matter is ignored, the attacker may forgo his anger—or in time, even, his
unconscious mind may find another object on which to fix
its tentacles . . ."

H.D. was a diligent student, and patient: "I over-stressed
or over-compensated; I purposely and painfully dwelt on certain events in the past about which I was none too happy,
lest I appear to be dodging the analysis . . ." And as diligent
students go, she was not about to simply hero-worship: "I was
a student," she wrote, "working under the direction of the
greatest mind of this and of perhaps many succeeding gener-
ations. But the Professor was not always right."

H.D. particularly wanted to explore with Freud a series of
disastrous personal events that had occurred during and immediately after World War I, events that had culminated in
a semi-breakdown and in a strange mystical experience on
the island of Corfu in the spring of 1920. During the war her
older brother had been killed at the front, her flat had been
bombed (she was living in London), her marriage to the
writer Richard Aldington had been on the verge of collapse,
and she had lost a child in miscarriage. After the war, in
1919, her father, a noted American astronomer, died, she herself almost died of double pneumonia while pregnant a second time, and her six-year-old marriage to Aldington finally
did collapse. But let her tell it in her own words:

> For things had happened in my life, pictures, "real
> dreams," actual psychic or occult experiences that were super-
> ficially, at least, outside the province of established psycho-
> analysis. But I am working with the old Professor himself. I

want his opinion on a series of events. It is true, I had not discussed these experiences openly, but I had sought help from one or two (to my mind) extremely wise and gifted people in the past and they had not helped me. At least, they had not been able to lay, as it were, the ghost. If the Professor could not do this, I thought, nobody could. I could not get rid of the experience by writing about it. I had tried that.

. . . I was alone outside London in the early spring of that bad influenza winter of 1919. I myself was waiting for my second child . . .

The second child, for some reason, I knew, must be born. O, she would be born, all right, though it was an admitted scientific fact that a waiting mother, stricken with that pneumonia, double-pneumonia, would not live. She might live—yes—but then the child would not. They rarely both live, if ever! But there were reasons for us both living, so we did live. At some cost, however! The material and spiritual burden of pulling us out of danger fell upon a young woman whom I had only recently met—anyone who knows me knows who this person is. Her pseudonym is Bryher and we all call her Bryher. If I got well, she would herself see that the baby was protected and cherished and she would take me to a new world, a new life, to the land, spiritually of my predilection, geographically of my dreams. We would go to Greece, it could be arranged. It was arranged, though we two were the first unofficial visitors to Athens after that war. This was spring, 1920.

Bryher (Winifred Ellerman), the English writer, was twenty-six in 1920, eight years younger than H.D. An advocate of women's rights, Bryher was the product of one of Britain's most wealthy and influential families, a family that had sent her to a boarding school whose headmistress never ceased claiming that her aim was to "turn out the greatest number of girls conforming to an average pattern."[8] In Bry-

her's case, at least, the headmistress was to fail badly in her
aim. In her autobiography, which she wrote in 1962, Bryher
noted that in 1913, when she left school, women belonged in
the home. Speaking of herself and some of her young women
friends, she wrote: "Our rebellions took place in our
thoughts, it was only after 1920 that they passed into deeds."
She left home in 1920 firmly convinced that the task of her
generation "was to break the unhealthy taboos of the nineteenth century." For many years thereafter she attempted
just that, never to the delight of her celebrated family.

Bryher had always wanted to be a writer; when she did
publish her first book, *Development*, a slightly notorious po-
lemic about English boarding schools, she later said, "I had
committed the unpardonable Victorian sin and made myself
'conspicuous' (I enjoyed this very much)." But before she
actually took the step of writing she read the work of other
women writers. "There will always be one book among all
the others that makes us aware of ourselves; for me, it is *Sea
Garden* by H.D." After reading the poems, Bryher wrote to
H.D. and was invited to tea, this in 1918. "I had a friend at
last who talked to me about poetry and did not laugh at my
meager attempts at writing. (Not that I thought them meager at the time!) It was my first real contact with an artist,
and H.D. was the most beautiful figure that I have ever seen
in my life, with a face that came directly from a Greek statue
and, almost to the end, the body of an athlete." The following year, when H.D. was in hospital gravely ill, Bryher
thought, "I have just found you, suppose I lose you." She
said to H.D.: "I will take you to Greece as soon as you are
well."

They left in April of 1920. H.D. picks up the story:

. . . We had come from Athens, by boat, through the
Corinthian canal and up the Gulf of Corinth. Delphi and
the shrine of Helios (Hellas, Helen) had been really the main

objective of my journey. Athens came a very close second in affection; however, having left Athens, we were informed when the boat stopped at Itea that it was absolutely impossible for two ladies alone, at that time, to make the then dangerous trip on the winding road to Delphi . . . travel was difficult, the country itself in a state of political upheaval; chance hotel acquaintances expressed surprise that two women alone had been allowed to come at all at that time. We were always "two women alone" or "two ladies alone," but we were not alone.

In a hotel room on the Ionian island of Corfu, H.D. had her vision, or, as she put it, she began to see the "picture writing on the wall."

And there I sat and there is my friend Bryher who has brought me to Greece. I can turn now to her, though I do not budge an inch or break the sustained crystal-gazing stare at the wall before me. I say to Bryher, "there have been pictures here—I thought they were shadows at first, but they are light, not shadow. They are quite simple objects—but of course it's very strange. I can break away from them now, if I want—it's just a matter of concentrating—what do you think? Shall I stop? Shall I go on?" Bryher says without hesitation, "go on."

H.D. describes the vision itself in a long and detailed account in *Tribute to Freud*. The vision was of such intensity that toward the end of it she had the sensation of drowning, knowing that to free herself she must "drown completely and come out on the other side, or rise to the surface after the third time down, not dead to this life but with a new set of values, my treasure dredged from the depth. I must be born again or break utterly."

She did recover. Bryher and she left Corfu, returned to London and then traveled to the United States, where Bry-

her received word from her family that she was to return
home to live with them, or else. Bryher reports that had she
been analyzed at the time (she would be later, in Berlin, by
Hanns Sachs), she would not have panicked, but she did, by
swiftly arranging a marriage of convenience with Robert Mc-
Almon. He wanted to live in Paris, to write and to publish
books; she needed a husband. Bryher proposed to him the
day after their meeting: "I put my problem before him and
suggested that if we married, my family would leave me
alone. I would give him part of my allowance, he would
join me for occasional visits to my parents, but otherwise we
would live strictly separate lives." McAlmon, a homosexual,
agreed. Sylvia Beach, owner of the famous Paris bookshop
Shakespeare and Company, and a close friend of Bryher's, reports that later, in all the Paris cafés and boîtes that Mc-
Almon frequented, he insisted that he hadn't known the marriage was to be in name only. He established Contact Editions
with Bryher's considerable monies and published books by
Gertrude Stein, Hemingway, H.D., and others. Bryher and
H.D. settled in Switzerland with H.D.'s young daughter,
Perdita.

Freud translated H.D.'s mystical picture writing on the
wall, which had haunted her for thirteen years, as "a desire
for union with my mother. I was physically in Greece, in Hellas (Helen). I had come home to the glory that was Greece";
H.D.'s mother's name had been Helen. This theme of mother-
search was a recurring one in the analysis. In the beginning,
when Freud had pounded with his fist on the headpiece of
his consulting-room couch and had said, "The trouble is—I
am an old man—*you do not think it worth your while to love
me,*" H.D. had been taken aback and her skepticism came
forth:

   The impact of his words was too dreadful—I simply felt
nothing at all. I said nothing. . . . Why had I come to

Vienna? The Professor had said in the very beginning that I had come to Vienna hoping to find my mother. Mother? Mamma. But my mother was dead. I was dead; that is, the child in me that had called her mamma, was dead. Anyhow, he was a terribly frightening old man, too old and too detached, too wise and too famous altogether, to beat that way with his fist, like a child hammering a porridge-spoon on the table.

And another time,

when I painfully unravelled a dingy, carelessly woven strip of tapestry of cause and effect and related to him, in over-careful detail, some none-too-happy friendships, he waved it all aside, not bored, not grieved or surprised, but simply a little wistful, I thought, as if we had wasted precious time, our precious hours together, on something that didn't matter. "But why," he asked, "did you worry about all this? Why did you think you had to tell me? *Those two didn't count.* But you felt you wanted to tell your mother."

H.D. does not comment directly in her book on how she responded to Freud's theory that she perhaps had a mother problem. In fact, it very much seems that between analyst and analysand there was "an argument implicit in our very bones." H.D. seems to have been disappointed that during their sessions they did not concentrate more on "abstruse transcendental problems." She wrote, "We touched lightly on [them], it is true, but we related them to the familiar family-complex." Of major concern to H.D. was the threat of the coming war, World War II. She felt that only by dealing with the horrors she had gone through during World War I could she possibly cope with another. That is why she had sought out the Professor. But the Professor, whose job it was to discover unconscious motivation, may very well have had in the back of his mind, and probably did, his famous "Psychology of Women" lecture, which he had written just the year before and in which he strongly reiterated his penis-envy-in-women theory, the situation that he thought governed every aspect of a woman's life:

> The desire after all to obtain the penis for which she so much longs may even contribute to the motives that impel a grown-up woman to come to analysis; and what she quite reasonably expects to get from analysis, such as the capacity to pursue an intellectual career, can often be recognized as a sublimated modification of this repressed wish.[9]

H.D., nothing if not an intellectual, had been willing to delve into the family complex and in fact did, at first. However, the growing threat of war, which hovered over their analytic sessions, she finally felt too broad in its implications to be considered only through her "personal Phobia":

> I had begun my preliminary research in order to fortify and equip myself to face war when it came, and to help in some subsidiary way, if my training were sufficient and my aptitudes suitable, with war-shocked and war-shattered people. But my actual personal war-shock (1914–1919) did not have a chance. My sessions with the Professor were barely under way, before there were preliminary signs and symbols of the approaching ordeal. . . . With the death-head swastika chalked on the pavement, leading to the Professor's very door, I must, in all decency, calm as best I could my own personal Phobia, my own personal little Dragon of war-terror . . .

Freud too could not ignore the reality of the outside world, but, interestingly, his response was a very personal one. He said to H.D., at one of their last sessions, "What will become of my grandchildren?" H.D. felt a sudden gap, a severance, a chasm or a schism in consciousness, which I tried to conceal from him. It was so tribal, so conventionally Mosaic. As he ran over their names and the names of their parents, one felt the old impatience, a sort of intellectual eye-strain, the old boredom of looking out historical, genealogical references in a small-print school or Sunday-school Bible. . . . He was worried about them (and no wonder), but I was worried about something else.

In the end, H.D., who had come to Freud for an answer, "to lay, as it were, the ghost," recognized that the great man was not, after all, at least not at that particular moment in history, the oracle she sought—"war closed on us." She *had* grown to love him, the classic transference phase had taken place, but not in psychoanalytic terms; her love was not that for a father figure but that for a fellow human who was going through a very grave period of personal trial. On one of her last days in Vienna she walked to Berggasse 19 through an unusually quiet city, the streets empty of people, the chalked swastikas everywhere; a year earlier Freud's books had been publicly burned. Freud's maid Paula

peered through a crack in the door, hesitated, then furtively ushered me in. . . . The Professor opened the inner door after a short interval . . . "But why did you come? No one has come here to-day, no one. What is it like outside? Why did you come out?" . . . I did not know what the Professor was thinking. He could not be thinking, "I am an old man— *you do not think it worth your while to love me.*" Or if he remembered having said that, this surely was the answer to it.

H.D.'s book is also her answer. Her tribute to Freud is described by an English analyst-poet in the foreword thus: "This book celebrates the meaningfulness of human individuality. It is a poem or a poetic prose entity, a dramatized

integrated unique message and a communication of one spirit
to another."

H.D. left Vienna in 1934. She and Freud corresponded in
a series of tender letters until his death; this excerpt from one
of Freud's last letters to her is typical of the general tone:
"What you gave me, was not praise, was affection and I need
not be ashamed of my satisfaction. Life at my age is not easy,
but spring is beautiful and so is love."

To go from Freud's humanistic words to this country's
current sprawling and technological sexual revolution—ironically, Freud's legacy—necessitates a mind-boggling jump.
"America," Freud had said in 1909, "is the most grandiose
experiment the world has seen, but I am afraid it is not going
to be a success."[10] During one of H.D.'s last sessions with
Freud, he, old and ill, soon to be forced to flee to London,
there to die in exile, said to her, "I struck oil. It was I who
struck oil. But the contents of the oil wells have only just
been sampled. There is oil enough, material enough for research and exploitation, to last fifty years, to last one hundred years—or longer. My discoveries are not primarily a heal-
all. My discoveries are a basis for a very grave philosophy."
Eleven years later, in 1945, H.D. wrote: "[Freud] himself—
at least to me personally—deplored the tendency to *fix* ideas
too firmly, to set symbols, or to weld them inexorably . . .
He struck oil; certainly there was 'something in it'; yes, a vast
field for exploration and—alas—exploitation lay open." In
1962, Bryher, an advocate of psychoanalysis, who knew
Freud and to whom Freud in his letters to H.D. always sent
warmest wishes, wrote:

> The gay excitement of the early days [of psychoanalysis] died
> with the founders, the second generation was engaged in
> obtaining official recognition, they aspired to become part of
> the Establishment. They succeeded and yet because in the
> deepest way they thus betrayed some of their leader's ideas,

they tended in compensation to make laws of what Freud had
suggested were points of investigation.

As will be noted in the next chapter, in the United States
(where Freud's work took firmest foothold), certain of today's psychoanalysts have made of Freud's "grave philosophy" a universal "heal-all."

It will be recalled that in Freud's 1920 case history of his
eighteen-year-old lesbian patient he suggested that perhaps a
woman analyst might succeed with lesbian patients where he
could not. Analyst Helene Deutsch, one of Freud's early female disciples, recorded, in 1921, the history of one of her
lesbian patients. The patient, a married woman with several
children, was suffering from terrible periods of depression
that had led to several suicide attempts. She considered
herself lesbian, but she did not engage in any actual sexual
practices; she was drawn strongly to women and when she
hugged and kissed certain of them she became sexually
aroused. She couldn't say why her relationships had never
gone beyond the platonic; Deutsch reports that "she only
knew that her inhibitions against [homosexuality] were too
strong—inhibitions which she rationalized on the basis of social shyness, family duty, and fear of psychic subjugation."[11]
The fear of subjugation, Deutsch concluded, was a fear on
the patient's part of being masochistically attached to her
mother (the patient's mother had been a stern and distant
woman whom the patient had hated all her life).
   Transference did take place, and strongly. The female patient fell in love with the female analyst. "Her transference
to me was very pronounced," Deutsch writes, "and was characteristic of that type whose actions as well as conscious responses over a long period of time reveal nothing except tenderness, respect and a feeling of safety. The patient was very
happy and felt as if she had at last found a kind, understand-

ing mother, who was making up to her all that her own mother had denied her."

When revival of the mother relationship had taken place and had been worked through, Deutsch felt that a revival of the father relationship was in order. She referred the patient to an analyst "of the fatherly type," but, as with Freud, "Unfortunately, the transference did not advance beyond respect and sympathy, and the analysis was interrupted after a short time."

About a year later Deutsch met the woman and

saw that she had become a vivid, radiant person. She told me that her depressions had entirely disappeared. The wish to die which had been almost continuously present and her nostalgia had apparently receded completely. At last she had found happiness in a particularly congenial and uninhibited sexual relationship with a woman. The patient, who was intelligent and conversant with analysis, informed me that their homosexual relationship was quite consciously acted out as if it were a mother–child situation, in which sometimes one, sometimes the other played the mother—a play with a double cast, so to speak. Moreover, the satisfactions sought in this homosexual love play involved chiefly the mouth and the external genitalia. No "male–female" contrast appeared in this relationship; the essential contrast was that of activity and passivity. The impression gained was that the feeling of happiness lay in the possibility of being able to play *both* roles.

The result of her analysis was evident. Everything that had come to the surface so clearly in the analytic transference was now detached from the person of the analyst and transferred to other women. The gratifications denied her in the analytic situation could now be found in the relationship with the new objects. It was evident that the overcoming of her hostility toward the analyst had brought with it the overcoming of her anxiety and, consequently, a positive libidinal relationship to women could appear in place of the anxiety and hostility which had caused the neurotic symptoms—only, of course, after the mother-substitute object had paid off the infantile grievances by granting her sexual satisfactions.

Deutsch goes on to repeat that there were no more depressions, as there had been prior to the analysis, and no more suicide attempts. The woman remained content with her "positive libidinal relationship." In summing up the case Deutsch writes: "The analytic treatment had not brought about the further and more favorable solution of the mother attachment, that is, a renunciation of her homosexuality and an inclination toward men."

It is to be asked, and seriously so, whether it is not solution enough for a depressed, suicidal person, like this Viennese woman, to turn into a vivid, radiant, nonsuicidal being. Today this question *is* seriously asked, and answered in the affirmative by certain psychotherapists who believe that lesbianism is not necessarily antipathetic to mental health. As will be seen, other therapists maintain that an inclination toward men is the only "solution."

CHAPTER FOUR

Post-Freud American Confusion

ALTHOUGH it is popularly believed that the American psychotherapeutic community as a whole considers lesbianism to be
a psychological illness, by no means is this the case. Among
the many different schools of psychotherapy that have sprung
up in this country since Freud, there is no meeting of minds
on the "sickness theory," the belief that lesbianism is a mental disorder and as such needs "curing" ("cure" being a
change to heterosexual ways).

It should be noted that the "curing" of homosexuals is a
peculiarly American preoccupation. In England, the psychotherapeutic community generally rejects the idea. The findings of the famed government-appointed Wolfenden Committee, whose 1957 report led to a legalization of homosexual
acts between consenting adults in England, concluded that
a change in sexual orientation in adults was seldom possible.
In France, where psychotherapy is not as readily acknowledged as it is in the United States, study of homosexuality
is seldom undertaken. Eastern European countries, with
some exceptions, have tended to dismiss psychotherapy as a
bourgeois institution. Third World countries have never been

known to devote much time to "curing" certain of their citizens of their sexual orientations. Only in the United States have people turned in droves to psychotherapists for answers. Why? One of this country's more controversial psychiatrists, Thomas Szasz, sees it this way:

> Our secular society dreads homosexuality in the same way and with the same intensity as the theological societies of our ancestors dreaded heresy. . . . Thus has the physician replaced the priest, and the patient the witch, in the drama of society's perpetual struggle to destroy precisely those human characteristics that, by differentiating men from their fellows, identify persons as individuals rather than as members of the herd.[1]

The division of thinking in the American psychotherapeutic community on the "sickness theory" is clearly expressed by two differing psychiatrists:

Frank S. Caprio: "The vast majority of lesbians are emotionally unstable and neurotic." "Lesbianism is capable of influencing the stability of our social structure." "Our modern attitude should be one of understanding—regarding homosexuality as an illness in the sense that it represents a form of sexual immaturity, a type of existence that carries with it complications and ultimately results in frustration and loneliness."[2]

Harry Benjamin: "Homosexual behavior cannot possibly be interpreted as evidence of a 'psychopathic personality.' Too many homosexuals are well balanced people and too many definite psychopaths are completely heterosexual." "Such a concept belongs in the medical wastebasket, with the errors of the past. To my mind, it ranks with the 'toxicity' of the menstruating woman, or the 'vice' and harmfulness of masturbation."[3]

Most lesbians never enter psychotherapy. Those who do, do so because they are unhappy—at best, a vague term. Such

women are usually depressed, anxious, and in some cases suicidal—factors that have prompted most people in therapy to
seek help. Some lesbians who do enter therapy say they want
to change their sexual orientation; some say they do not, but
they do want professional help with their feelings of unease.
Once the decision to seek help is made a lesbian is faced with
a confusing range of contradictory psychotherapeutic schools
from which to choose. The various schools are too numerous
to be given detailed delineation here; for our purposes it is
sufficient to divide the community into those therapists who
believe that "cure"—a change to heterosexual ways—is ad-
visable and possible, and those who believe that change is not
necessary and frequently not possible. The "curers" feel
that a lesbian's unhappiness stems directly from her sexual
orientation, and thus a lesbian consulting such a therapist
will spend her time concentrating on *changing* her sex life.
The "non-curers" feel that a lesbian's unhappiness stems
from the pressures she must withstand in a society that disapproves of her sexual life, and thus a lesbian consulting such
a therapist will concentrate on ridding herself of guilt feelings and *adapting* to her sex life.

As for the matter of what causes lesbianism, there is no
agreement among psychotherapists. Some of those who believe that lesbianism is a psychological illness generally lay
the cause at the feet of the lesbian's mother or father (the
mother is rejecting, thus the daughter seeks the mother in
other women; the father unconsciously manifests a seductive
attitude toward the daughter, thus the daughter, frightened
of incest, fears all men). There are, of course, many variations on the parental-relationship theme. Other theories that
are held, to name only a few: disappointment by a male; a
refusal to accept woman's traditional societal role; narcissistic
regression—that is, in loving one's own sex one is in reality
loving oneself; and so on. Those therapists who hold that lesbianism is not necessarily a psychological illness don't bother

much with cause; they tend to say that whatever prompts heterosexual behavior also prompts homosexual behavior.

Treatments vary greatly. For example, among the change-is-necessary therapists are the so-called "neo-Freudian" psychoanalysts. Therapy consists of fairly traditional psychoanalysis, delving into the patient's past, into her childhood experiences and family relationships, during a long-term and expensive series of sessions on the couch. Some of these psychoanalysts claim a twenty-five percent cure rate for male homosexuals (there are no statistics for female homosexuals); such cures, they say, take at least three years and often longer. These analysts operate from the premise that only by altering a patient's feelings can behavior be changed.

Other believers in the possibility of cure are the behaviorists. They operate from the premise that behavior is determined not from within but from without, from conditioning, and therefore it is not feelings that need altering but actions. Some behaviorists use the treatment method called "aversion therapy," a short-term treatment that seldom lasts more than six months. Aversion therapy with homosexual patients consists of inducing revulsion or fear in connection with homosexual stimuli. In part, for example, a patient is aroused sexually (through provocative photos of women or some such) and while thus aroused is administered an electric shock or a nausea-producing drug. The theory, obviously, is Pavlovian; after a while, when a lesbian patient digs a woman, she will either fear getting physically shocked or she will be repulsed to the point of throwing up. This same treatment is used on patients who want to stop drinking, smoking, or overeating. Behaviorists claim varying percentage rates of cure. Often it works, they say, often it works temporarily, and sometimes it doesn't work.

Still other therapists who believe in cure are the so-called eclectics. They borrow from various psychotherapeutic schools, a little bit of classic psychoanalysis, a little bit of behavior therapy, a little bit of directed psychotherapy, perhaps some group therapy, all mixed together to form a method of treatment of their own. Claimed rates of cure vary from twenty-five to fifty percent.

All of these therapists (the ones mentioned by no means exhaust the "cure" school) agree that their job is made easier and success is better guaranteed if (1) the patient is highly motivated in her desire to be heterosexual; (2) the patient is young, preferably under thirty; (3) the patient has had some heterosexual experience, or at least interest, in the past. When these therapists are bombarded by homosexual-rights groups who claim that homosexuals are not sick and don't need curing (such groups are particularly vehement regarding aversion therapy, calling it "a form of torture," "brainwashing," "Clockwork Orange!"), the therapists answer that they exist only to aid those homosexuals who come to them for help, those who *want* to change their sexual orientation. Other therapist-advocates of the "sickness theory" point out that the American Psychiatric Association's "Diagnostic & Statistical Manual of Mental Disorders" lists homosexuality as one of the mental disorders; gay rights groups and sympathetic professionals are agitating in an effort to revise this manual.*

The psychotherapists who believe that cure is not necessary and often not possible work from the premise that

---

* In December 1973 (as this book was going to press), the American Psychiatric Association, in a landmark decision, voted to delete homosexuality from its official list of "mental disorders." The Association now officially differentiates between those homosexuals who are content with their homosexuality and demonstrate no impairment in social functioning, and those homosexuals who are distressed by their sexual orientation and do demonstrate some impairment in social functioning. The latter now fall under the Association's category titled "sexual orientation disturbance." The former do not fall under this category. In other words, the APA no longer lists homosexuality per se as a mental disorder, and considers it to be a "sexual orientation disturbance" only for certain homosexuals.

lesbianism is not a psychological illness; they feel that whatever suffering prompts a lesbian to seek therapy stems not from her sexual behavior as such but from the fact that this behavior is socially condemned. Thus, therapy—usually directed talk sessions—concentrates on the removal of societal-imposed guilt feelings and the attendant inner conflict, with a goal of establishing an identity free of fragmentation. Adaptation to one's sexual orientation is the end goal of such therapy, not change. Lawrence LeShan, a psychotherapist typical of a newer breed in the profession, explains his method this way:

> "Curing" the homosexual has never been my goal. What I am interested in is how the individual feels about herself as a person. Does she see herself as lovable, as potentially creative and capable of loving? Is she living the best that is in her —is she glad to be who she is and is she making the most use she can of all her talents and strengths? Both homosexuals and heterosexuals can lead lives of quiet despair and self-destruction—or they can in their love relationships, in whatever form these may take, be expressing a profound sense of self and a capacity to give lovingly to another person.[4]

These therapists seem to speak more of love than of sex and seem to be agreeing with Freud's statement that "we are bound to regard the choice of an object of the same sex as a regular type of offshoot of the capacity to love . . ."[5]

Among psychotherapists, the division of thinking regarding homosexuality leads to an immense amount of professional backbiting, often of bitter proportions. Those who think that cure is possible accuse their opponents of being wild-eyed radicals interested in overthrowing the "system," by which they usually mean the family. At the very least the curers call the others apologists for homosexuality, and at the very most they charge them with being homosexually inclined themselves, with personal axes to grind. Those who don't believe in cure say that the cures claimed by their opponents are phony, that there doesn't exist enough follow-up information to show that the patients stayed cured. Or they say that the patients were not homosexual to begin with. Or they accuse their opponents of being moralists in the guise of scientists, narrow-minded conformists who turn societal disapproval into scientific theory.

Since the psychotherapeutic community disagrees so violently as to whether homosexuality is or is not a sickness, why does the American public insist, in overwhelming numbers, that it is? Disregarding, for the moment, deeply entrenched religious and moral disapproval, it is of importance to note that the majority of popular books and articles on homosexuality (where the public gets its information) written by therapists have been written by those who endorse the sickness theory. Such books are usually based on the study of "a sample" of homosexuals—either the private patients of the author or the patients of a group of therapists who hold the same attitude toward homosexuality as does the author. The findings and theories based on the study of the sample are extended to serve as universal truths about all homosexuals. There is, of course, nothing wrong with a therapist publishing his particular findings. However, a problem arises when such findings are published in a book meant for the general public (a popular book) and not in a book or professional journal meant for the psychotherapeutic community. The specific problem has to do with the marketing of such popular books. Dust-jacket copy usually calls the book "definitive"; advertising copy uses headlines such as, in one case, "Once a Homosexual, Always a Homosexual? No."[6] In turn, such books become news to popular journalists, and in the case of the above book, The New York Times ran a front-page news story that was headlined "More Homosexuals Aided to Become Heterosexual."[7]

Long after the publicity of such a newly published book

dies down, the book continues to be quoted in the media—print or TV—by reporters who are pressed by deadlines and have no time for gathering together all the isolated and contradictory research from specialized fields that is published only in professional journals, non-mass-marketed books, or read as papers at scientific conferences. At the very most, such reporters may run off for a quick "update" interview with the therapist who wrote the original book.

It has been charged that *Time* magazine heavily based its lengthy essay on homosexuality (January 21, 1966) on the views of only one therapist, Edmund Bergler, who endorsed the sickness theory in his book *Homosexuality: Disease or Way of Life*. The charger said that *Time's* essay "warned readers that whatever pity they might have in their hearts for homosexuals they were nevertheless not to let this emotion becloud the realization that they were here face to face with 'a pernicious disease.' "[8] It will be remembered that Bergler is the gentleman who was frightened of a "whisper campaign" as a result of Kinsey's statistics on homosexuality. Bergler called his own personal theory of lesbianism "oral regression"; he believed that lesbians cannot cope with being weaned from the bottle or the breast and therefore run after another woman's clitoris, which they unconsciously identify with the nipple. In so doing, he felt, they wish to be disappointed and are archmasochists, and even those who claim to be happy in their life styles are not, because a clitoris is not a nipple.[9]

Because of the publicity surrounding these popular homosexual books written by therapists the general public gets half a picture of homosexual research—actually, something more like one one-hundredth of the total picture.

Popular magazines and TV interview shows also tend to present a lopsided picture. The very first issue of a popular and serious-looking sex magazine, *Sexual Behavior*, ran an article titled "Lesbian Relationships" which presented the views of one therapist, Harvey E. Kaye, who has studied lesbians. Kaye is a psychoanalyst who believes in cures. His theory is that lesbians suffer from a "close-binding, overly intimate" father and that their lesbianism is "not a conscious and chosen preference. It is a reaction to a crippling inhibition of heterosexual development." Although Kaye, unlike someone like Bergler, did occasionally qualify his statements in the article, a lay reader was not made aware that various schools of thought exist among psychotherapists. Kaye ended his article by addressing lesbians in a manner quite common to articles of this sort: "You only pass this way but once."[10] The article, by using a photograph of an older butch-looking woman and her younger femme-looking lover, perpetuated the lesbian-couple stereotype. Although there are relationships of this sort, the butch–femme phenomenon is by no means representative of all lesbian relationships.

Then there is the example of television's in-house sociologist, David Susskind. Susskind invited to one of his shows a group of lesbians and then proceeded to pronounce them all sick. To a barrage of hisses and guffaws from his guests he sputtered, But how can you ignore the "great body of medical evidence"? Obviously he and his television helpers had gathered together only a small percentage of the available evidence. Susskind is not much better on the subject of male homosexuality. When one of the guests said that gay males were more tolerated than gay females (in itself a statement subject to dispute), Susskind countered with "Well, that's because they perform a function—hairdressing, decorating . . ."[11]

Examples of this sort of media half-information are legion. One nontherapist sex researcher, who worked with the Kinsey team, says that serious researchers look upon the therapists who write popular books and articles as not very professional. He feels that such writings lead to continual misrepresentation of material; the material is too varied, too contradictory, in constant flux, and none of it is near being definitive. He claimed that whenever a new popular book by a therapist appeared, he and his colleagues sat around laughing their heads off. As an example, he referred to a book by a therapist in which the therapist quoted Lady Bird Johnson's reaction to the homosexual scandal revolving around then presidential aide Walter Jenkins. Lady Bird had said that Jenkins' homosexuality was a shame, obviously he was "overworked" at the White House.

This researcher, who made his remarks during a university class on homosexuality but refused to be quoted by name, also had some rather harsh things to say about the conduct of his own colleagues, the nontherapists. He said that in general a career in sex research is looked upon as a strange choice, that people are constantly wondering why such individuals have chosen such a field, are they professional voyeurs? And in the case of those whose specialty is homosexuality, could it be that they themselves are homosexual? In an effort to combat this latter idea, he claimed, some of his colleagues—for the most part white, middle-class, middle-aged males—were constantly defending their choice of occupation, even among themselves. He used as example one man who brought to a conference on transsexuals his wife and introduced her by saying, "Gentlemen, this is not a transsexual, this is my wife." In this context, it is not amiss to point out that many popular sex books on homosexuality written by men are dedicated to "my loving wife, without whom . . ." and so on.

No one is neutral on the subject of sex. When Kinsey tried to assemble a staff of objective researchers for his project, he had a difficult time of it. His colleague Wardell Pomeroy reports that the major stumbling block was that Kinsey wanted interviewers who, although born and raised in this country and exposed to our censoring attitude toward sexuality, would nonetheless never evaluate what others did sexually. An interviewer should "not be prone to moral evaluation, as far as humanly possible, because there were few areas of research where the investigator's own system of morals was so challenged and so crucial as in the study of human sexual behavior." Kinsey turned down one noted sex researcher with these words:

"I don't think you want to work for us."

"But I do," the researcher insisted.

"Well," Kinsey observed, "you have just said that premarital intercourse might lead to later difficulties in marriage, that extramarital relations would break up a marriage, that homosexuality is abnormal and intercourse with animals ludicrous. Apparently you already have all the answers. Why do you want to do research?"[12]

It should be pointed out that most of the popular writing done by psychiatrists, psychologists, or psychoanalysts on the subject of homosexuality has been done from the point of view that considers the male of the species as representative of the species as a whole; thus the material on male homosexuality far outweighs that on female homosexuality. This situation has led to the earlier quoting of Frank S. Caprio as representative of those psychiatrists who endorse the "sickness theory," rather than the quoting of some of the bigger guns in the field who have written popular books endorsing the theory. These men—Irving Bieber, Lawrence J. Hatterer, and Edmund Bergler—limited their books to the male homosexual. At the time of this writing, the *only* mass-marketed book written by a psychiatrist devoted solely to lesbianism was Frank S. Caprio's *Female Homosexuality*. The book was written in 1954 and has been in print ever since; it has been widely read and widely quoted, and for lack of other general books on the subject it has taken on, for the public, something of a definitive appearance. For this reason, we examine it here.

Caprio has written a lot of popular sex books, among

which are titles like *Why Grow Old?*, *Medical Items of Interest*, *Marital Infidelity*, and *The Sexually Adequate Female*. As has been noted, Caprio feels that lesbianism is a sickness "capable of influencing the stability of our social structure." He specifically believes that narcissism is the primary drive behind lesbianism. "Homosexuality is an extension of auto-eroticism (cooperative masturbation)." "The desire for cunnilingus in a woman is a projection of an *unconscious* desire to suck the nipples of her own breasts."[13]

All right. That's an opinion. Caprio does quote the theories of other therapists, but *only* the theories of those who consider, as he does, lesbianism to be a psychological illness in need of curing. The opponent school is not once mentioned. It is as if the controversy in the psychotherapeutic community did not exist.

Here are some statements from the book: "Lesbians are basically unhappy people." "Lesbians seem to hold on to the philosophy that life without love of some kind is meaningless . . ." "[Lesbianism] is contrary to a woman's basic needs. Women unconsciously prefer to fulfill their maternal role and to be loved by a man." ". . . no matter how talented or brilliant some lesbians may be, their emotional life is childish and immature."

Here are some of the adjectives and phrases strewn throughout the book: lesbians are lonely, unhappy, frustrated, insanely jealous, insecure, guilty, unstable, maladjusted, compulsive obsessional neurotics. They are love-starved daughters of cold mothers; they relish seducing and enslaving innocent young girls; they are hypochondriacs; they suffer from nervous breakdowns, alcoholism, suicide tendencies, drug addiction, and dissipation. To all intents, lesbians seem to be very sick individuals indeed.

Caprio's opinions are based on his study of his patients, on information given to him by his fellow therapists, and on information gathered when "I circled the globe with the specific purpose of accumulating scientific information dealing with the prevalence and practices of lesbianism in various parts of the world." His worldwide explorations seem to have centered on interviewing prostitutes, and, "wherever necessary," he "engaged the services of a taxi driver who acted as an interpreter." What this book contains, then, is a lot of data about a limited number of patients and prostitutes. Since, as has been noted, the great majority of lesbians are not patients and are not prostitutes, Caprio's statements, such as "The vast majority of lesbians are emotionally unstable and neurotic," stem from consideration of a very small percentage of women who are lesbian. One is reminded of Ernest van den Haag's much quoted statement: when a colleague said to him, "All my homosexual patients are sick," he replied, "So are all my heterosexual patients."[14]

Caprio, like Krafft-Ebing, includes a number of lesbian case histories in his book. And, like Krafft-Ebing, not only does he present his own cases but he quotes from outside sources. One of Caprio's sources is *Life Romances* magazine.

It's quite impossible to believe that a serious psychiatrist doesn't know how articles in romance magazines are put together. They're piped, of course, pulled out of thin air. But even if, by some highly improbable chance, the doctor didn't know how romance magazines operate, the case we will mention (Caprio uses *two* cases from romance magazines) is so patently ridiculous that he as an "expert" in the field should have at least questioned it. It's a fake, from beginning to end.

The case concerns a young American woman, Joan Alpine, who relates her story in what psychiatrists call an "autobiographical confession." Her case was said to have been given to *Life Romances* from the private files of her psychiatrist, a Dr. J.L.T. Actually, there's no doubt that the thing was written by a hack writer who did a lot of library research. For one thing, the writer read his Krafft-Ebing. Early on in Joan's story she says, "When I was ten, I remember I put a whole folder of matches in milk and drank it, trying to make myself sick enough to get some parental sympathy." By sheer coincidence, in Case No. 154 of *Psychopathia Sexualis* Krafft-Ebing reports the tale of a Mrs. M., a forty-four-year-old lesbian mother of four: "It is noteworthy . . . that one day when ten years of age [Mrs. M.] fancied her mother did not love her. Thereupon she put a lot of sulphur matches in her coffee and drank it to make herself ill, in order to draw her mother's love to herself."[15] Not only did the *Life Romances* writer do his research, he was professional enough to adapt the material for his audience: unlike a European kid, Joan Alpine, an American, would drink milk.

Of equal interest is the fact that Joan, poor thing, suffered from every conceivable thing any medical authority has ever put forth as a theory for what causes lesbianism. The authorities have through the years believed in one or another of the theories, as the writer's library digging showed him, but no authority, ever, has maintained that any one lesbian suffers from all of them. Joan Alpine wins hands down as Super Dyke of all time. She suffered from an unloving mother; a father who wished she had been a boy; jealousy of a beautiful sister; jealousy of a younger brother; fear of childbirth pains; a mother who warned that men were brutal beasts; evil years in a girls' school; desertion by a beautiful girl on whom she had an adolescent crush; seduction by a plain girl (who had, of course, learned her tricks in Paris); a crush on an English teacher (who had graceful hands); years of promiscuity; enslavement by a pure butch type; guilt for her father's fatal heart attack, thinking it was punishment for her sins; abandonment by her mother; more guilt when she read (in a newspaper, of course) of the butch's suicide: "No, no, no!" she gasped; inability to turn to religion for solace. So she turned to books about lesbianism, especially to esoteric volumes not at all readily available to the five-and-ten salesgirl that she was, books like Dr. Magnus Hirschfeld's *Sexual Pathology*. Then at long last she reached her final destination, the office of a psychiatrist: "My future is in your hands,

Doctor. May God forgive my past!" Luckily her doctor also believed in God; he ends his comments on the case with a ringing quote from Genesis: "Joan's mightiest hope is that she is praying to God to turn her feet into the 'way that is straight'—that God will give her a husband she loves and who loves her, to fulfill the Bible's natural edict in Genesis: 'And God created man in His own image, in the image of God created He him; male and female created He them; and God said unto them, Be fruitful and multiply.' "

The awfulness of this fakery is not the fact that publications like *Life Romances* exist; that can be dealt with. What cannot be understood is the fact that an established psychiatrist, who was accepted by the public as an "expert" in this field, chose to reprint in a purportedly serious book a patently untrue case history. Why did he do it? Even more serious is the fact that from 1954 until the time of this writing—almost twenty years—Caprio's work was the *only* in-print popular book by a psychiatrist devoted solely to the subject of female homosexuality.

The book is full of other silly things pawned off as "definitive" findings. One final evidence of the good doctor's expertise: his view on lesbian seduction, something he believes in strongly and goes on and on about. "Many seductions take place in ladies' restrooms, particularly if the lesbian is of the overt masculine type. The aggressive lesbian seeks opportunities to make advances under circumstances that favor a seduction." Ladies' rest rooms favor seduction? Come now, Doctor. Surely this is a projection of the practices of certain male homosexuals, the whole tea-room scene. "Quickies" in toilets have little to do with female sexuality. A woman's rocks are rarely so anonymously gotten off.

It is because of books like Caprio's that some female homosexuals become radicalized overnight. It is even worse for male homosexuals, by the mere fact that they have been more "studied" and more written about. In 1954, a group of

West Coast homosexual men who led stable lives and were successful in their occupations became sick and tired of hearing that they were mentally ill. They approached a Los Angeles psychologist, Evelyn Hooker, and asked her to conduct a scientific investigation into homosexuality, offering themselves as subjects. None of the men had ever sought psychotherapeutic help and all of them felt there was no need to. However, being intelligent and aware citizens, they did not cavalierly dismiss the thought of scientific research into the phenomenon of which they were a part. Hooker, after careful consideration, accepted their proposition.

From this small beginning has grown a vast amount of research and theorizing about the nonpatient male homosexual. No such body of information exists on the female homosexual. Hooker's twenty years of study, with these men and others, have led her to believe that the forms of homosexuality are as various as the forms of heterosexuality and that some homosexuals can lead well-adjusted lives devoid of any pathology. She also suggests that on a psychological level homosexuality is in all probability a "deviation in sexual pattern which is within the normal range."[16]

Her most famous single study, much quoted and somewhat argued about, she conducted in the late fifties. She administered three commonly used psychological tests (including the Rorschach ink blot) to thirty homosexual and thirty heterosexual men of the same age, education, and intelligence. She gave the anonymous results to three judges who were experts in the analyzing of such tests. The judges were unable to say who was homosexual and who was not. But the most surprising finding, even to Hooker herself, was how many of the homosexuals, according to the tests, had what our society considers well-adjusted personalities. In fact, the judges found that two thirds of the homosexual men were average to superior in their adjustment, which tended to show, at least in this particular sample, that some homosexuals fall into the category that is labeled normal.

Hooker has also theorized that some of the characteristics people think peculiar to homosexuals—a preoccupation with their homosexuality, a cutting self-deprecating humor, extreme sensitivity, sometimes self-doubt and self-hatred—are in fact defensive reactions to a hostile society, reactions common to all rejected minority groups. Along these lines, an interesting symposium took place in Israel recently. A group of Israeli and American Jewish intellectuals and community leaders gathered to consider the differences between American Jews, who are a minority group, and Israeli Jews, who are a majority group. It was noted that self-acceptance, self-confidence and perhaps an overdose of chauvinism was evident among Israelis, undoubtedly due to majority status, and was not particularly evident in American Jews.[17] In this context, there's no doubt that many lesbians who move only in lesbian circles do so to buoy their identity in an atmosphere where that identity has majority status.

Starting with only a handful of male subjects, Hooker now has readily at hand several hundred nonpatient homosexual men to call upon for research purposes. Sex researchers around the country sometimes call on her to test out specific theories. One of the lighter moments in sex research (a field that is not rife with light moments) occurred when a group of East Coast researchers discussed the fact that Havelock Ellis's old theory (first put forth by Ulrichs) that male homosexuals could not whistle had never really been tested out. Let's ask Hooker, the researchers said. They called her and she in turn spent a few days on the telephone asking her subjects to whistle. Most of them couldn't. An old theory seemed to be on the way to affirmation. However, when Hooker later asked an equal number of heterosexual men to whistle it was found that they too, for the most part, could not.[18]

Havelock Ellis also mentioned that green seemed to be a favorite color of male homosexuals. A homosexual who read

Ellis's book wrote to him and said he couldn't whistle, his favorite color was green, but he also couldn't spit. Was this significant? As far as is known, America's sex researchers have not tested out the spitting theory.[19]

Hooker has accumulated a vast amount of serious research about the nonpatient male homosexual. She has a long-term grant from the federal government, so presumably her research will continue. There is no comparative work going on with lesbian nonpatients.

Hooker served as chairwoman of the National Institute of Mental Health's Task Force on Homosexuality, whose mandate was "to review carefully the current state of knowledge regarding homosexuality in its mental health aspects and to make recommendations for Institute programming in this area." The task force was composed of fifteen well-known behavioral, medical, social, and legal scientists. Their final report was issued in 1969. It concluded, among many other things, that:

> Homosexual individuals vary widely in terms of their emotional and social adjustments. Some persons who engage in homosexual behavior function well in everyday life; others are severely maladjusted or disturbed in their functioning. There are those whose total life is dominated by homosexual impulses and those whose sexual behavior is just one component in their total life experience.[20]

In answer to those who say that there are no happy homosexuals, Hooker has said, "Chances of being unhappy in our society are very great. I am convinced that homosexuality and unhappiness do not invariably go together."[21]

Hooker's work, of course, has been challenged by the therapists who believe in the sickness theory. It is to be noted that nowhere does Hooker say that *all* homosexuals are well-adjusted personalities, whereas her opponents tend to assume that all homosexuals are ipso facto maladjusted individuals.

It is also to be noted that Hooker has *not* written a popular book based on her work.

While it has been possible, in a book of this sort, to present no more than an overview survey of the many and contradictory present-day psychological theories and treatments of lesbianism, it is quite impossible, without oversimplifying, to summarize the many and contradictory researches into homosexuality that are being conducted by scientists in specialized laboratories; these scientists—be they endocrinologists, geneticists, or animal behaviorists—work within narrowly confined, highly technical disciplines. Their findings constitute important, although partial and self-admittedly tentative, theories in the total picture of homosexual research. Some of the more fascinating research into homosexuality going on today is being conducted by those endocrinologists who are investigating the distribution of the female and male sex hormones within individuals (females and males) and the effect that distribution has on sexual behavior.

In several recent tests adult female homosexuals were found to have, in their blood and urine samples, higher levels of male sex hormones than did a like number of adult heterosexual women tested. There was no evidence to determine whether the lesbians tested were born with this hormonal "imbalance" or whether it had developed as a result of their homosexual behavior.

These studies are extremely tentative, and investigators urge extreme caution, pending further confirmation. Most of the investigators do admit that they are working on the hypothesis that homosexuality may be caused by the biochemical makeup of an individual, but the hypothesis is, at the moment, just that, an hypothesis.

This testing of adult homosexuals has stemmed from established research that has shown the important role the sex hormones play in prenatal life. Briefly, during fetal development male and female sex hormones (chemical substances) are present. The amounts in which the types are present determine what sort of sex organs the fetus will develop—i.e., whether a genital male or a genital female will eventually be born, or indeed an individual with both sets of sex organs, an hermaphrodite. Also of revelance to those investigating adult homosexuals are the many animal studies that show that the amounts in which the male and female sex hormones appear at this time in animals not only affect the eventual sex differentiation but also affect the central nervous system, specifically the developing brain tissues which in later life will determine whether sexual behavior will be what we call masculine or feminine. In other words, there is evidence, but based only on animal studies, that the amounts in which male and female sex hormones are present during prenatal development "program" the brain for later sexual behavior. An overdose of male hormones administered to a pregnant female guinea pig, for example, will cause the female offspring to express male behavior—i.e., they will mount other females. The same test, with the same results, has been conducted on monkeys.

These animal studies and their potential application to human beings play havoc with all the research (e.g., Harlow's monkey studies, discussed in Chapter One) that has pointed to sexual behavior as a result of conditioning, of the influence of environmental factors, rather than as a result of something that is inborn, a result of hormonal or chromosomal makeup (the nurture-versus-nature question). John Money and a number of different colleagues at Johns Hopkins University Medical School have spent many years studying just this question.

Money's early studies of hermaphrodites led him to the conclusion that sexual behavior is learned, a result of rearing. Hermaphrodites tended to take on either feminine or masculine behavior according to whether they were raised as girls or boys. Later studies have led him to alter this theory. One of his more famous studies concerned a group of girls who in their mother's wombs had accidentally been the recipients of an overdose of male hormones. The girls were born with enlarged clitorises, and as they grew up their behavior was aggressive, behavior we label tomboy. Other studies of individuals "masculinized" in the womb have shown the same results. At the moment Money feels that sexual behavior is determined from both cultural *and* prenatal hormonal distribution factors. His work has shown him the intersexual possibilities of humans, and, rather than labeling behavior masculine or feminine *per se*, he postulates that since individuals are made up of many different mixes of male and female hormones their behavior is simply one degree or another of what is culturally considered normal femininity or normal masculinity.[22]

The repercussions of the animal studies, of Money's work, and the recent endocrinological testing of adult homosexuals, clearly are mind-boggling. If further studies should confirm that there is indeed a universal hormonal "imbalance" in adult homosexuals and if yet further study should show that the "imbalance" is not a result of homosexual behavior but is established during prenatal development, well, the psychotherapeutic community, for one, will have to pack up its theories and leave them for the historians to footnote. Krafft-Ebing and Havelock Ellis, who felt that homosexuality was inborn (though their theories were not based on hormonal studies), and even Freud, who hinted that the biochemists might hold some answers, might be proven to have been on the right track after all.

However, this is all simply intriguing speculation. As one of the endocrinologists working in the field has said, "The major importance of our finding is that it reopens the door. We don't yet know the underlying causes of homosexuality, but we must not close our minds to the possibility of a biochemical explanation."[23]

If, at this point, there are any lay readers who are *not* con-

POST-FREUD AMERICAN CONFUSION

fused by the many contradictions that exist in the scientific community in regard to lesbianism, it would seem that they are holding on to preconceived notions. Are all homosexuals simply immature, as some psychoanalysts have it? Are others mature, well-adjusted individuals, as Hooker and other professionals have it? Is a woman lesbian because of her hormonal makeup? Did the lesbian who lives down the street have a rejecting mother? Did her father figuratively seduce her? Is she simply rejecting the female role as it exists in a sexist society? Is she simply narcissistic, as Caprio has determined, loving other women as an image of herself? Is she simply a nonconformist, as Szasz and R. D. Laing would have it—shunned by a moralistic society? Is she a vivid, radiant human being living to her full capacity, but could she be even more vivid and radiant if she switched to men, as Deutsch suggested? Is she a neurotic mess because she digs women? Is she a neurotic mess because society treats her like a freak? Is she just one variety in the vast number of complexities human beings come in? Is she just a commonplace human being who deserves neither honor nor abuse? Or is her life capable of undermining our American way of life?

Pick a number. No matter your choice, you'll find "scientific" support to back your conclusion. The psychotherapists and researchers have by no means solved the "problem" of homosexuality. What science has shown is that an individual's sexuality can fall anywhere between the polarities of what *society* considers masculine or feminine behavior. *Why* it falls in one particular place is still, as one of the greatest therapists, Freud, maintained, a "mystery."

Despite all of the various researches into homosexuality that have had as a goal a definitive explanation of the phenomenon, a final statement has proved elusive. Sex researchers of various schools—who agree on very little—handle this problem with a universal call for yet more research, es-

pecially into female homosexuality. Those researchers who
are not narrowly boxed into dogmatic theory tend to agree
that a major difficulty in conducting more research is the
fact that sampling methods are sorely deficient. The National Institute of Mental Health's Task Force on Homosexuality suggested in its final report the establishment of a
Center for the Study of Sexual Behavior that would bring
all current information from all disciplines into one broad
evaluation center. As one of its goals toward further research
it was suggested that the center develop "better sampling
methods to cover the total range of homosexual phenomena.
This range should include homosexual individuals who do
not come into contact with medical, legal or other social control or treatment sources and who therefore have been least
studied."[24] The Institute for Sex Research at Indiana University, at the time of this writing engaged in several major
homosexual studies on nonpatients, agrees. The Institute's
head, Paul Gebhard, has said, "We [miss] those who can't
afford to be seen in homosexual gathering places or who have
stable relationships. I think that having a circle of homosexual friends and entertaining at home is probably the most
common social pattern."[25] Although the goal to reach those
homosexuals who are "least studied" is a logical one, it would
seem to be far from realistic. Invisible homosexuals are difficult to reach. Unless there is a change in the social climate
to make "coming out" more desirable, it is likely that further
research into homosexuality will not yield what the researchers are after; at the very most what we will have is yet
more research about special visible groups of homosexuals.
The vast majority will remain unstudied, untabulated, living
lives circumscribed by the monumental collective legacy of
negativism with which each, in her or his own individual
way, must deal. The interview that follows shows how one
young woman, unstudied, untabulated, has, as she puts it,
"come to terms" with her lesbianism.

INTERVIEW 2

THE WOMAN interviewed here is in her early thirties. She teaches at a state university; her field is archeology. Like the woman interviewed at the beginning of this book, she has chosen to hide her lesbianism. However, unlike the first woman interviewed, who discovered her lesbianism years before the advent of the gay liberation movement, this young woman discovered hers during the height of the movement. The two women are—what? Lovers? Friends? Companions? Partners? Mates? Although all these words apply to their relationship, no one of them accurately pinpoints their total relationship. Our language is bereft of a word to describe women who are sharing and building a life together, one fact among so many others that attests to how deep is the nonrecognition status of lesbians in our society.

How did you meet the woman you're living with?
I seduced her. You're surprised because she's older and more experienced at these things? I invited her to dinner, we talked about politics, and eventually I took her to bed—or made her take me to bed.

And it's been happily ever after ever since?
Yes.
Am I right in thinking that this is all very new to you?
Yes and no. I've never lived with a woman before, but I've had one other affair with a woman, a lesbian, who's a pretty well-known actress; she's a big blowzy sex symbol. We used to laugh about that a lot. I was with her only a few months. A very intense relationship. My present relationship started three years ago. But for the most part my affairs have been with men. Short-term except for one—many frenzied short affairs.
Would you consider yourself bisexual?
It's impossible to be bisexual unless you're having a lot of meaningless one-night stands—because if you're involved with someone you're being either hetero- or homosexual at that particular time. Right now I'm lesbian. I'm willing to make, in fact I have made, a commitment of some years. It's a strong commitment. Nevertheless there are distinct questions. That is, I am not sure that I couldn't under the right circumstances have a serious heterosexual relationship. I mean if my current relationship ended, I *might* be open to men again. My fantasies still sometimes involve men. I've never had any very satisfactory sex with men. But now that I've found my sexuality—and I owe this to my two female lovers—I think, just possibly, I could have good sex with men; emotional rapport I'm not at all sure about. Perhaps some people would consider this bisexuality. Right now, though, my sex life and my emotional life are totally lesbian.
How open are you about this lesbianism?
Not very, although I see a line of greater honesty emerging. My close friends, of course, know—perhaps that's a definition of "close friend." My family does not know, and I can't imagine telling them.
Are you content about this?
Well, about a year ago a gay male friend and I discussed

the possibility of marrying—as a cover for our families and our professional lives. Ultimately we decided it wasn't necessary, since no one is getting married these days anyway. It does bother me that my family can't know that my lover is my lover. We've always been a close family; now I have to be vague with them. As my ego gets stronger, I may make my true life more apparent. It's been difficult for me to accept my lesbianism; I never wanted to be a lesbian; it's really only in the last couple of years that I've come to terms with myself about it.

How did you come to terms?

Well, it happened sometime between my affair with the Sex Symbol and my present one. When I was growing up I was terribly concerned about being in the mainstream. You know, I really wanted to be a golden girl. All right, I wasn't a blonde, so I couldn't literally be a golden girl, but I could have a successful husband, a slim waistline—and a career. In that order. I bought the whole thing: a career without a husband was unthinkable. I remember, the first time I was in graduate school so many of my female friends were incredibly torn—they were into medieval history, or some such, and at the same time into all that earth-mother stuff. To compensate. To say, Look, we're still women. We cooked a lot and served everything in earthenware bowls—do you know what I mean? Those of my friends who decided to have children all went the natural-childbirth way. Somehow very Mary McCarthy, isn't it? And yet we were much younger than The Group. We were terribly torn. Those who said, Fuck it, my work's important, it doesn't make me less a woman, were the weirdies. Half-women. I remember, at the tea to welcome graduate students the head of the department said—and he spoke so politely that no one got aggressively angry, only faces flushed, consciousnesses had not yet been raised—he said, "I notice that there are a number of women here. I might as well tell you right now that you're here under great odds; you had to be exceptional to be admitted at all. We don't take many women. It's not that we have anything against women, but what we're trying to do here is graduate professional scholars and we've found that women tend to marry without finishing." What he meant, of course, was that he'd rather not have us there at all since he was in the business of graduating professional scholars, not of sheltering prospective wives—implying that it was fine that our goals were to become wives, not scholars, but he'd rather we did it elsewhere. I stuck to it, but with one eye focused on that savior, that successful man.

And it's no longer focused thus?

No. I thought I wanted a Harvard husband, but I really wanted to find the Aphrodite head—or another Troy.

Have you?

Well, Professor Love* found Aphrodite first. I still hope to do something comparable.

And you feel a husband and children would be in the way?

For me, yes. I'd have trouble playing second fiddle to a man and then changing my head to be conductor of a serious project. It's a question of taking yourself—and your work—seriously.

When did you realize you might be lesbian?

After my affair with the Sex Symbol my sexuality was very much alive, totally awakened. During the beginning of that affair, and after, I went back to sleeping with a lot of men, trying desperately to be attracted to men. I hated the *thought* of being a lesbian, not the *reality* of it. I was very confused. That golden-girl stuff creeping in again. But I found sex with men fruitless and I finally abandoned it. I felt I was quite probably lesbian. But. But where do you find lesbians? I had met my first female lover socially. We didn't

---

* A reference to American archeologist Iris Love who, in 1970, found Praxiteles' long-missing marble bust of Aphrodite of Cnidus (350 B.C.) moldering away in the basement of the British Museum.

hang around gay bars or anything like that. It was very much one to one. Anyway, I was sitting around wondering how I would ever get into the scene, and one night I tuned into the middle of a radio program of women talking about the women's movement. The conversation turned to lesbianism—as it always did in those discussions—and one after another of the women said, Well, I'm a lesbian, I'm a lesbian, I'm a lesbian. And they gave a few phone numbers to call if you wanted to join their new women's liberation group. Well, I immediately called, not unaware of the humor of the situation, and was told to go to a consciousness-raising group in my area. Two of the women who had been on the radio show came to the group, and sure enough they were dykes—one has since become rather famous—but they came just to that one meeting. All the other women in the group were new, confused, scared. About a lot of things. Actually the group is a fabled one; it was written up in *The New Yorker* as the most disastrous consciousness-raising group on record. If any of the women were lesbian they were terribly much in the closet. And I wasn't about to reveal myself when all the conversations were how do you act on dates with men.

Do you mean you went to a women's meeting specifically to find lesbians?

Yes. A good lesbian is hard to find.

And did you find any?

Some. But by the time I got seriously involved in the movement itself I had already met my lover—*not* at a women's meeting.

How involved did you get in the movement?

I sort of led one foray that caused a stir and did succeed somewhat in its aims. I say "sort of led" because the group I was with frowned on "leaders." But in fact I found myself taking over and plunging through. If I hadn't, it would have fizzled. I'm no longer active, but I do support most of the aims. I guess I'm a fellow traveler in a sense. I find the projects take an interminable amount of time and usually for very little good. You're constantly dealing with a vast cross section of people, and I guess I just don't like cross sections. But time is really the factor. And the movement is sometimes more strident than is politically wise—and it's sometimes oppressive to lesbians. There's still a tremendous fear that most women have about being labeled lesbian. I do think a natural outgrowth of women's liberation will be more widespread lesbianism. Not that straight women will be converted, but women who have always felt lesbian feelings won't be so frightened of acting on them.

Are you involved in the gay liberation movement?
No.
How do you feel about this movement?
Well . . . the way I feel about not having been active in the peace movement. I feel guilty. I feel that I'm being a good German. I feel I should be active in political dissent, I feel I should be doing something about the Jews in Russia. The same with the gay movement. But I really feel that to be effective I'd have to learn a great deal about social organizing. So much of what goes on is wasted effort, and to be really committed is a full-time job. It's not beating your head against a brick wall, because the wall has given in some instances, but it's like—oh, it's like batting your head against the Great Wall of China. You make a little hole and you still have that whole damn wall.

Are you concerned about what straight men and women think of lesbians?
I really don't give a damn what uninformed people think. Well, maybe that's not true—since I've been gay I've noticed that nice liberal people make an awful lot of anti-homosexual jokes. I went to visit my family recently, and they—if I were paranoid—they kept making all sorts of gay jokes. Until I became a closet homosexual I really had no idea how ridiculed homosexuals were—and the jokes are so stupidly standard-

ized. I saw a play the other night, about a stand-up comedian, and the comedian was into a thing about how most homosexual jokes are made about male homosexuals and very few are made about lesbians. Why? he asked. Because the lesbians would beat you up, that's why. The audience roared. It's all so programmed.

How do you relate to homosexual men?

I feel comfortable with them. When I was straight I used to think of homosexual men as a great waste. A waste of male flesh. And I used to get upset at those who were overtly homosexual; by "overtly" I don't mean that they held hands in public, but they had certain mannerisms that I was raised to think were unmanly.

What about butch-type women?

I'm not interested in a man *manqué*—in being one or knowing any. I'm not into lesbianism because I like men.

How do you relate to heterosexual men?

These days I'm relating to them in an entirely different way—unafraid, unfrazzled. Perhaps this is typically lesbian—I'm not sure. Since being satisfied that I'm a lesbian or at least that I'm involved happily in a long-term lesbian relationship, I've not slept with any men, nor have I been seriously attracted to any. Although—let me backtrack—I did have a one-week stand at the very beginning of this affair. As an antidote, I suppose; to make certain. Men are beginning to play an ever less important role in my life. I always notice some condescension even when they are trying to be pleasant and especially when they are trying to flirt. Actually, my attitude toward men has changed drastically. Previously, even men who didn't interest me got careful ego-building treatment. If anything, I'm more honest with men now. The feeling that they'd reject me for the slightest independent thought is gone. And good riddance. The amount of energy I've spent on being sexy and coy and dishonest! It's strange, the more independent I act with men now—I say whatever the hell I please because I'm not in any way dependent on them—the more charming they seem to find me. These days it seems that an awful lot of straight men are afraid of dependent women, and I seem very independent; thus the attraction.

Do you feel superior to heterosexual women?

No. But I do feel superior to my former self. Because I'm having a fulfilling relationship. And I wouldn't rather have it with a man. I do think the relationships of most heterosexual women are at their own expense.

Have you any thoughts about role playing in lesbian relationships?

At the beginning of a relationship one person may be more knowledgeable or otherwise more dominant. As a relationship continues, it's my experience that "power" equalizes and, ideally, it becomes a relationship of equals. I think this is all but impossible in a heterosexual relationship—the equalization.

When you were straight, what did you think of homosexuality?

To go way back, when I was seventeen we used to discuss that everyone had homosexual tendencies, that it was just a matter of acting on them. A new college friend was visiting me and she told me that she was bisexual. I was in fact shocked and immediately said, "Well, I'm *not*." Actually I wasn't anything at the time. Presexual, really. Later, when we were seniors we discussed her lesbianism, which was very active. We didn't discuss my presexuality, which was still with me. I was definitely frigid—that's the only way you could say it, I mean with my clothes on. At one point my friend more or less suggested that we have an affair, and I said, "I don't really need any more problems." That really was my objection, that I had so many problems with growing up, I didn't need yet another. I didn't see why I should open up the avenue to being a homosexual in a society that frowned on it. I didn't have any moral antipathy. I later developed various antipathies, but at that time I didn't know enough about sexuality to have any prejudices.

Would you say that at that point you considered homosexuality an aberration, not in the mainstream of society?

Definitely not in the mainstream. An aberration I won't say. Perhaps I thought of it as that, but it wasn't a thing that bothered me. It was mainly that I still wanted to be that golden girl.

Does this friend you mentioned know about your lesbianism?

Yes. When I wrote to her she had an I-told-you-so attitude which was rightful actually. Our friendship had been terribly entangled. At one point we were with the same man. It had more to do with our relationship than with the man. In this same letter she said she still digs men—sometimes. But her long-term relationships have been with women. She'd say her primary orientation is lesbian. She likes sex, she has a lot of experience with it and she doesn't want to limit herself. I remember, when we were nineteen she was having an affair with a girl of seventeen. I felt the girl was emotionally mixed up in a lot of ways and that my friend was taking advantage of her. You know, perverting her from the straight and narrow, or at least giving her more problems than she could handle—no, I think the first is exactly what I mean. Because here was this impressionable young girl . . . Funny, isn't it?

What did you mean when you said your friendship had been terribly entangled?

That was in graduate school. I was twenty-one and she was leaving for the summer. She introduced me to this man she had had an affair with several months earlier. Their affair was over, they were still friends, and we were supposed to get together for the summer, he and I. And, well, we did. I guess mainly on my part because it was just before my twenty-second birthday and I was a virgin and I was determined not to become twenty-two and still be unlaid. I really didn't like the man very much, in fact I couldn't relate to him in any very good way. But we both sort of felt programmed by her, we felt it was very necessary. I had terrible guilt feelings—not about the sex but about having an affair with this man who was my friend's, although she had absolutely said that he wasn't. It was strange. Tremendous guilt. I insisted that he not tell her we were seeing each other. And things like that.

What was the relationship with this man like?

There was no emotional rapport whatsoever. It was only once when we were high on grass that I had any insight into his emotional makeup at all. And now I think that was an incorrect insight. The sex was very pleasant, he was very skilled, and I always thought of him as a technician. There was never any orgasm, but everything else was very pleasant. And he tried very consciously to make it so. I was usually drunk. Now, why I was drunk I don't know. Anyway, there we were at one point at a sort of nadir in my comprehension of my life—my girl friend, this man, and I, on a bed, he mostly caressing me. And I felt my friend was very left out, so I kissed her cheek. I don't know how self-deluded I was, but at the time I thought how alone she was in that situation and it was a very friendly, certainly a very childlike kiss. On the cheek. And she reacted to it as if it were something more. But I backed off. The next day she and I talked after he had gone. She was presuming on that innocent kiss—as it was, I think. She was presuming that it meant that we were to have some sort of deep close relationship, perhaps of a sexual nature, much more than I was prepared for at the time. I was frightened and I threw her out and I did it very nastily and I wasn't angry when I did it. I purposely tried to be cruel so she wouldn't come back, but she did come back and I threw her out again. I think that this violence of mine and her reaction to it might well have meant that there was some underlying sexual feeling that I still can't say for sure was there. After that I became militantly heterosexual.

Have you ever had a fulfilling relationship with a man?

Once. We almost married. And yet I remember he kept saying that one day he'd come and I wouldn't be there; I'd have run off to Mérida or somewhere. I had no idea where Mérida was and I don't know why he felt that, because I didn't feel like running off at all. But I was jumpy in the relationship and I suppose he sensed it. I kept thinking of the future; was he that successful man I'd always dreamed of? He was about to go off to England to teach, and I was prepared to go with him. But then he decided to go and teach in a small college in the Middle West; this was very popular then—coming from a major university, you would throw that up and go off to some small semirural community to teach. I would say that within a week of his decision I broke off the relationship.

When did the actress come along?

Long after this man I've just told you about. After about two years of idiocy—sleeping around, retreating into a shell, frenzy. Innumerable one-night stands, two-week stands. A mess.

How long did this affair last?.

Only a few months. But terribly intense. It was the first time I was into a relationship in the present. I totally abandoned myself to it. That really was the greatest service that relationship did for me. I was able to get into it and stay there as it was happening instead of sitting off to the side wondering if it would last—if she were "husband material." She had a lot of guilts about it being my first such affair. Actually, much of the affair had to do with my getting over her —she was involved with another woman. Whereas my present relationship has to do with building. There was a tremendous emotional tie to this first lesbian affair, but it began with a sexual attraction. She was gorgeous, sexy—fantastic.

I became very dependent on her, more than I ever had on anyone else. She was so different from me. She was fast and loose and a boozer. Still, she saw there was a great need and she tended it.

You say she was involved with another woman. If she had not been, would you have wanted to try for a lasting relationship—as you say, a "building" one?

I can't answer that question because I never had the chance to consider it. Her other lover was living with someone else whom she'd lived with for years and years and felt certain obligations to. Part of the Sex Symbol's liking for me was that she wanted to feel as strong with me as her other lover felt with her—I think. There was tremendous approach/avoidance on her part. On the one hand she wanted to use me and on the other hand she didn't want to hurt me and on the other hand she wanted to see me and on the third or fourth hand she thought she shouldn't. It was complicated, strange—yet good. Incidentally, a few years later she left the other woman and now lives with someone else—who looks like me.

You said earlier that your sexuality was totally awakened after this first lesbian affair. What do you mean?

Well, I had orgasm number one, two, three, four, five . . . Then I tried to match that with men, at the beginning of this affair and after, and I *faked* orgasm number 501, 502 . . . It's not simply that I'm more honest with my female lovers or that their egos are stronger—I *tried* to fake an orgasm with my first woman, you know, it's all I knew to do, and she *knew*, something no man ever had. She had done it herself with men. I remember she smiled, hugged me and said, "There's no need for that, that's not what it's all about, relax." And I did. And my second female lover always knows what I feel or what I want—not just sexually—even if I try to dissemble.

Would you say that you've accepted your lesbianism and are happy about it?

Who's totally happy? I am happier than I've ever been, however. My work is going very well; I've just begun teaching and I'm learning that my work can be as important as a lover's—something no man I've known could accept. I'm working better because of the encouragement and example of my lover, who is her own woman. In this relationship I've been transformed into someone who lives in the present and plans for the future but isn't full of anxiety about whether that future will be as envisioned. I know it's quite possible that this relationship could come to an end as do most relationships, but there's no reason to think that it could happen soon, or even for a lot of years. The life that we foresee in the next years looks to be exciting and fulfilling—and it's something I would never have had the courage to undertake alone. Nor am I just hanging on to some man's coattail to share the excitement vicariously. Oddly enough, it's a fulfillment of all those dreams I had when I was sixteen and thought anything was possible—before I started thinking in terms of putting my husband's needs before my own—even though I thought I could work surrounded by kids and wifely duties. Thinking, incidentally, as one is programmed to think.

I take it you don't want children.

I did until just a few months ago. Now I have one, a fantasy child, who is quite fulfilling. Her name is Atalanta, she's three years old and she's a biochemist. She's won a Nobel Prize. She still goes to school, though she spends most of her time in her lab. She appears whenever there's a need for her. She also disappears whenever she's in the way. Goes to visit Grandma. Very handy. But to be serious. Well, actually, it *is* serious. I do feel at this moment the fantasy has largely fulfilled the urge to have a child, which was quite strong not too long ago. Perhaps in the future. I really can't say; and I may not bear the child myself. For the moment the fantasy is fulfilling in itself. Can't you just hear the shrinks?

I suppose your lover knows of this fantasy?

Sure. We have a great time with the child. Although my

lover isn't particularly overjoyed by the fact that Atalanta's a biochemist. She's recently gotten her interested in poetry.

I see.

Do you? Understand, we *know* she's a fantasy. The irony is half of the fun. You must meet her sometime.

You know, of course, that there are those who would come down very hard on you for such a fantasy.

Of course. But it's *my* life, isn't it? And it's a joke, of course. You know that business about anything is possible? A few years ago I had a failure of nerve. It was during the second period when I was sleeping around with anyone. I was tired, I wanted to get out of the fight. I wanted to get out so I wouldn't have to fight, wouldn't have to choose, wouldn't have to decide things for myself. I was tired and frightened and thought I wanted some man to do the thinking and deciding. It's hard to take on the world alone, especially if for years, as a woman, you've been told left and right that it's somehow not "nice." But on some level I just couldn't accept the stereotype. Some shrinks would say, Fantasy, fantasy, anything is *not* possible, it's adolescent. They're wrong, of course—very wrong. And there's a new school of psychology that would agree with me. But the point I'm trying to make is that as a lesbian I have to take responsibility for my own life. As does my lover for hers. We sink or swim together, and yet separately. I have enormous faith that I can continue to run my life in concert with hers—and I no longer can conceive of taking a secondary position in a relationship.

Does this mean that a future relationship with a man is not possible?

It would be possible, I suppose, with a man who accepted a woman as equal. The women's movement is spawning some surface equality, but it will take a long time before total equality is taken for granted. Until then, half a relationship is just not enough.

All this seems to point to the fact that you're a lesbian be-

cause of unsuccessful relationships with men. I take it, then, that you don't think you were born a lesbian.

I don't know enough about biochemistry to answer that. You might ask Atalanta. A lot of people do say that women become lesbians because they can't catch a man. I'd say I couldn't find a man worth catching. I'm lesbian partly because of unsatisfying sexual and emotional relationships with men and partly because of the reinforcement of warm emotional and sexual relationships I've had with two women. Two very different women.

Part II

HISTORIC WITNESSES

Look for a long time at what pleases you,
and longer still at what pains you.

—COLETTE

CHAPTER FIVE

Sappho and the Lesbian Ghetto

SAPPHO of Lesbos, the ancient Greek poet, once ventured a prediction; she wrote:

> I have no complaint
>
> Prosperity that
> the golden Muses
> gave me was no
> delusion: dead I
> won't be forgotten.[1]

What she meant, of course, was that she would be remembered as a poet, as the masterly lyricist that she was. As it has turned out, however, it is not primarily as a poet that Sappho is remembered, but as a lover of women, such a famous lover of women that her name, in the form of "sapphist," and her island, in the form of "lesbian," have come to be generic terms. No one in Sappho's day, least of all herself, had reason to predict such an outcome: the lesbian ghetto as we know it had not yet come into being. In Sappho's day, a Lesbian was, simply, a resident of the island of Lesbos—female or male. The ghetto would begin some six hundred years after Sappho's death. She would be relegated to it as a charter member, designated to act as its high priestess, her splendid reputation to suffer mighty vicissitudes through the centuries, her name, once cheered, to be laughed at, leered at, sneered at, and worse.

The slide in Sappho's reputation had nothing to do with the quality of her poems—no one has ever questioned their literary worth. Her extant oeuvre, small and fragmented as it is, constitutes one of the masterpieces of man/womankind. Rather, the slide had to do with the manner in which the general attitude toward lesbianism changed from acceptance in her day to ridicule later, and finally, with the official recognition of Christianity in the Eastern Roman Empire, to censure. It also had to do with the fact that she was a woman.

In Sappho's day (c. 612–558 B.C.) her poems were known and sung throughout the Greek world. No woman of the time was more celebrated. Coins were minted in her honor, statues erected in tribute. She was pretty much a household word, with no opprobrium attached; when she died she was given a noble burial. A century or so after her death she still had her champions, the likes of Socrates and Plato. Socrates called her "lovely," in the sense of having a lovely soul, not a pretty face, and placed her among the "wise men and women of old."[2] Plato wrote: "Some say the Muses are nine, but how carelessly! Look at the tenth, Sappho from Lesbos."[3] But by the time of Aristotle (384–322 B.C.) things had begun to change. Aristotle wrote, quoting the philosopher Alcidamus: "The Mytilenaeans honored Sappho—although she was a woman."[4]

". . . although she was a woman." Women didn't count for much in Aristotle's day. They fell into three categories, and their duties, according to Demosthenes, were simply to exist for men: "Hetaerae [courtesans] we keep for the sake of pleasure; concubines (i.e., female slaves) for the daily care of our persons; wives, to bear us legitimate children and to be the trusted guardians of our households.'"[5] The place of wives was in the home; deprived of education, they participated not at all in the period we recognize as the great flowering of Greek civilization, except, of course, to bear the offspring of the flowerers. In fourth-century Athens women had no say in politics, they were minors in court, they could own no property, their marriages were arranged.

In contrast, two centuries earlier, during Sappho's time, Asian Greek women of the aristocracy had all of the freedoms denied their later Athenian sisters. This was especially true on Lesbos, the island in the Aegean Sea hard by the coast of Turkey, where Sappho was born. The island's main town, Mytilene, was a vigorous and prosperous community where the arts flourished. In broad surveys of Greek history the cultural flowering of Lesbos and other Asian Greek settlements, in reality a small renaissance, is seldom detailed, in logical deference to the importance of the later Athenian age. But a flowering there certainly had been. And Sappho was at the center of it. Women of the day were free to be educated in the same manner as their brothers, they were free to participate in politics, they could own property and conduct legal business, they were not bound solely to domestic duties, they were free to love whomever they pleased—really an immense amount of social freedom that allowed them to participate actively, if they so chose, in the flowering of the times. Sappho and a surprising number of other women poets of the late sixth century—for example Myrtis, who was an important influence on the early work of Pindar, a fellow Theban—so chose.

Sappho has often been portrayed (even by today's lesbian activists)[6] as a rebellious feminist who screamed out at the strictures that circumscribed the lives of Greek women. Clearly this was not so. There was no need to scream out in her day, for there were no strictures at which to scream. Had Sappho lived some two centuries later, in Athens, it is doubtful that we ever would have heard of her; her social position, that of an aristocrat, would have forced her into the category of wife—and into silence. We have only to note that the most famous woman of fourth-century Athens was not an independent artist, but an appendage: Phryne, the sculptor Praxiteles' favorite model, and whore. Even a century earlier the most famous woman in Athens was another appendage: the legendary Aspasia (whose name means Welcome!), mistress to the statesman Pericles. Aspasia, although essentially an appendage, was no dummy. It is said that Socrates liked to talk to her; she never would have caught his ear had she been a wife. As her famous lover is said to have said at the time: "The best reputation a woman can have is not to be spoken of among men either for good or evil."[7] From a feminist viewpoint, being the most intelligent and sought-after of *pleasure-givers*, as was Aspasia in her time, does not a whole woman make. An appendage is an appendage is a whore. Whatever status Aspasia had in Athenian society derived from the fact that she had caught the most famous man of the times, certainly an avenue trod by womankind down the ages. A few years ago, an American critic took the poet H.D. to task for writing about independent Greek heroines, real and mythological, Sappho among them, who felt that men were dangerous to love. In commenting on H.D.'s choice of Greek women, the critic asked: "Where are the faithful wives and loving sweethearts who abound in classical history and mythology? Where is Aspasia, who subordinated her genius to that of her lover Pericles?"[8] The key words here, of course, are *"subordinated her genius."**

How to deal with Sappho in Aristotle's day? Her poems

---

* It should be noted that some scholars of Greek culture have argued that Athenian wives did not have such a bad time of it, since in one matter they reigned supreme: the running of a household. That these women were uneducated, unable to vote, and without legal rights, these scholars consider minor matters.

were still very much sung, but she simply did not fit into any of Demosthenes' categories of women. She hadn't been a wife. She hadn't been a slave. That left only courtesans, and accordingly, without facts, the Athenian comic poets, those who wrote what we call Middle Comedy, treated Sappho as a joke in their plays, portraying her as a prostitute, something she had never been. This was the first of the myths about Sappho, one that would stick for centuries. Natalie Clifford Barney, who loved to write aphorisms, once wrote: "Greek women had to become courtesans in order to be listened to."[9] As did Sappho, posthumously.

Sappho's lesbianism was not a factor in the ridicule heaped upon her by the Athenian comic poets in the fourth century B.C. Her free-wheeling, nondomestic, nonappendage life, and the fact that she had spoken openly of this life, set her enough apart from the silenced Athenian women—that is, enough apart from the then cultural average—to warrant ridicule. It was only in Roman times that her lesbianism became the focal point for ridicule, and shortly thereafter for censure.

In the second century A.D., six hundred years after Sappho's death, Lucian of Samosata, a Greek writer living in Rome, satirized Sappho and her colony of women in his much-read work *Dialogues of the Courtesans*. Two courtesans, Leaena and Clonarium, are having a conversation. One whore to another:

"We've been hearing queer things about you, Leaena. They say Philippa, that millionaire lady from Lesbos, feels about you the way a man does and that the two of you have been making love, doing lord knows what to each other. What's this—blushing? Tell me, is it true?"

"Yes, Clonarium. But I'm so ashamed of myself! It's all so unnatural!"

"In the name of Venus, what's it all about? What's the woman after? What do you two do when you make love to each other, anyway? See? You're not really my friend. You wouldn't have kept a thing like that secret from me."

"You *are* my friend; there isn't another girl I like as much. But this woman is so like a man it's frightening."

"I don't know what you're talking about—unless you mean she's one of those Lesbians. I hear that the women on that island look just like men and that they never go through the act with men; they make love to other women the way men do."[10]

With these few paragraphs (only part of the dialogue is quoted here) Lucian standardized a lot of thinking about women who love other women, thinking that has been seconded down the centuries. In this ancient work we have Philippa of Lesbos, one of Western literature's first tough strutting butches. She paves the way for a long literary tradition of role-playing lesbians. Although Philippa is intended to be a satirical portrait of Sappho, the butch–femme phenomenon never made the slightest appearance in Sappho's poems. We also have women who love other women labeled "Lesbians"; in Sappho's day, as has been noted, a Lesbian was simply a resident of the island of Lesbos. We also have the beginning of some long-believed myths: lesbians look like men; lesbians make love like men; lesbians are ashamed of their loving. And we have the beginning of a controversy that is still with us: lesbianism is unnatural. Not one of these statements, not even a hint, is to be found in Sappho's poems. Finally, the practice of lumping lesbians with whores in an atmosphere of general debauchery, when writing about them, stems from these times. (The comic poets of the fourth century B.C. who declared Sappho a prostitute declared her a heterosexual one.) This habit of thinking of lesbians in the same context as whores is still with us; as has been noted, in the most discussed popular sex book of the late sixties, *Everything You Always Wanted to Know About*

Sex, the author covers lesbianism in his chapter on prostitution. The roots of tradition are deep, and unfortunately they are rarely examined.

It was with the official recognition of Christianity in the Roman Empire that ridicule of Sappho turned to censure. Lesbianism, perfectly acceptable in Sappho's lifetime, had become in early-Christian/Roman times perfectly unacceptable—in fact, cause for burning.

The first burning of Sappho's songs, as nearly as it can be dated, is said to have taken place in the Eastern Roman Empire around A.D. 380. It is said that her poems were destroyed along with other masterpieces of antiquity during a period of ecclesiastic housecleaning. It was a time when the Christians feared a return to paganism and a time when the newly Christianized Roman emperors were beginning to proclaim edicts making male homosexuality a crime punishable by death. About twenty years earlier, in the years 361–363, Julian the Apostate, Emperor of Rome, who, like Socrates, had praised Sappho's beautiful soul, tried to bring back the glory of antiquity. To the early Christians this meant a return to paganism. Twenty years after that, prompted by a revival of Arianism (the heresy that denied the divinity of Christ, believing him only a superior being, an intermediary between God and the world), the Church and the state convened the First Ecumenical Council of Constantinople, at which paganism was outlawed. The Council had been called by Emperor Theodosius the Great, ruler of the East, who proclaimed one of the first edicts making homosexuality a crime punishable by death, and who would, a few years later, in 390, massacre seven thousand human beings at Thessalonica in revenge for an insurrection. The Council named Gregory Nazianzen Bishop of Constantinople, and it was during his tenure that Sappho's poems were set to flame. Today Gregory Nazianzen is listed as one of the four great Greek Doctors of the Church.

The second burning of Sappho's poems is said to have
taken place in the eleventh century in the West during another period of ecclesiastic housecleaning. This time a widespread atmosphere of debauchery led to the burning, an atmosphere that reached as far as the papal throne in the
person of Pope Benedict IX, whom history remembers for the
"notorious homosexual orgies" he hosted. Reform-minded
Popes followed Benedict, and during the tenure of one of
them, Gregory VII (1073–1085), the masterpieces of antiquity, Sappho's poems included, once again were converted
to ashes. Pope Gregory VII was canonized in 1728.

Burned first in the East and then in the West, Sappho's
poems had been splendidly silenced—or so it seemed. Fortu-
nately for the sake of literature and, it could be said, for the
sake of lesbianism, the burnings did not totally succeed.

As Sappho's work was burned twice, so it was recovered
twice—first in the West, in Italy, during the early Renaissance, and later in the East, in Egypt, at the turn of the nineteenth century. "Recovered" is perhaps too definitive a word.
All that was found was bits and pieces. It is estimated that
of her nine books of poetry—an ennead, some twelve thousand lines—we possess today only some six hundred lines:
one complete poem, one perhaps complete poem, and the
rest fragments. The English writer John Addington Symonds,
in very *fin-de-siècle* style, has said of this loss, "We muse in
a sad rapture of astonishment to think what the complete
poems must have been."[11] Moses Hadas, the Greek scholar,
put it more succinctly: "Perhaps the greatest single loss in all
literature is the work of Sappho . . ."[12]

During the early Renaissance, Italian antiquarians who
were hunting for lost Latin and Greek texts by the ancients
found Sappho quoted in some of these texts. For the most
part, the quotes were only fragments of her poems, lines used
to illustrate points of grammar or to point out the specific

uses of particular words. But in two of the unearthed ancient essays Sappho had been quoted at length to show her mastery of style.

The one complete surviving poem by Sappho was found in the essay *On Composition*, written by Dionysius of Halicarnassus in the first century B.C. In the essay, Dionysius spoke of ancient writers whose literary style was of excellence; he picked Hesiod as the best of the epic poets, Euripides as the best of the tragic poets, and Sappho as the best of the lyric poets.

The poem of Sappho's that he quoted to prove his thesis is known as the "Ode to Aphrodite." In it Sappho speaks of her love for a young woman who does not return that love, and appeals to Aphrodite for help:

> Prayer to my lady of Paphos
>
> Dapple-throned Aphrodite
> eternal daughter of God,
> snare-knitter! Don't, I beg you,
>
> cow my heart with grief! Come,
> as once when you heard my far-
> off cry and, listening, stepped
>
> from your father's house to your
> gold car, to yoke the pair whose
> beautiful thick-feathered wings
>
> oaring down mid-air from heaven
> carried you to light swiftly
> on dark earth; then, blissful one,
>
> smiling your immortal smile
> you asked, What ailed me now that
> made me call you again? What

was it that my distracted
heart most wanted? "Whom has
Persuasion to bring round now

"to your love? Who, Sappho, is
unfair to you? For, let her
run, she will soon run after;

"if she won't accept gifts, she
will one day give them; and if
she won't love you—she soon will

"love, although unwillingly . . ."
If ever—come now! Relieve
this intolerable pain!

What my heart most hopes will
happen, make happen; you yourself join forces on my side!

When British translators of the eighteenth and nineteenth centuries first rendered this poem into English, the
young woman with whom Sappho had been in love magi-
cally became a young man. Here is J. Herman Merivale's
1833 heterosexual version of the poem, a version typical of
the renderings of the time:

Immortal Venus, throned above
In radiant beauty, child of Jove,
O skilled in every art of love
        And artful snare;
Dread power, to whom I bend the knee,
Release my soul and set it free
From bonds of piercing agony
        And gloomy care.
Yet come thyself, if e'er, benign
Thy listening ears thou didst incline
To my rude lay, the starry shrine

Of Jove's court leaving,
In chariot yoked with coursers fair,
Thine own immortal birds that bear
Thee swift to earth, the middle air
    With bright wings cleaving.
Soon they were sped—and thou, most blest,
In thine own smiles ambrosial dressed,
Didst ask what griefs my mind oppressed—
    What meant my song—
What end my frenzied thoughts pursue
For what loved youth I spread anew
My amorous nets—"Who Sappho, who
    Hath done thee wrong?
What though he fly, he'll soon return—
Still press thy gifts, though now he spurn:
Heed not his coldness—soon he'll burn,
    E'en though thou chide."
—And saidst thou thus, dread goddess? Oh,
Come then once more to ease my woe;
Grant all, and thy great self bestow,
    My shield and guide![13]

Another poem found in the early Renaissance is thought
to be almost complete. It is the most famous of Sappho's
poems, looked upon by the leerers as her juiciest. It was
found quoted in On the Sublime, the classic essay of literary
criticism attributed to Longinus (A.D. 213–273) but thought
to have been written earlier, in the first century A.D., by an
ancient critic whom scholars have been unable to identify.
The "Sublime" of the title literally means height, greatness
of thought. Longinus points out who of the ancient writers
reached this sublimity, quoting Homer's description of a
storm and Sappho's description of a lover. This linkage of
Homer and Sappho by the ancients is not unusual. They
were commonly spoken of as "The Poet" and "The Poetess,"

without benefit of name, and everyone knew who was meant.

This poem of Sappho's shows how she—a lover—reacts when a man pays attention to the young woman with whom she is in love:

> He is more than a hero
>
> He is a god in my eyes—
> the man who is allowed
> to sit beside you—he
>
> who listens intimately
> to the sweet murmur of
> your voice, the enticing
>
> laughter that makes my own
> heart beat fast. If I meet
> you suddenly, I can't
>
> speak—my tongue is broken;
> a thin flame runs under
> my skin; seeing nothing,
>
> hearing only my own ears
> drumming, I drip with sweat;
> trembling shakes my body
>
> and I turn paler than
> dry grass. At such times
> death isn't far from me

It is worth quoting some of what Longinus had to say about this poem:

Do you not marvel how [Sappho] seeks to gather soul and body into one, hearing and tongue, eyes and complexion; all dispersed and strangers before: now, by a series of contradictions, she is cold at once and burns, is irrational, is sensible . . . so that it may not appear to be a single passion which is upon her, but an assemblage of passions? All the symptoms are found severally in lovers; to the choice of those which are conspicuous, and to their concentration into one, is due the preeminent merit here.[14]

British translators had a heyday with this poem. Of course, it must be taken into account that Sappho is difficult to translate, not only because of the flexibility of ancient Greek but also because of the fragmentary condition in which her poems have come down to us. However, it was known that she composed her poems spontaneously, sung to the accompaniment of a lyre, and thus she used everyday speech. There are enough clues in the fragments to show that the poems are candid, strong, passionate, and never pretentious. Mary Barnard's 1958 translations, which we use throughout this chapter, are done in the intense but simple style that was Sappho's. Dudley Fitts says, "Like the Greek, it [one of Barnard's translations] is stripped and hard, awkward with the fine awkwardness of truth."[15]

The first English translations of the poem in question had nothing stripped and hard about them. The translations seem to have come not from a study of Sappho and her art but rather from the psyches of the translators. The early renderings were either silly, preciously baroque, or downright lurid. One of these early translations (1711) is that of Ambrose Philips, and it can be dispensed with quickly. Here is his version of the ending of the poem:

> In dewy damps my limbs were chilled,
> My blood with gentle horror thrilled:
> My feeble pulse forgot to play:
> I fainted, sank, and died away.[16]

To the credit of the English, Philips later became known as "Namby-Pamby."

What can't be dismissed so readily is Swinburne's 1866

loose rendering of this poem, in which we have nothing of
Longinus's assessment of Sappho "gathering soul and body
into one," but rather Sappho wallowing in a hothouse of
lust, Sappho as a woman-devouring woman, a sadistic bitch,
most assuredly an exciting fantasy to the masochistic mind
that was Swinburne's. Swinburne called his version a paraphrase and titled it "Anactoria." Here are some excerpts:

> My life is bitter with thy love; thine eyes
> Blind me, thy tresses burn me, thy sharp sighs
> Divide my flesh and spirit with soft sound,
> And my blood strengthens, and my
>   veins abound. . . .
>
> I feel thy blood against my blood: my pain
> Pains thee, and lips bruise lips, and vein
>   stings vein. . . .
>
> I would my love could kill thee; I am satiated
> With seeing thee live, and fain would have
>   thee dead. . . .
>
> Ah that my lips were tuneless lips, but pressed
> To the bruised blossom of thy scourged white breast!
> Ah that my mouth for Muses' milk were fed
> On the sweet blood thy sweet small wounds
>   had bled! . . .[17]

Because Swinburne's *Poems and Ballads, First Series*, in
which this poem appeared, caused such a critical uproar on
its publication in 1866, he wrote a defense of the volume.
Noting that contemporary translations of Sappho were awful, he said that it was his purpose not to do a direct translation of her poems, which he held sacred, but rather to get
into the spirit of the poet. What he did, of course, was
merely present his own spirit. It is once again, as in Lucian's

Dialogues of the Courtesans, a case of a man assuming that Sappho's relationship to her women friends was that of a tough butch perpetrating violent affection on her flock of passive young women. One of Swinburne's friends, on reading "Anactoria," told him, "That is not Sappho." To which the poet replied, "It is as near as I can come; and no man can come close to her."[18] But many have insisted on trying.

Sappho's poems remained mangled in inept English translations until well after they were recovered for the second time, at the turn of the nineteenth century, at Oxyrhynchus, in Egypt. This time the discoverers were two young Oxford scholars, Bernard Pyne Grenfell and Arthur Surridge Hunt.

In 1897, Oxyrhynchus, today called Behneseh, an area 120 miles south of Cairo, was mostly an abandoned stretch of desert dotted with many quite high rubbish mounds, the debris of centuries. Most archeologists digging in Egypt at the time bypassed Oxyrhynchus for more promising grounds. But Grenfell and Hunt, armed with the knowledge that Oxyrhynchus was once a thriving Greek colony that had become a Christian stronghold in the fourth century A.D., were convinced that the rubbish heaps were worth investigating. They were not wrong. The find was one of the extraordinary events in the history of papyrology (the study of ancient Greek and Latin texts).

Painstaking ferreting through the layers of rubbish yielded unimagined jewels: a satyr play by Sophocles, a biography of Euripides, poems by Pindar, fragments of poems by Alcaeus (Sappho's friend), and many poems by Sappho herself. So much was unearthed during the digs (1897–1906) that editing took years.

Originally, the unearthed literary works were written on six-by-nine-inch sheets of papyrus which were then pasted together to form one continuous sheet of some twenty-five to thirty feet. This sheet was then rolled around a piece of wood to form a scroll, a book. With the formal recognition of

Christianity in Oxyrhynchus in the fourth century, interest in Greek literature died. Whole libraries were discarded, simply thrown onto rubbish heaps. Hunt comments: "The right-minded man would tend to replace Sappho with the Psalms and satisfy his appetite for history and romance with the lives of the saints and martyrs."[19] The papyrus rolls were seldom thrown away whole; they were usually torn into strips. In turn, the papyri suffered damage from the elements. It is remarkable that anything survived; we have the dry climate and sands of Egypt to thank. Digging in the mounds in 1897 was done only to a depth of ten feet; below that depth all was mush, a result of the creeping Nile.

When the bushels of unearthed papyri were shipped back to England the editing began, and it was, to say the least, no easy task. What the scholars were faced with was tons of mutilated pieces of papyrus. They sorted and pieced together, a process quite as painstaking as the actual digging in the mounds. When Sappho scholars examined her newly discovered verses, they found that those which were love lyrics were all addressed to women. This led them to reexamine the finds of the early Renaissance and finally, slowly, very slowly, to a straightening out of that pronoun in the "Ode to Aphrodite." The lyric being a personal form, there is no question that Sappho is speaking in her own voice in her poems. With the Oxyrhynchus finds, there was corroborative evidence which tended to confirm that the person with whom Sappho had been in love in that poem was most assuredly a woman.

Nonetheless, many Sappho experts have refused to concede. It's curious, because these same men have been diligent in tracking down and correcting other myths about Sappho's life. Only when it comes to the question of her love life do they hesitate. They somehow feel it their duty to deny or excuse her lesbianism. From reading their arguments one gets the feeling that they feel that the beauty of her poems would be negated should this love of hers for women be taken as a matter of course.

One such guardian of Sappho's moral purity, David M. Robinson, a noted Sappho "expert," wrote, as late as 1963:

It is against the nature of things that a woman who has given herself up to unnatural and inordinate practices which defy the moral instinct and throw the soul into disorder, practices which harden and petrify the soul, should be able to write in perfect obedience to the laws of vocal harmony, imaginative portrayal, and arrangement of the details of thought. The nature of things does not admit of such an inconsistency. Sappho's love for flowers, moreover, affords another luminous testimony. A bad woman as well as a pure woman might love roses, but a bad woman does not love the small and hidden wild flowers of the field, the dainty anthrysc and the clover, as Sappho did.[20]

Sappho would have smiled at this. Actually, given the climate in which she lived, she would have had a difficult time in understanding what the Johns Hopkins professor was talking about. "Unnatural and inordinate practices"? This phrase would have had no meaning in her day.

To further prove Sappho's "purity," Professor Robinson concluded that her poems are never erotic, that only "bad women" would run on and on with erotic imagery. Surely by "erotic" the professor must mean heavy talk of things genital, and, yes, there are no explicit "cunts" and "comes" in Sappho's works. But surely this is a modern definition of eroticism. In Sappho's day the definition of eroticism was not narrowly focused on the genitalia. Her people, the Aeolians, made an art of elegant and voluptuous living. There existed no puritan ethic to call the voluptuousness into question. Passion and sensuality, perhaps a more civilized definition of eroticism, run consistently through Sappho's works.

Not all of the critics have been as quaint as Professor Rob-

inson. Others have tried to skirt Sappho's lesbianism by saying that the available men during her day were off fighting
wars, so naturally she turned to women (the favorite *faute
de mieux* excuse). Another has said that poets often *write*
more than they *do*. Still another has pointed to the fact that
she wrote numerous songs honoring wedding ceremonies,
thus showing that she was not opposed to marriage (implying that lesbians are innately opposed to *other* people's marriages—a myth). And yet others have argued that Sappho
was, if anything, bisexual.

It is only the bisexual theory that deserves serious consideration. It is said that in her late teens Sappho was exiled to
Sicily for participating in a political plot to stem the activities of the tyrant Pittacus, who was trying to overthrow the
aristocracy of Lesbos. This is assumed to be true, not only
because women of the time were active in politics but also
because Sappho's good friend at the time was a fellow poet,
Alcaeus, one of the instigators of the political plot. At the
time that Sappho is said to have been exiled to Sicily there is
documentation to prove that Alcaeus was exiled to Egypt.
Alcaeus, a homosexual, was a colorful free spirit—hard-
drinking, hard-fighting, hard-playing, equally celebrated for
his sensitive poems and his political activism. He is the only
person to write of Sappho who actually knew her—that is,
only his words have come down to us. Much of Alcaeus'
work is lost to us; of his feeling for Sappho we have only this
rather unedifying scrap: "Lady of the violet hair, holy,
sweetly smiling Sappho."[21] Most scholars say the "violet
hair" refers to actual flowers, not color.

It is also said, however, that Sappho was not at all political, that she went to Sicily of her own accord (or more likely
was sent by her parents) to escape the political turmoil on
Lesbos. Whatever the reason, it appears that she did live in
Sicily for a few years, and since the arts flourished on this
island of Greek colonies she probably found the experience

one to her liking. She continued with her poetry while in "exile" (after her death a statue was erected in Syracuse in her honor), and when she finally did return to Lesbos, perhaps sometime in her middle twenties, she came as an established poet. She also returned, legend has it, as a wife and mother. There are no solid facts that point to the existence of a husband; most scholars contend that the husband was a figment of the imaginations of the comic poets. But more to the point, no husband appears in any of her surviving poems. The question of a daughter is more complicated. A "daughter," Cleis, does appear in the poems. Some scholars have claimed that the word "daughter" simply refers to one of the women with whom Sappho surrounded herself on her return to Lesbos. Another school says that the poems in which Sappho mentions a daughter were in reality written by another poet. Yet another school feels that if Sappho said "daughter" she meant daughter. Be this as it may, Sappho's husband, if indeed such existed, did not return with her to Lesbos. Once she was home from "exile" her life was lived exclusively among females.

The reason the bisexual theory has held ground so strongly is not because of the supposed early marriage but because of a much read work by the Roman poet Ovid (43 B.C.–A.D. 17). Although in one work Ovid wrote that Sappho's sensual poems constituted a veritable course of instruction in female homosexuality, in another work he about-faced and neatly killed her off in a heterosexual suicide. This he did in *Heroides*, a series of tales of famous women who had been starcrossed in love. Ovid, taking his "facts" from the fourth-century-B.C. comic poets, portrayed a fifty-five-year-old Sappho as madly in love with a twenty-year-old ferryman, Phaon, who rebuffed her, causing her to chase him around the Aegean, finally to the island of Leucadia, where, from atop a cliff, heartbroken, she threw herself into the sea.[22] The myth stuck for centuries, repeated in dozens of literary works, and although it is now discredited it is still found printed as fact.

The centuries-long controversy over Sappho's sexuality is, in the end, absurd. Her poems show that she was an intensely passionate woman to whom sensuality of any sort, even her inordinate love of flowers, was the very essence of her being. That this sensuality could have encompassed affairs with men, and even an early marriage, is quite possible. Any number of lesbian women throughout history have been married, are married, have had heterosexual affairs. However, in some people's minds there still seems to be a need for a definition of just what a lesbian woman is; the generally accepted definition is: a woman whose *primary* sexual and emotional feelings are fulfilled by other women and not by men. One only has to turn to Sappho's love lyrics to see where her primary affections lay.

When Sappho returned from Sicily, she set up housekeeping on Lesbos in what is said to have been a large house, the rooms of which opened onto an unroofed center courtyard. Near the house was her fine rose garden. The house was in the country, within walking distance of Mytilene. This part of Lesbos was hilly, rocky, and gorgeously sunny most of the year: a land of silent olive groves, vineyards of renown, hidden coves backed by tall pines, and vast carpets of the most various wildflowers—all of it under the exceptional Aegean sky, the special blue wondered at even today.

The island was rather a paradise, and to it, from near and far, came a number of aristocratic young women to sit at the feet of Sappho. They came for the express purpose of learning the composition of poetry and music, oral verse accompanied on a lyre—song. To receive the full benefit of Sappho's poems it is best to read them aloud.

There were at this time a number of religious festivals in which participation was limited to women. The most important of the festivals were those dedicated to Aphrodite, the goddess of love and beauty, and those that honored the goddess of the wild, the protector of women, the huntress Artemis, described by one writer as "a young and lovely huntress roaming the woods and mountains, delighting, like her brother Apollo, in music and the dance, free and unattached, 'chaste Dian,' owing no obedience to any male."[23]

Participation in these women-only festivals was an essential part of any well-bred young woman's life, and since the ceremonies demanded song and dance, the women had to be trained in these arts. The most exceptional of the women came to study with Sappho. Her colony, in which men were banned, was in reality a sort of special school dedicated to the cult of Aphrodite and the cultivation of the Muses. Sappho composed poem after poem addressed to Aphrodite. The goddess appears in the verses under a variety of names— Queen of Paphos, Cytherea, Cypris, Cyprian. In this song Sappho appeals to Aphrodite to grace her colony:

> You know the place: then
>
> Leave Crete and come to us
> waiting where the grove is
> pleasantest, by precincts
>
> sacred to you; incense
> smokes on the altar, cold
> streams murmur through the
>
> apple branches, a young
> rose thicket shades the ground
> and quivering leaves pour
>
> down deep sleep; in meadows
> where horses have grown sleek
> among spring flowers, dill
>
> scents the air. Queen! Cyprian!
> Fill our gold cups with love
> stirred into clear nectar

Sappho called her students her "hetaerae," a word which meant intimate companions, close friends; it wasn't until the glory days of Athens that "hetaerae" came to mean courtesans, women who served the pleasure of men. Life at the colony was an outdoor life. Sappho's hetaerae rose before dawn to gather flowers with which to salute the sun. Garlanding was an important part of the day's activities. Here is Sappho giving advice to one of her young women:

> Tomorrow you had better
>
> Use your soft hands,
> Dica, to tear off
> dill shoots, to cap
> your lovely curls
>
> She who wears flowers
> attracts the happy
> Graces: they turn
> back from a bare head

Worship of Aphrodite took place outdoors, in groves, often at twilight, as these two fragments show:

> In the spring twilight
>
> The full moon is shining:
> Girls take their places
> as though around an altar
>
> And their feet move
>
> Rhythmically, as tender
> feet of Cretan girls
> danced once around an
>
> altar of love, crushing
> a circle in the soft
> smooth flowering grass

The young women of Sappho's colony were trained in music and dance and most importantly in the composition of poetry. But of almost equal importance Sappho stressed the cultivation of *charis*, grace, in both the aesthetic and physical sense. A roughhewn talented woman was all well and good, but if she lacked *charis* she was somehow incomplete.

Sappho herself is said to have been beautifully graceful. From a few coins, from a few statues, from a few vase paintings, and from a very few written descriptions of her (written after her death), we know that she was probably small in stature, not at all Amazonian, and probably dark in coloring. She had long hair worn knotted at the nape of her neck. She dressed carefully in purple and gold, often with leather sandals dyed to match. As was the custom of the day, she wore kohl on her eyelids and was heavily perfumed. Flowers were very much a part of her wardrobe, worn twined in her hair. She was what our society calls a feminine woman. Fiercely individual, deeply sensuous, she delighted in the use of mind and body, and was every inch an Aeolian. The Aeolians have been described by John Addington Symonds, perhaps a bit too romantically:

> There seems to have been something passionate and intense in their temperament, which made the emotions of the Dorian and the Ionian feeble by comparison. Lesbos, the centre of Aeolian culture, was the island of overmastering passions; the personality of the Greek race burned there with a fierce and steady flame of concentrated feeling . . . Nowhere in any age of Greek history, or in any part of Hellas, did the love of physical beauty, the. sensibility to radiant scenes of nature, the consuming fervour of personal feeling assume such grand proportions and receive so illustrious an expression as they did in Lesbos.[24]

In her love lyrics Sappho spoke frankly of the joys and sorrows of women loving other women. A search for the beautiful bound her to her hetaerae. The poems could be as simple as these three fragments:

If you will come

I shall put out
new pillows for
you to rest on

I was so happy

Believe me, I
prayed that that
night might be
doubled for us

The gods bless you

May you sleep then
on some tender
girl friend's breast

or as impassioned as this poem addressed to one of the young
women who left the colony:

I have had not one word from her

Frankly I wish I were dead.
When she left, she wept

a great deal; she said to
me, "This parting must be
endured, Sappho. I go unwillingly."

I said, "Go, and be happy
but remember (you know
well) whom you leave shackled by love

"If you forget me, think
of our gifts to Aphrodite
and all the loveliness that we shared

"all the violet tiaras,
braided rosebuds, dill and
crocus twined around your young neck

"myrrh poured on your head
and on soft mats girls with
all that they most wished for beside them

"while no voices chanted
choruses without ours,
no woodlot bloomed in spring without song . . ."

   To another of her hetaerae, Gongyla by name, Sappho addressed these verses of longing:

Be kind to me

Gongyla; I ask only
that you wear the cream
white dress when you come

Desire darts about your
loveliness, drawn down in
circling flight at sight of it

and I am glad, although
once I too quarrelled
with Aphrodite
                    to whom
I pray that you will
come soon

Thank you, my dear

You came, and you did
well to come: I needed
you. You have made

love blaze up in
my breast—bless you!
Bless you as often

as the hours have
been endless to me
while you were gone

One of Sappho's favorites was the young woman Atthis.
Atthis came to the colony when quite young, and it appears
that her passionate attachment to Sappho lasted a number
of years. Toward the end of their affair Atthis fell in love
with one Andromeda, a woman said to have headed a rival
colony to Sappho's. Sappho was not pleased:

I hear that Andromeda—

That hayseed in her hay-
seed finery—has put
a torch to your heart

and she without even
the art of lifting her
skirt over her ankles

Sappho thinks longingly of her lost Atthis in this series of
fragments:

But you, monkey face

Atthis, I loved you
long ago while you
still seemed to me a
small ungracious child

I was proud of you, too

In skill I think
you need never
bow to any girl

not one who may
see the sunlight
in time to come

After all this

Atthis, you hate
even the thought

of me. You dart
off to Andromeda

Afraid of losing you

I ran fluttering
like a little girl
after her mother

We are primarily concerned here with Sappho's love lyrics, and although it is true that they comprise the bulk of
what remains of her work, she did speak of other things. In
the following fragment, which deals with the myth of Niobe
and Leto, Sappho seems to be commenting on the state of
motherhood. Niobe, so the myth goes, was arrogantly proud
of her seven strong sons and seven fine daughters and was insanely jealous of the adulation that Thebans showered on
Leto, a woman who had produced only one son and one
daughter. Leto, offended, appealed to her two offspring, the
powerful Apollo and Artemis, who avenged their mother by
killing off all fourteen of Niobe's children. Niobe, sick with
anguish, was turned to stone. Here is Sappho's somewhat
cheeky comment on the affair:

Before they were mothers
Leto and Niobe
had been the most
devoted of friends

To a wealthy woman of no learning Sappho could be icy,
as in the following fragment. (Pieria was the original home
of the Muses; Sappho felt that those who knew nothing of
the Muses went through life half formed.)

Rich as you are

Death will finish
you: afterwards no
one will remember

or want you: you
had no share in
the Pierian roses

You will flitter
invisible among
the indistinct dead
in Hell's palace
darting fitfully

This next fragment is an example of the songs the popu-
lace commissioned Sappho to compose for wedding ceremonies:

Lament for a maidenhead

FIRST VOICE: Like a quince-apple
ripening on a top
branch in a tree top

not once noticed by
harvesters or if
not unnoticed, not reached

SECOND VOICE: Like a hyacinth in
                  the mountains, trampled
                  by shepherds until
                  only a purple stain
                  remains on the ground

Of old age we have this melancholy thought:

Tonight I've watched

The moon and then
the Pleiades
go down

The night is now
half-gone; youth
goes; I am

in bed alone

And of death these two very different verses:

We know this much

Death is an evil;
we have the gods'
word for it; they too
would die if death
were a good thing

I have often asked you
not to come now

Hermes, Lord, you
who lead the ghosts
home:
        But this time
I am not happy; I
want to die, to see

the moist lotus open
along Acheron

Bùt it is of love that Sappho sang and sang:

To an army wife, in Sardis:

Some say a cavalry corps,
some infantry, some, again,
will maintain that the swift oars

of our fleet are the finest
sight on dark earth; but I say
that whatever one loves, is.

This is easily proved: did
not Helen—she who had scanned
the flower of the world's manhood—

choose as first among men one
who laid Troy's honor in ruin?
warped to his will, forgetting

love due her own blood, her own
child, she wandered far with him.
So Anactoria, although you

being far away forget us,
the dear sound of your footstep
and light glancing in your eyes

would move me more than glitter
of Lydian horse or armored
tread of mainland infantry

In writing of Sappho, one longs for firmer archeological
evidence, for a biography written by a contemporary, for
more poems. So much of the confusion that has followed
Sappho through the years stems from the fact that we really
know very little of her actual life. For example, of her early

childhood we know only that she was born to aristocratic parents and that she was educated in the same manner as the boys in her family. Because of this dearth of facts, Sappho has taken on the properties of a myth. There are even those who think that she was a member of that legendary group of women the Amazons. She wasn't.

Although historical evidence is slim, it appears that tribes of women, called Amazons, did exist in ancient Greek settlements in Asia Minor. In addition, early European explorers to Africa and South America, particularly Brazil, brought back tales of such all-women tribes on those continents. But it is mainly from Greek mythology and Greek art that we know of these women. Legend has it that they were born of a strange mating—that of Ares, the god of war, and Harmony, a peace-loving nymph. Greek sculpture and Greek vases depict these women as extremely healthy, robust, big-boned women with short hair and a minimum of clothing. They were excellent hunters, excellent equestrians, and formidable warriors. It is said that they burned away one breast to easier facilitate the use of bow and arrow and spear. They lived a communal life, in which men were banned. They ensured the continuance of their societies by mating once a year, during a spring festival, with the males of neighboring tribes, keeping only the female children that resulted. Male babies were either sent to their fathers, killed outright, or maimed in some way to act as household servants. Between the spring rites, it is said, the Amazons' sex lives were lesbian.

The two major myths about the Amazons concern the exploits of Hercules and Theseus. Hercules came to Amazon territory to take away the sash of their Queen, Hippolyta; this adventure was the ninth of his twelve labors. Hippolyta welcomed him warmly and agreed to give him the sash without benefit of battle. However, Hera (Zeus's wife and one of mythology's more angry and jealous women) convinced the other Amazons that Hercules had come to steal away their

Queen, not just her sash. The Amazons attacked; Hercules, thinking Hippolyta had double-crossed him, killed her, and fled with the sash.

Theseus did not come for Hippolyta's sash; he came for her. Legend has it that he came shortly after Hercules (some versions of the myth say it was Hippolyta's daughter Antiope whom Theseus abducted, for Hippolyta was dead, so two versions of the myth exist). Theseus took Hippolyta to Athens, where she became a devoted wife and bore him a son, Hippolytus, he who had so much trouble with Theseus's second wife, Phaedra. Shortly after the birth of Hippolytus the Amazons invaded Athens in an attempt to rescue their Queen. Theseus defeated them. Interestingly, in the poem by H.D. "She Contrasts Herself with Hippolyta," the poet tampers with the legend, suggesting that Hippolyta was by no means a devoted wife and that she did in fact detest Theseus and longed to return to the wild ways of the Amazons.[25]

Legend also has it that it was the Amazons who founded at Ephesus, in 550 B.C., the first shrine to Artemis, the virgin goddess of the hunt. Artemis is a lesbian figure in Greek mythology, a protector of wild things, always surrounded by a band of devoted woodland nymphs. One of the most devoted was Camilla, whose father, pursued by enemies, had heaved her, tied to a spear, across a river to be protected by Artemis. Camilla was brought up in the woods, wore a tiger skin, refused many offers of marriage, and remained faithful to Artemis.

Sappho was no myth. Nor should she be thought of mainly as the high priestess of the lesbian ghetto. If ever it should be decided to eliminate the lesbian ghetto, by allowing women who love women exit to claim their full identities, perhaps the high priestess should be the first offered such exit. Sappho was a poet who loved women. She was not a lesbian who wrote poetry.

CHAPTER SIX

The Belle Époque: Rénee Vivien, Natalie Clifford Barney, Colette

IN THINKING of Sappho's colony one is reminded of the French boarding school Pensionnat des Ruches, situated outside Fontainebleau and run by that extraordinary Frenchwoman Marie Souvestre. Talented young women of the late nineteenth century flocked to the school. One such was Dorothy Strachey Bussy, Lytton Strachey's sister and Gide's translator, who many years later wrote the roman à clef *Olivia* (she wrote it under the pseudonym "Olivia") in which the fictional headmistress is a thinly disguised Souvestre and in which lesbianism is the major theme. Later, Souvestre moved to England to head Allenswood, an equally celebrated young women's boarding school near Wimbledon. Eleanor Roosevelt attended Allenswood from 1899 to 1902, and Souvestre's liberated ways influenced her greatly.[1] Souvestre, like Sappho, fostered the development of grace in her charges. Evenings she invited her special students into her flower-filled study, which contained somewhat daring art works, including sculpture by her friend Rodin. There the young women read poetry aloud, and under the steady eyes of their silver-haired headmistress they stretched their minds beyond the limited scope of woman's pre-World War I state. Both Souvestre's schools and Sappho's colony had as their drawing card exceptional charismatic headmistresses and produced, for the most part, some very exceptional women. Natalie Clifford Barney attended the Fontainebleau school, and, extraordinarily enough, she and the poet Renée Vivien traveled to Lesbos at the turn of the century to set up a women-only colony of poets on the island, "inviting those from far and wide who are vibrating with youth, love and poetry."[2] The undertaking of this Sappho-like experiment was a fiasco. Even in the hands of two women as extraordinary as Natalie Clifford Barney and Renée Vivien, two thousand years of condemnation of lesbianism proved too much to handle. But it was more complicated than that. . . .

In 1900, Paris was gay, in all senses of the word. This was the Belle Époque, the city's leisurely era of elegance brought so abruptly to a close by World War I. At the time, the city was filled with a fashionable international society; within that society there existed a special coterie of very unconventional women. These "Baronesses of the Empire, canonesses, lady cousins of Czars, illegitimate daughters of grand dukes, exquisites of the Parisian bourgeoisie, and also some aged horsewomen of the Austrian aristocracy,"[3] as Colette has described them, rubbed elbows—and more—with Parisian demimondaines and with young expatriated English and American heiresses. The society was small; everyone knew everyone else; the women were always meeting at one or another of the many salons, recitals, and costume balls that characterized the period. The times were prosperous and the women were a moneyed crew; their immense leisure led many of them to busy themselves with entertaining, being entertained—and having love affairs with one another. Some of the women, actually rather a large minority, wrote. Two such were Natalie Clifford Barney and Renée Vivien, then in their early twenties.

Barney's writings, few of them translated into English, form a curious package. There is some poetry, a novel and a few plays, but in the main they consist of autobiographical works and *pensées*—collections of random thoughts and aphorisms: "He who confuses reproduction and love spoils both of them; marriage is the result of this mess." "It isn't because I don't think about men that I don't care for them. It is because I do think about them."[4] Barney, intelligent and witty and truly bilingual, became respected in certain French literary circles. But as she once said: "My life is my work. My writing but the result."[5] Vivien, on the other hand, became the pure artist. Of all the women poets who have looked to Sappho as heroine, none has written so openly, so erotically and so prolifically of lesbian love. And none has been so bizarre a personality. Half English and half American, Renée Vivien was born Pauline Tarn in 1877 in London. When she was twenty-three she settled in Paris, and, like Barney, she wrote in French. Little of her poetry—thirteen volumes written at seemingly breakneck speed between 1900 and her strange death in 1909—has been translated into English. Her early poems are languorously sensual and full of wide-eyed, earnest rebellion, much as was her early life . . .

. . . *Sous ta robe, qui glisse en un frôlement d'aile,*
Je devine ton corps,—les lys ardents des seins,
L'or blême de l'aisselle,
Les flancs doux et fleuris, les jambes d'Immortelle,
Le velouté du ventre et la rondeur des reins.

La terre s'alanguit, énervée, et la brise,
Chaude encore des lits lointains, vient assouplir
La mer lasse et soumise . . .

Voici la nuit d'amour depuis longtemps promise . . .
Dans l'ombre je te vois divinement pâlir.**[6]*

The later poems, preoccupied with solitude and death, are
sharper, tortured, funereal; again they reflect her life. A decadent, an aesthete, a late disciple of the poets Verlaine and
Baudelaire, Vivien ended as a true *poète maudit*, dying of
self-imposed starvation at the age of thirty-two. Barney, born
in 1877 in Dayton, Ohio, and raised in Cincinnati and Europe, was in no way the *poète maudit*. She lived an extraordinarily full life in Paris for the better part of seventy years,
dying there in 1972 at the age of ninety-four.

The two women met in Paris in 1900. Vivien was new in
town. Barney was already a fixture in that special society described by Colette; she was in fact in the midst of a mad affair with Liane de Pougy, one of the city's famed courtesans.
Pougy was also a writer, of sorts; Barney is the main character, Flossie, in Pougy's book *Idylle saphique*. This was the
first time Barney figured in a work of fiction, but by no means
the last. Still to come were her appearances as the amazon in
Lettres à l'amazone, written by her friend the scholarly decadent Rémy de Gourmont; as Laurette in *L'Ange et les pervers*,
by her friend Lucie Delarue-Mardrus; as Evangeline Musset
in Djuna Barnes's little-known and hilarious *Ladies Alma-*

---

* . . . Under your gown, which glides like a wing's caress,
  I fathom your body,—the eager lilies of your breasts,
      The pale gold of your underarm,
  Your flanks gentle and flushed, your legs, those of a goddess,
  The velvet smoothness of your belly and the fullness of your loins.

  The earth flags, listless, and the breeze,
  Still warm from far distant beds, comes to envelop
      The weary and submissive sea . . .
  The so long intended night of love is here . . .
  In the darkness I see you grow exquisitely pale.

  (This literal and inadequate translation and the others in this chapter are by
  the author, and will have to serve until and if some poet attempts to offer us
  Vivien's poems in English.)

nack; and as Valérie Seymour in Radclyffe Hall's once notorious *The Well of Loneliness.*

Barney and Vivien's tumultuous love affair, unfaithful on both sides, lasted only a few years. During that time they each produced several books with lesbian themes, and they tried twice to set up a colony of women poets who would inspire one another. Their initial Sappho-type experiment took place in Paris. As live-in chaperons the two had an elderly male professor of ancient Greek and a straight-laced middle-aged French governess. It wasn't long before the old professor and the governess, to outside eyes a decidedly ill-matched couple, became lovers. This caused much hilarity among the young poets, causing Barney to remark, "These representatives of heterosexual love were hardly examples to convert us."[7]

The women were a brash and rather insolent duo. Parents were far away, money they had, educated they were. And Paris offered them a special ambiance in which to operate. They spent their days writing. Vivien, who was determined to do a French translation of Sappho's poems (she kept a copy of Wharton's English work on the poet always nearby), was studying Greek with the live-in professor. Vivien's literary launching had taken place a short time earlier. She had published her first volume, *Études et préludes,* when she was still known as Pauline Tarn. She chose the pseudonym R. Vivien. No one in the literary establishment knew who this was. The book was dedicated to "N——," and the poems were addressed to "Lorelei." Shortly after publication a noted literary critic who delighted in the discovery of new poets held a lecture to launch his latest find. Barney and Vivien attended. The critic opened the lecture by saying that never had he read such fervent love poems, obviously written by a very young man to his very first mistress; in the audience Barney and Vivien exchanged amused glances. Later, when the critic, in grand theatrical voice, quoted one of the more graphic of the poems, detailing the young man's ardent passion, Vivien and her Lorelei, unable to control their laughter, fled the lecture hall.

Shortly after this lecture, word reached the literary world that R. Vivien, that "very young man," was in fact a very young woman, an Anglo-American woman who lived and wrote in Paris. Interviews were sought, and in more than one case the poet, who enjoyed subterfuge, had the ménage's chaperon impersonate her when the interviewers arrived. The sculptor Rodin she met herself, agreeing to pose for his bust of a woman poet. Rodin, like the painter Klimt, had always been fascinated by lesbians; reproductions of his erotic lesbian sculpture and drawings seldom appear in art books, but some of the real things can be seen in Paris's Musée Rodin. The writer Pierre Louÿs was also a welcome guest. He gave the women copies of his *Chansons de Bilitis* and in Vivien's copy he inscribed the Keats verse "For ever wilt thou love, and she be fair."[8] *Chansons de Bilitis*, first published in Paris in 1894, is a collection of prose poems about an ancient Greek woman, Bilitis, who travels to Lesbos and is convinced to remain there by a group of young women: "Women alone know how to love. Stay with us, Bilitis, stay. And if thou hast an ardent soul, thou wilt see thy beauty, as in a mirror, upon the bodies of the women thou lovest."[9] The book, when first published, was pawned off as "translated from the Greek," but the prose poems are in reality Louÿs's own erotic expansions of Sappho's fragments.*

Although Vivien and Barney were surrounded by women who sported dinner jackets, neckties, and monocles, they were, as was Sappho, what society calls feminine. In early photographs Vivien looks rather like a young Anaïs Nin. Tall and willowy, with slender animated hands and soft light-brown eyes, she wore her long ash-blond hair piled precari-

---

* The American lesbian organization the Daughters of Bilitis, founded in 1955, takes its name from the Louÿs book.

ously atop her head. Colette reports that she spoke with a
lisp and was "afflicted with an angelic clumsiness." At private
parties she drank herself into oblivion, and she had a vocabu-
lary that did not actually shock—most of the women in her
circle were quite familiar with the words—but, coming as
they did from her youthful laughing self, did jar. It was only
later that she came to look the haunted melancholy poet.

Barney was a teetotaler. Shorter in stature than Vivien,
light in coloring, she was a woman who looked at the world
through knowledgeable eyes. Elegant, humorous, a master of
French, an expert horsewoman, she was soon to become a
legendary hostess.

The couple's Sappho-like Paris experiment never really got
off the ground. Vivien had plunged into grief on learning of
the much too early death of her good friend, a woman we
know only by her first name, Violette, the Cincinnati girl-
hood friend of Barney who had initially introduced the pair.
With Vivien in despair, Barney suggested a trip to America.
There, among other things, they visited Bryn Mawr College
and showed their poetry to a Miss G. (The initial is used by
Barney in her memoirs; Miss G. undoubtedly was Mary
Gwinn, at that time English professor at the college and
lover of Carey Thomas, the school's famous president. The
pair appear, thinly disguised, in Gertrude Stein's long unpublished and only recently available early work *Fernhurst*.)

America did not help Vivien's depression; she was slowly
becoming obsessed by Violette's death. After a summer in
Bar Harbor, Vivien left for England to visit her parents, and
Barney stayed on with her family in Washington, D.C.

On her return to Paris, Barney went directly to Vivien's
new flat near the Bois de Boulogne. There she found the poet
in the arms of a tall "Walkyrie," an extremely wealthy baroness. Vivien kept this woman's name a secret, presumably
by order of the baroness herself, and Barney's autobiographical writings, which reveal almost everything else, are mum

about the name of the "Walkyrie." She was in fact a Rothschild.[10]

Barney tried her damnedest to win back Vivien, but to no avail. It seems that a member of the poet's household constantly foiled Barney's various plots, one of which included dressing up in drag with her friend the opera diva Emma Calvé and serenading Vivien under her window. In the midst of these campy plots and counterplots Barney was summoned to Monte Carlo, where her father lay gravely ill. She did not see Vivien for many months. When they did meet again it was at the Wagner Festival in Bayreuth, a must pilgrimage for any self-respecting Belle Époque Parisian. Their old attraction blossomed and they found themselves forging plans for a long journey; destination, Lesbos.

The Lesbos colony was a fiasco. When their ship pulled up to the island's wharf they heard a phonograph blasting a vulgar French tune. *"Viens poupoule, viens poupoule, viens . . ."* it went, falling uncomfortably on the sensitive ears of the increasingly melancholy poet and her Lorelei. On the island they found no Greek lovelies, no followers of Sappho, only a few medals that bore the poet's likeness. More importantly, they found a society not at all receptive to disciples of their island's most famous ancient citizen. Nonetheless, Vivien, who had always longed to visit Lesbos, and who, once there, had fallen in love with the place, announced that she never wanted to leave. Near the town of Mytilene they bought two villas with a connecting orchard and settled in. Vivien worked on her translation of Sappho, which she would publish in 1903. She celebrated the sensuousness of the island in many poems:

> *Du fond de mon passé, je retourne vers toi, Mytilène . . .*
>
> .   .   .   .
>
> *Reçois dans tes vergers un couple féminin,*
> *Île mélodieuse et propice aux caresses . . .*

Parmi l'asiatique odeur du lourd jasmin,
Tu n'as point oublié Psappha ni ses maîtresses. . . .

· · · ·

Quand, disposant leurs corps sur tes lits d'algues sèches,
Les amantes jetaient des mots las et brisés,
Tu mêlais tes odeurs de roses et de pêches
Aux longs chuchotements qui suivent les baisers. . . .*[11]

This second experiment to set up a women-only colony didn't even progress as far as the Paris colony, for just as the two instigators were deciding whom to invite, the Walkyrie beckoned. Barney couldn't figure out why her friend was so mysteriously tied to the baroness. This millionairess was known to have set up indigent young women in the past, but Vivien had her own fortune, so it was not for money that she ran whenever called. Colette reports that the poet told her she was frightened of the baroness, and in Vivien's mad moments, which were soon to commence, Vivien swore to Colette that the Walkyrie was going to kill her.

Back in Paris, the baroness demanded that Barney sign over to her one of the Lesbos villas. This caused the final split in Vivien and Barney's relationship. Lorelei hied herself to Neuilly and new loves, and La Scandaleuse, as Vivien had come to be called, ensconced herself in her macabre avenue du Bois apartment, number 23.

---

* From the depth of my past, I come back to you, Mytilene . . .

· · ·

Welcome to your orchards a female couple,
Melodious island conducive to caresses . . .
Amid the Oriental fragrance of heavy jasmine,
You have not forgotten Sappho nor her mistresses . . .

· · · ·

While stretching their bodies on your beds of dry seaweed,
The lovers sigh—words breathy, tired,
You enmesh your fragrances of roses and peaches
With the long whispers that follow kisses. . . .

It was at Neuilly, at the edge of Paris, in 1905, that Natalie
Barney began her famous at homes. She hosted these count-
less gatherings for some seventy years, first in Neuilly and
later, after 1909, in her renowned Saint-Germain-des-Près pa-
vilion at 20 rue Jacob. Over the years, Barney's salon and her
money encouraged any number of artists. She founded Bel
Esprit, a company of guarantors, which enabled Paul Valéry
to concentrate on his poetry. A similar project was launched
with Ezra Pound to do the same for T. S. Eliot, at the time
struggling on in his bank in England. Aside from the literary
and musical events for which she provided the setting, she
presided over some outrageously elegant dinner parties, at
one of which the diners were showered with rose petals re-
leased by a young boy concealed in a skylight; at others she
limited her guest list to women-only. Even a partial list of the
various guests at various times is quite staggering: the writers
Colette, Paul Valéry, Gertrude Stein, Ezra Pound, Edna St.
Vincent Millay, Radclyffe Hall, Rilke, d'Annunzio, Gide,
Apollinaire, and the Duchesse de Clermont-Tonnerre; the
composers Virgil Thomson and George Antheil; the harpsi-
chordist Wanda Landowska; the pianist Renata Borgatti; the
opera singer Emma Calvé; the dancers Isadora Duncan and
Ida Rubinstein; the actress Marguerite Moreno; the painters
Marie Laurencin and Romaine Brooks; the journalist Janet
Flanner; the critic Rachilde; the bookshop owners Sylvia
Beach and Adrienne Monnier. Dolly Wilde, Oscar's niece,
was an early visitor; Caresse Crosby and the Singer Sewing
Machine heiress, the Princesse de Polignac, showed up now
and again, as did Bernard Berenson. Proust visited only once,
alone, at midnight, wrapped in furs and scarves; he stayed
only ten minutes. One of Proust's characters, Baron Charlus,
the real-life superaesthete Count Robert de Montesquiou, no
slouch himself at entertaining, was a frequent visitor.

Barney's gatherings are legendary. Perhaps none was more
elaborately silly than one of her very first, a spring afternoon's

entertainment in her garden at Neuilly. The program opened
with a performance of Pierre Louÿs's Daphnis and Chloë
pastoral, *Dialogue au soleil couchant*. The shepherd Daphnis was played by a Frenchwoman who was dressed in a
scanty tunic of terra-cotta crepe de Chine, Roman buskins,
and a Tahiti-style wreath; she spoke her lines with a thick
Burgundy accent, rolling her *r*'s like a Russian. An amateur actress, Daphnis shivered throughout the performance—
partly from stage fright, partly from the cold spring air. No
sooner had this "Burgundian shepherd" left the scene to po-
lite applause than a gigantic white horse with a dark-skinned
woman astride it thundered center stage. The horse wore a
turquoise-studded bridle that belonged to the hostess. The
dark-skinned rider wore nothing. Later, Barney and her current friend, the writer Lucie Delarue-Mardrus, introduced
the Burgundian shepherd to the bareback rider, who was now
wrapped in a sari. Colette and Mata Hari shook hands.

Colette had met Barney a few months earlier. Chafing at
the chains that bound her to her first husband, Henri Gau-
thier-Villars, "Willy," under whose stern direction she had
written the *Claudine* series, and under whose rather perverse
sense of publicity she and another young woman, the actress
Polaire, were ordered to crop their hair and dress up as school-
girls to simulate the main characters in *Claudine à l'école*,
Colette was only too happy to accept Barney's invitation to
act in the pastoral, for which Willy reluctantly gave his permission. When Barney visited them, Colette sadly admitted
to her, "I'm ashamed that you've seen my bondage first
hand."[12]

For Colette the artistically ludicrous occasion marked a
turning point in her life. It was the first time she had been
out alone since her marriage (the following year she would
break with Willy); it was her first amateur theatrical (her
professional music-hall years were about to begin); and it
seems that it was her first entrée into that special society of

unconventional women. Soon she would set up housekeeping with Missy, the ex-wife of the Marquis de Belboeuf and the daughter of the Duc de Morny.

A shy but worldly and witty older woman, Missy smoked cigars, knew her wines to perfection, and usually wore a tuxedo. Colette, with cropped hair and wearing neckties imported from England, lived with Missy for five years. During this time (1906–1911) Colette, who made her living by miming in music halls, wrote four books on her own (the earlier *Claudine* books had carried Willy's name). Among the four is what is considered her first masterpiece, *La Vagabonde*. It was also during this time that she began to accrue a reputation as a scandalous young woman; in *La Vagabonde* she describes herself as a lady of letters gone to the bad. She shocked many of her friends by hanging around gay bars. But the biggest public scandal happened in 1907 during a performance of the pantomime *Rêve d'Égypte* at the Moulin Rouge, with Missy (who sometimes joined Colette on the stage) playing the male lead, Yssim. At the end of the performance Colette and Missy kissed passionately. The police banned further performances.

In most biographies of Colette and in the 1970 New York stage production *Colette*, based on her autobiographical writings, there is no mention of Missy. Colette's music-hall years are dealt with in great detail, but there is no mention of her lover of the time. Colette, perhaps more than most writers, understood and used her art to examine the fact that love manifests itself in a variety of ways. She hated hypocrisy. Her real life is in her writings, most of them so autobiographical. Her edited life comes to us in plays like the abovementioned. She was described at her state funeral as a "pagan, sensuous, Dionysiac" personality; she does not deserve to have certain stages of her life censored.

Colette had many lesbian friends throughout her life (though apparently Missy was her only long-term female lover). When she was seventy years old, one of her closest *copines* was the writer Renée Hamon, a woman who died very young. Renée Hamon's *Journal* recounts this conversation:

"Colette, I'm in love!"

"Ah! With whom?"

"With a woman."

"So? Is she nice?"

"Oh, she's a love. Beautiful to look at, intelligent, sweet-natured, and so prudent . . ."

"Now don't be carried away. Look out. You are a migratory bird. Don't be too quick to attach yourself."

"It's happened all the same. I'm going to live with her."

Colette looks at me, astonished.

"But that's very serious."

"Oh, yes. But I won't be seeing her all day."

"Very good. There is nothing like separation to preserve love . . ."[13]

When Colette first broke with Willy in 1906, having been deeply pained by the marriage—she did not establish literary rights to the four *Claudine* books until 1926—she moved into a ground-floor flat on the rue de Villejust, near the Bois de Boulogne. Her building's shady courtyard connected by way of a wrought-iron gate with the courtyard of another apartment house that fronted on the avenue du Bois, number 23. In the ground-floor flat of this building lived Renée Vivien.

Vivien was already going to pieces when Colette and she met. Increasingly mysterious and mystical, she lived in an eerie flat surrounded by gigantic Buddhas, heavy draperies hung on leaded windows, flickering candles, burning incense, constantly wilting lilies, and ever present bouquets of violets set out in honor of her dead friend Violette. In remembering this apartment, Colette said that it always smelled to her like a rich man's funeral. Wandering around clad in flowing black or purple, painfully thin, with dark circles under her eyes, Vivien looked the very model of the Baudelairian ideal, beautiful and sad, a white-faced doomed beauty whose flushed cheeks made her pallor all the more striking. She ate little, save for a bit of rice, weak tea, and fruit; alcohol—strong cocktails and champagne—had become her mainstay. She was dying, as did Swinburne's fictional heroine Lesbia Brandon, by inches. Lesbia Brandon had hastened her death by drinking cologne laced with opium; Vivien did not—although a rumor sprang up that she did.

Disgusted with life, she retreated further and further into her art. Death and solitude were her themes. She became known as La Muse-aux-Violettes and La Scandaleuse. Her final plunge into despair occurred when a critic printed some damaging gossip about one of her lesbian love affairs. Incensed, she broke with her editor and removed her books from circulation. There are several poems from this period of "martyrdom." Here is an excerpt from one of them, "Defeated":

> *Le couchant est semblable à la mort d'un poète . . .*
> *Ah! pesanteur des ans et des songes vécus!*
> *Ici, je goûte en paix l'heure de la défaite,*
> *Car le soir pitoyable est l'ami des vaincus.*

> *Mes vers n'ont pas atteint à la calme excellence,*
> *Je l'ai compris, et nul ne les lira jamais . . .*
> *Il me reste la lune et le proche silence,*
> *Et les lys, et surtout la femme que j'aimais. . . .*

> *Du moins, j'aurai connu la splendeur sans limite*
> *De la couleur, de la ligne, de la senteur . . .*
> *J'aurai vécu ma vie ainsi que l'on récite*
> *Un poème, avec art et tendresse et lenteur.*

Mes mains gardent l'odeur des belles chevelures.
Que l'on m'enterre avec mes souvenirs. . . .[*][14]

Natalie Barney, whom some have called cruel, or at least never self-deluded, has said that Vivien's life was nothing but a long suicide. To Colette, Vivien often lisped, ':Ah, ma pethith Coletthe, how disgusting this life is." In 1908, in London, Vivien took an overdose of laudanum in an unsuccessful suicide attempt. During this time and for the next year a friend, E. Sansot, received a number of her poems scrawled hastily in pencil and postmarked London, Paris, Amsterdam. In Vivien's last letter to Sansot, written on Hotel Savoy stationery, September 4, 1909, she pleaded with him to appraise her poems—"I am so frightened of ridicule."[15] She was now too ill to get about; what little energy she had, she saved for her poetry. Three days before her death in Paris, Vivien, the archpagan, was converted to Catholicism. Her fellow pagan Colette was hard put to explain this strange event: "She kept losing weight, always refusing to eat. In her spells of giddiness, in the aurora borealis of starvation, she thought she saw the flames of the Catholic hell. Someone close to her perhaps fanned the flames, or described them to her? Mystery. En-

---

[*] The setting of the sun is like the death of a poet—
Oh! weight of years and dreams lived!
Here, in peace, I taste the hour of defeat,
For compassionate dusk is the friend of the vanquished.

My verses have not attained the excellence of serenity,
This I have understood, and no one will ever read them again—
I still have the moon and the enveloping silence,
And the lilies, and above all the woman I loved. . . .

At least I shall have known the limitless splendor
Of color, line, scent—
I shall have lived my life as one recites
A poem, with beauty, tenderness, and calm.

My hands retain the fragrance of beautiful tresses.
Let them bury me with my memories. . . .

feebled, she became humble and was converted." The scholar
Mario Praz, a specialist in the period, who notes that a number of decadents, including Vivien's models Baudelaire and
Verlaine, and a number of homosexual artists have been
Catholic converts, theorizes that "this religion is merely a
disguised form of morbid satisfaction: repentance may be
nothing more than a mask for algolagnia" (pleasure derived
from suffering pain).[16]

When Barney heard that Vivien was ill, she went to her
carrying a bouquet of violets. Informed by the butler that
Mademoiselle had just died, Barney instructed him to place
the violets next to her body. (In 1949 she would endow a
Renée Vivien Prize for women poets.) Nor did Colette know
how close to death Vivien was; she was away on tour at the
time.

> I was by chance spared the sight of Renée dying, then dead
> [Colette wrote]. She carried off with her more than one
> secret, and beneath her purple veil, Renée Vivien, the poet,
> led away—her throat encircled with moonstones, beryls,
> aquamarines, and other anemic gems—the immodest child,
> the excited little girl who taught me, with unembarrassed
> competence: "There are fewer ways of making love than they
> say, and more than one believes."

In any evaluation of Vivien's poetry it must be taken into
consideration that she was utterly dedicated to her art and
that she was totally honest in baring her soul, brave even.
Some of her poems seem mediocre, but so, for that matter,
do some of her idol Verlaine's. There is little doubt that critics have avoided considering her work because of its lesbian
subject matter. There have been no critical works in English
on Vivien's poetry, and very few in French. Two French critics, acknowledging the fact that her lesbian subject matter
was looked upon by society as perverse, concluded that the
poems themselves were anything but perverse. One said that

"of all the women poets of the time, [Vivien] was the best and purest of artists; that is why her work is chaste."[17] The other called her work "pure passion, coming from the most intelligent perverseness."[18] Colette wrote, "Renée Vivien has left a great many poems of unequal strength, force, merit, unequal as the human breath, as the pulsations of human suffering."

Of concern here is Vivien's lesbian subject matter. No one since Sappho had spoken of lesbian love as had Renée Vivien, but what a world of difference there is in their approaches. After reading through Vivien's poems, most of them so funereal in tone, where death triumphs over life and solitude over love, it is difficult, in picking up Sappho's poems, to realize that they deal with the same subject matter. Take, for example, the manner in which they speak of flowers. Sappho sings joyfully of the tiny wildflowers of the field and of the happiness she feels entwining them in a loved one's hair. Vivien's flowers are somber violets—remembrances of the dead Violette—and icy wilting lilies. Instead of twining them in her lover's hair, Vivien in a harsh moment once said to Natalie Barney, "Ah, my fine lily! You too will wither away one day."[19] Critic Mario Praz has noted that "the image of white lilies crushed by cruel hands"[20] runs throughout Vivien's work—a telling remark. A tragic melancholy hangs over Vivien's poems; an enthusiasm for living, over Sappho's. Sure, Sappho suffered when Atthis left her for another woman; sure, she was pained when she saw a loved one in the company of a young man; but this suffering and pain was, it could be said, of a normal kind, that of an abandoned lover who still loves, an all too common human happening. Nowhere in Sappho's poems is there a plea for tolerance of her manner of loving. This is not true of Vivien's poems. We cannot cavalierly say that Vivien's tortured self and the resulting bitterness of her late poems were all society's fault for not accepting her way of loving. She was much too complicated a person for such facile evaluation; she did, after all, write in the tradition of the decadents whose poetry renounced the "hideous" realities of life. Much of her despair had to do with her two (and perhaps more) unhappy love affairs, with Barney and the wealthy baroness, along with the early death of her friend Violette. However, Vivien's final plunge into despair occurred when she was not quite strong enough to stand up to published gossip about her love life, and withdrew her books from circulation; there was no such gossip in Sappho's day. But on the other hand we have the example of Colette, who was strong enough to overcome events like the scandal of the Moulin Rouge. Colette was a friend of Vivien, but a reluctant friend; she was dismayed by Vivien's descent into alcohol and melancholy. But Colette, being Colette, a realist and a humanist, wrote of her friend's state: "Like all those who never use their strength to the limit I am hostile to those who let life burn them out." Vivien was not a survivor.

Barney was.

CHAPTER SEVEN

The 1920s: Radclyffe Hall's "Obscene" Best Seller

To JUDGE from the many memoirs of Paris in the 1920s, the city was home to a number of well-known women who were lesbian. Renée Vivien was dead; Colette had left her music-hall days behind; many of the baronesses and lady cousins of czars had died off, or at least had dropped their titles. The leisured times of the Belle Époque were gone; in its place there appeared a convulsive post-World War I period, a time in which women in general were experiencing a new sense of independence; even the heterosexual ones cropped their hair, turned to severe suits and neckties, smoked, drank, and swore ostentatiously in public—all of the characteristics once associated only with lesbians, now adopted by hetero-sexual women as symbols of an unfettered life. As the young heroine in Compton Mackenzie's lesbian satire, *Extraordinary Women*, predicts to her grandmother, "When the war is over you will find that women will be entirely different from what you have known. It is very much in the air, I can assure you, this change."[1] As for the lesbian women, so many of whom had served in the war, the English writer Radclyffe Hall comments, in her 1928 novel *The Well of Loneliness*:

"a battalion was formed in those terrible years that would never again be completely disbanded. War and death had given them a right to life, and life tasted sweet, very sweet to their palates. Later on would come bitterness, disillusion, but never again would such women submit to being driven back to their holes and corners. They had found themselves . . ."[2]

Those lesbians who found themselves in Paris in the twenties eventually made their way to Natalie Clifford Barney's salon, now ensconced and flourishing at 20 rue Jacob. Radclyffe Hall and her lover Una, Lady Troubridge, showed up in 1927.

It was during this Paris stay that Hall made her final decision to write what would become the most notorious of lesbian novels. Much of her decision to embark on the book had to do with meeting Barney and her circle. Hall began writing in Paris, at the Hotel Pont-Royal; she used the famous blue writing paper favored by her friend Colette. Some of the most vivid scenes in *The Well of Loneliness* are those that take place in Paris. Hall based several of her fictional women on the real women she knew in the city. Valérie Seymour in the novel is Natalie Barney, an accurate portrait. Others who figure—in highly fictionalized form—are the French writer the Duchesse de Clermont-Tonnerre, who wrote voluminous memoirs under her maiden name, Élisabeth de Gramont, and the American expatriate painter Romaine Brooks. Though minor characters in the book, they were both important figures in Barney's circle, and they deserve, especially Brooks, more than a mention here.

It was the Duchesse, a handsome, extremely intelligent woman who, after having her long hair bobbed, visited Gertrude Stein one evening and influenced Stein immediately to ask Toklas to give her a haircut, too. Sherwood Anderson came by after the shearing and reacted favorably, telling Stein that she now looked like a monk, not at all a bad thing to look like. Hemingway was not so pleased. He said that

Stein looked like "a Roman emperor,"[3] a look not at all to his liking. Picasso, whose famous portrait of Stein had been painted when she wore her long hair swept into a crown, was angry at first, but later he said, shrugging, "After all, it is all there."[4]

Romaine Brooks painted a splendid portrait of the Duchesse, which can be seen in the Smithsonian Institution's National Collection of Fine Arts in Washington, D.C. Brooks also did a portrait of Lady Troubridge, a bold work in which Troubridge appears in tail coat and monocle, caressing two sleek champion dachshunds. The portrait was banned from a 1925 London showing of the painter's works.

Romaine Brooks's portraits are strong statements, not at all standard superficial society portraits. Montesquiou was moved to dub her "Thief of Souls." Many of the portraits are of cultivated homosexuals—Barney, Cocteau, Lady Troubridge—and aside from their artistic quality they serve as extraordinary visual documents of the homosexual milieu in which she traveled.

Until 1971 Romaine Brooks was virtually unknown in the United States. In that year the Smithsonian, to which Brooks left the majority of her paintings and drawings, mounted a large exhibition of her works and published an important catalogue. The show, much abridged, traveled to the Whitney Museum of American Art in New York. *The New York Times* art critic Hilton Kramer said at the time that the artist

> proves to be a painter of remarkable powers. Her portraits are at once very strong and very cold. Her figure paintings— especially the female nudes—are impressively eerie, suggesting a kind of icy eroticism . . . [There] is in Romaine Brooks's painting a force, even a vehemence, that can only be described as masculine. . . . [The] artist's own self-portrait, painted in 1923, is unmistakably the work of a woman who has been disabused of most of the illusions life had to offer.[5]

Romaine Brooks was born Romaine Goddard in 1874 of American parents, and her childhood, which she relates in her mostly unpublished memoirs, *No Pleasant Memories*, was nightmarish. Living in the south of France, shackled to a mad mother and a certifiably insane brother, she was finally allowed to go to Rome when she was twenty-four to study painting. The only woman in classes at the Scuola Nazionale and Circolo Artistico, she was the butt of crude jokes from her classmates; they had a habit of tacking obscene drawings to her easel. When her mother died in 1902, she found herself in possession of a fortune. She set up a studio in London and began to devote herself to painting. She married John Ellingham Brooks, a homosexual, and then promptly left him with an annuity, after which she chopped off her hair and started to wear male attire. Later, she made her way to Paris.

She was one of the talented exotics in Paris. An admirer of d'Annunzio, she helped him with his creditors, painted his portrait, and also, very much in keeping with the times, spirited off one of d'Annunzio's woman friends, the notably beautiful eccentric dancer Ida Rubinstein. Rubinstein, terribly tall, terribly thin, with stark long black hair and pearl-white skin, is the model Brooks used for her unearthly nudes.

There is an interesting affinity between Brooks's drawings and Renée Vivien's poems. The drawings, eerie forays into Brooks's unconscious, heavily sexual, reminiscent in a way of Leonor Fini's work, are signed in their bottom corners not with Brooks's signature or initials but with a drawing of a full-spread wing anchored down by a heavy chain—certainly a symbol to which Renée Vivien could have related only too well. Sometime in the mid-twenties, despite her success, which included the Cross of the Legion of Honor from the French government, Brooks retreated from Paris' *haut monde* and insisted, as had Renée Vivien, that society had ostracized her. She began to call herself a *lapide*, an outcast, and it was at this time that she painted her extraordinary self-portrait, a haunting revelation of an isolated being.

It was Natalie Barney who contacted the Smithsonian regarding Brooks's paintings, which for years had been moldering away forgotten in different studios. The women had met in 1915, and their friendship lasted until the painter's death in 1970 at the age of ninety-six.

Of the 1971 U.S. revival of Romaine Brooks's work, Hilton Kramer wrote that the exhibition was "yet another reminder that the history of American art in this century is still to be written."[6] The life of Romaine Brooks is yet another reminder that the social history of lesbianism has never really been fully documented.

But to return to Radclyffe Hall's novel. When she came to write The Well of Loneliness, her fifth novel, she already had a modest literary reputation. Her books were all very mainstream, English good-reads.* Adam's Breed, which had just been published in England, was well received, winning two important literary prizes. Lady Troubridge reports that her friend had long wanted to write a serious novel about female inversion, as lesbianism was commonly called at the time (it was also called sapphism), and felt that only an "invert" could write incisively on the subject.[7] Hall's avowed intention was to speak in behalf of what she felt was a misunderstood and misjudged minority of women. It was no easy decision for so accepted a novelist to embark on such a novel. There was no precedent in mainstream English fiction that dared to say that lesbianism should not be condemned. It was, of course, perfectly acceptable to write works with les-

---

* The first novels, The Forge and The Unlit Lamp, appeared in the same year, 1924. They were followed by A Saturday Life (1925), Adam's Breed (1926), The Well of Loneliness (1928), The Master of the House (1932), and The Sixth Beatitude (1936). A volume of short stories, Miss Ogilvy Finds Herself, appeared in 1934. The volumes of poetry are 'Twixt Earth and Stars (1906), Poems of the Past and Present (1910), Songs of Three Counties and Other Poems (1913), and The Forgotten Island (1915).

bian themes if the lesbianism itself was condemned, or satirized. This was not Radclyffe Hall's intention.

She was, of course, correct to have wavered in her decision
to write the book. The following year, in November of 1928,
two months after the book's publication, she found herself
in London's Bow Street Police Court (wearing a man's dark-
colored fedora with a sprig of white heather tucked into its
band), listening helplessly as her decidedly tame novel went
through the process of being judged obscene. In making the
decision, Chief Magistrate Sir Chartres Biron said:

> The mere fact that a book deals with unnatural offences
> between women does not make it obscene. It might even
> have a strong moral influence. But in the present case there is
> not one word which suggests that anyone with the horrible
> tendencies described is in the least degree blameworthy. All
> the characters are presented as attractive people and put
> forward with admiration. . . .[8]

Radclyffe Hall, who had said nothing throughout the sensational proceedings, kept her silence. But when the magistrate continued, accusing the author of maligning certain
Englishwomen of "standing and position"—who had served
their country during World War I as ambulance drivers—by
portraying them as "addicted" to the "unnatural" practices
in question, she remained silent no longer. She cried out, "I
protest. I emphatically protest."

To which the magistrate, angered by her interruption, said,
"I must ask you to be quiet."

"I am the author of this book—" she shot back.

"If you cannot behave yourself in court I shall have to
have you removed."

Radclyffe Hall sat down. As she did so she looked to the
visitors' section and nodded to Lady Troubridge, with whom
she had lived for twelve years. Then she again faced the magistrate and called out to him her last word: "Shame!"[9]

The next morning, November 17, the first confiscated copies of *The Well of Loneliness*, 247 of them, were flung into a furnace in a cellar of Scotland Yard.

A melodramatic episode. An episode that easily could have come straight out of *The Well of Loneliness*, a melodramatic book. And yet a moving and essentially brave episode in the history of public lesbianism—much as was the book itself. Neither Hall nor her publishers, Jonathan Cape, expected the furor the book's publication caused, and except for the circulation-conscious mind of a London newspaper editor the book never would have become a landmark in the history of literary obscenity trials, nor would it have become the sensational international best seller that it did.

The events that led to the novel's suppression started three months before the trial. The book was published in England in August, it was duly reviewed—quite favorably— and it was selling well. Then, a few weeks after publication, on a summer weekend, totally unexpectedly, London's popular newspaper the *Sunday Express* printed a startling photograph of the author. She was dressed in drag, dykey as all get out. Her left hand was in the pocket of her men's trousers, her other hand held a burning cigarette, her hair was extremely short, and she wore a bow tie. She looked like a haughty, arrogant man about town. Alongside the photograph was a banner headline an inch and a half high. It read: A BOOK THAT MUST BE SUPPRESSED.

The article that followed, a classic in sensational journalism, a full-blown broadside of self-righteous indignation, was written by the editor of the paper, James Douglas. He had taken five columns to call the book an "intolerable outrage" and to demand that it be withdrawn from circulation. He told his readers: "The English people are slow to rise in their wrath and strike down the armies of evil," but he for one was certain they would rally. He called on them to protect their religion, to protect their children, to protect the country itself, and certainly not least to protect England's glorious tradition of great literature, all of these God-and-Country appeals couched in grandiloquent prose that reeked of sexual titillation.

It was surefire stuff. A very professional job. One critic noted that the sophisticated people of England consisted of about two percent of the population and that papers like the *Express* busied themselves with exposing to the remaining ninety-eight percent the wickedness of the sophisticates.[10] Certainly the decadent dandy in the photograph—a woman, by God—qualified for membership in the wicked two percent.

The newspaper attack read, in part:

. . . this pestilence [homosexuality] is devastating the younger generation. It is wrecking young lives. It is defiling young souls.

I have seen the plague stalking shamelessly through great social assemblies. I have heard it whispered about by young men and young women who do not and cannot grasp its unutterable putrefaction.

. . . this novel forces upon our society a disagreeable task which it has hitherto shirked, the task of cleansing itself from the leprosy of these lepers, and making the air clean and wholesome once more. . . .

I know that the battle has been lost in France and Germany, but it has not yet been lost in England, and I do not believe that it will be lost . . .

. . . It is a seductive and insidious piece of special pleading designed to display perverted decadence as a martyrdom inflicted upon these outcasts by a cruel society. It flings a veil of sentiment over their depravity. It even suggests that their self-made debasement is unavoidable, because they cannot save themselves.

This terrible doctrine may commend itself to certain

schools of pseudo-scientific thought, but it cannot be reconciled with the Christian religion or with the Christian doctrine of free-will. Therefore, it must be fought to the bitter end by the Christian Churches . . .

If Christianity does not destroy this doctrine, then this doctrine will destroy it, together with the civilisation which it has built on the ruins of paganism. . . .

It is meet and right to pity them, but we must also pity their victims. We must protect our children . . .

I would rather give a healthy boy or a healthy girl a phial of prussic acid than this novel. Poison kills the body, but moral poison kills the soul. . . .

Finally, let me warn our novelists and our men of letters that literature as well as morality is in peril. Fiction of this type is an injury to good literature. It makes the profession of literature fall into disrepute. Literature has not yet recovered from the harm done to it by the Oscar Wilde scandal. It should keep its house in order.[11]

The article caused a sensation, especially the line about giving young people a phial of prussic acid rather than the novel. Dozens of writers came to Radclyffe Hall's defense. Aldous Huxley, for one, offered to provide editor Douglas with a child, a bottle of prussic acid, and a copy of *The Well of Loneliness*, and if Douglas chose to give the child the acid Huxley himself would erect a handsome marble memorial to him, to be built immediately after the editor's execution.[12]

The publishers, Jonathan Cape, were more cautious. They feared prosecution and submitted a copy of the book to the then Home Secretary, William Joynson-Hicks, a man known as "Preposterous Jix," offering to withdraw the book should Hicks request it. Hicks did, of course, request the book's withdrawal. Cape withdrew the book, but then turned around and shipped the plates to Paris, to the Pegasus Press, which published the book and shipped copies back to England for

sale. Whereupon the director of public prosecutions brought
the case to trial.

Norman Birkett, K.C., who was to act, eighteen years
later, as one of the two British judges at the International
War Crimes Tribunal at Nuremberg, handled the defense
for Cape. Birkett opened with these words:

> Nowhere is there an obscene word or a lascivious passage.
> It is a sombre, sad, tragic, artistic revelation of that which is
> an undoubted fact in this world. It is the result of years of
> labour by one of the most distinguished novelists alive, and it
> is a sincere and high minded effort to make the world more
> tolerable for those who have to bear the tragic consequences
> of what they are not to blame for at all.[13]

But it was an uphill battle. When Birkett tried to call the
thirty-nine witnesses waiting to testify as to the merit of the
book, the Chief Magistrate disallowed the evidence with
these words:

> A book may be a fine piece of literature and yet obscene.
> Art and obscenity are not dissociated at all. There is a room
> at Naples to which visitors are not admitted as a rule, which
> contains fine bronzes and statues, all admirable works of art,
> but all grossly obscene. It does not follow that because a
> work is a work of art it is not obscene.[14]

The group of uncalled witnesses included the literary critic
Desmond MacCarthy, the biologist Julian Huxley, promi-
nent medical men, educators, clergymen, editors, booksellers,
librarians, and a string of respected writers, among them
E. M. Forster, Virginia Woolf, Leonard Woolf, and Vita
Sackville-West.

Birkett, who was working for the publishers, had not consulted Radclyffe Hall. Clutching at straws, and prompted by
Cape, he introduced the plea that the relations between the

women described in the book amounted to no more than casual friendship and had nothing to do with love and sex. The author, thunderstruck by this statement, lunched with Birkett and was in tears throughout the meal. Her whole purpose in writing the book, she told him, was to bring some truth to the subject, to say at last what everyone knew, that there were women worthy of respect who loved other women —and here was the defense advocate saying that the women were merely casual friends. In later years Birkett consistently came to the defense of *The Well of Loneliness*. He stated categorically that the book was ordered destroyed not because it was obscene—it wasn't, even if one read it as he had, word for word, always keeping in mind the Obscene Publications Act of 1857 under which the book was tried—but because the author had not condemned the women of whom she wrote.

It's interesting to note that Compton Mackenzie's satire of lesbians, *Extraordinary Women*, was published a few days before the trial, and that Virginia Woolf's fantasy *Orlando*, in which the main character (based on Vita Sackville-West) changes back and forth from a man to a woman, was published a few days after the trial. Neither of these books was touched by the legal authorities. *The Well of Loneliness* was destroyed on the basis that it did not condemn lesbians. In *Extraordinary Women* lesbians are the butt of the joke, perfectly acceptable, and in *Orlando* the sex changes were, well, pure fantasy. But, in addition, Radclyffe Hall was an out-of-the-closet real-life lesbian who made no bones about it and thus furnished James Douglas with the extraordinary photograph of herself that started the whole mess. Compton Mackenzie was no dyke. Nor, as we will see in the next chapter, was Virginia Woolf—well, not exactly.

The ban against *The Well of Loneliness* held in England for thirty-one years. Outside England the book had little trouble; it was published in fourteen countries and sold well.

The trouble it did have was in the United States, where a copy fell into the censoring hands of a self-appointed public servant of the time, John S. Sumner, head of the powerful New York Society for the Suppression of Vice. Actually, the book didn't fall into Sumner's hands at all. It was intentionally sold to him by the American publishers.

The publishers, Covici-Friede, a brand-new firm in 1928, had picked up the American rights to the book when the older established firm Alfred A. Knopf, which had earlier contracted for the book and had even set the type, withdrew it upon learning the results of the London trial. Donald Friede, a flamboyant promotion-minded publisher, saw the mileage to be had from a book banned in England. Friede assumed he would have trouble with the censors and as a precaution hired as attorney Morris Ernst, who was just on the threshold of his celebrated career in censorship law. It was Ernst who suggested selling a copy of the book to the Vice Society's Sumner, thus inviting a test case.

Sumner, who had spent many years in and out of American courts with his personal crusade against nasty books, considered *The Well of Loneliness* "literary refuse."[15] Accordingly, he had detectives seize 865 copies of the book on January 11, 1929. On January 23 he submitted two copies of the book to Magistrate Hyman Bushel of New York City's West Side Court, and on February 21, in the Tombs Court, Bushel found the book obscene, noting that the courts had "the duty of protecting the weaker members of society from [such] corrupt, depraving and lecherous influences."[16]

Ernst immediately appealed Bushel's decision and, with Friede, launched an all-out promotional campaign in behalf of the banned book, a campaign that perhaps was more exploitative than justified. But it worked. Friede had the book printed and distributed out of state; it became an immediate best seller. Ernst and his firm prepared an impressive fifty-one-page brief, a classic in the annals of obscenity prosecu-

tions. The appeal, on April 19, 1929, in the Court of Special
Sessions, was successful: *The Well of Loneliness* was decided
not obscene at all, its subject matter adjudged "a delicate social problem" having nothing to do with obscenity.

In Boston, just the day before this favorable decision, Donald Friede had not been so fortunate. Two years earlier, when
he had been with the publisher Horace Liveright, Friede had
been convicted in Boston for the distribution of another "obscene" book, Theodore Dreiser's *An American Tragedy*. The
appeal of this conviction, on April 18, 1929, was not successful. Friede remained convicted and *An American Tragedy*
remained banned in Boston.

Dreiser, who had had so much trouble with the vice societies, was among the seventy-four prominent Americans,
solicited by Ernst, who protested the banning of *The Well
of Loneliness*. The list included Hemingway, Dos Passos,
Sherwood Anderson, Edna Ferber and Sinclair Lewis among
other writers, along with distinguished critics, doctors, and
clergymen. This protest, unlike the protest of the English
witnesses, was considered on appeal. In London the appeal,
on December 14, 1928, had been dismissed—in ten minutes.

Obscene in England, not obscene in the United States.
Perhaps the last word on this matter should go to Bernard
Shaw. Although he raised his voice often in behalf of the
book, when asked to be one of the defense witnesses for the
London trial he had disqualified himself by saying that his
testimony would be worthless since he himself was immoral.

Radclyffe Hall never really recovered from it all. Worn out
by the proceedings, humiliated in the popular press, gossiped
about socially, she retreated to the south of France, to Saint-
Tropez, a then quiet spot suggested by her friend Colette.

Among the many press insults she had suffered was a satirical booklet called *The Sink of Solitude*. The booklet did
pulverize rather nicely James Douglas's *Express* attack on the
novel and Home Secretary Joynson-Hicks' prosecution of it:

I warn Mr. Douglas that there is a limit to the patience of
the Great British Public who read this pamphlet. I say deliberately that his newspaper is not fit to be sold by any news-
boy or borrowed in any railway carriage, because it inculcates,
nay it encourages, the habit of abusing words. This filthy
vice stalks hydra-headed in our midst, crawls in our tubes and
buses, and haunts our breakfast tables. I would rather give
Sir William Joynson-Hicks a copy of the *Sunday Express* than
a dose of prussic acid.[17]

The booklet also contained a less successful verse lampoon
of the novel. But what most affected Hall were the biting
caricatures of her and the equally biting comment on the
novel which ticked it off as a trivial and vulgar work that tried
to glorify the "pathetic post war lesbians with their mannish
modes and poses."

Lady Troubridge reports that in an attempt to amend this
insult Hall wrote her next book, *The Master of the House*,
published in 1932. It is a deeply felt religious work about a
carpenter's son in Provence, a tale of a modern Christ figure.
Troubridge also reports that during the writing of this book
Hall suffered from bleeding hands, something they both
thought to be the stigmata.

The two women shifted residences constantly after that—
England, France, Italy—and they continued to raise dogs, a
lifelong interest, wherever they went. It was in Florence, in
1936, that they at last seemed to find an ambiance in which
to settle. Troubridge was related to an old Florentine family,
and they moved easily in society. Their deepening Catholicism found ready expression. The large homosexual colony
welcomed them. And Hall's literary reputation in Italy was
a good one. One Italian, d'Annunzio, then very much a her-
mit holed up in his Villa Vittoriale, resented the treatment
the English had given *The Well of Loneliness*, and as a sort
of recompense, he gave to Hall the silver medal he had been

given by the British Literary Society. It was inscribed *"Gabriele d'Annunzio, poeta e voce d'Italia."* Harold Acton reports that d'Annunzio also gave Hall a laurel wreath, which she kept under a glass dome.[18]

The few good years in Florence were short-lived. The war came, and with their return to England Hall suffered a series of illnesses, including a botched eye operation. In March of 1943, at the age of sixty-three, she became acutely ill, and six months later, after a painful battle with cancer, she was dead. During Hall's final illness Lady Troubridge, of course, was at her side, as she had been for twenty-seven years. Hall's farewell letter to her, which she found after her friend's death, read: "God keep you until we meet again . . . and believe in my love, which is much, much stronger than mere death . . ."

The London *Times* obituary of Marguerite John Radclyffe Hall does not mention Una, Lady Troubridge. But by the time Troubridge died, twenty years later in Rome at the age of seventy-six, things had changed somewhat. The *Times* printed an obituary tribute to her, mentioning her and Hall's deep and rare lifelong friendship: "Few who remember London and the Continent in the twenties and thirties will fail to recall the appearance of these two friends, both so striking-looking in their different ways." And, in speaking of the novel that had catapulted them to prominence, the *Times* went on to say that few would forget "the heresy hunt of a work of considerable art which excited the Philistines to one of their periodic displays of outraged morality."[19]

It is not as a work of art that *The Well of Loneliness* has survived, but as a social document, as a long, impassioned plea for the acceptance of lesbianism. It is the story of a woman who recognizes her homosexuality, struggles against it, and finally accepts it, only to be condemned by society. It's a huge book. In its American paperback edition, which has gone through fifteen printings, it runs 437 pages of eye-straining type. There is no question that the novel is an honest book, a deadly serious book, one with which the author took great pains. It's full of plot and rich with characters, gays *and* straights, the latter a fact critics failed to recognize. At times the writing is quite good. But, for the most part, the book is highly sentimental, too often veering into maddening melodrama—overwritten, mushy, silly. Had Hollywood been a little braver at the time of the book's publication, it could have made one hell of a tear-jerker. (One hesitates to cast the heroine.)

In writing the novel, Hall took a step backward in what was a growing literary reputation. She had a message to put across, and the propaganda obscured the literary merit. As she said at the time of the trial:

> I wrote the book from a deep sense of duty. I am proud indeed to have taken up my pen in defence of those who are utterly defenceless, who being from birth a people set apart in accordance with some hidden scheme of Nature, need all the help that society can give them.[20]

Perhaps the most just comment on the book was the London *Times Literary Supplement* review at the time: "This long novel, sincere, courageous, high-minded, and often beautifully expressed as it is, fails as a work of art through divided purpose . . ."[21]

Radclyffe Hall felt that lesbianism was a congenital phenomenon. In the book she pleaded that women who were lesbian were bent that way through no fault of their own, having been born that way. She argued that the suffering—and her characters *do* suffer—was due to society's condemnation, to its inability to recognize that these women comprised a section of humanity, a special section, to be sure, but one that was as valuable as any other. When she wrote the book, despite the advent of Freud, the congenital theory was still accepted in many medical circles. Havelock Ellis, the early sex liberator, who supported the theory, wrote a brief preface for the novel. This prompted one commentator to call him a psychopath.[22] As for the general public, they still felt that lesbianism was simply immoral behavior, no more, and, as such, sinful. This thinking was reflected in the courts when the London magistrate declared, ". . . there is not one word which suggests that anyone with the horrible tendencies described is in the least degree blameworthy."

It's difficult to imagine a liberated lesbian of today relating to the book, except as an historical curio, and it comes as a surprise to hear the totally hip young woman in Kate Millett's 1971 film *Three Lives* tell of how she read *The Well of Loneliness*, "digging" it.

It remains to be said that if one is looking for lesbian sex scenes, *The Well of Loneliness* is not the place to look. The book is not in the least clinical. In fact, it probably qualifies as the longest fictional coming out ever written: not until page 313 of the American paperback edition does the main character, Stephen Gordon, actually go to bed with someone, and when she does it's described like this: ". . . and that night they were not divided."

It was Lady Troubridge who titled the book *The Well of Loneliness*, meaning, of course, the isolation suffered by those ostracized by society. Ever since, moralists, and not a few post-Freud psychiatrists, have misinterpreted the title, gloating on its aptness, in statements like "The book is well named as homosexuals for the most part are lonely and unhappy people."[23] This is not what Radclyffe Hall meant.

CHAPTER EIGHT

The Tell-All 1970s:
Gertrude Stein, Virginia Woolf

HOMOSEXUALS have long gossiped about who among the famous was or is gay. Most heterosexuals have found such lists preposterous; they accept the ancient Greeks, the evidence is too overwhelming to be denied, but when it comes to Jesus, George Washington, and Wild Bill Hickok—as one such published list of three hundred[1] claims—they have tended to balk. And when so many of Hollywood's manufactured sex symbols—male and female, beginning with Rudolph Valentino[2]—are pointed out as homosexual, they pshaw in disbelief. It has been suggested that if the general public realized how many outstanding women of our times are lesbian, this realization would, if not change their attitude toward lesbianism, at least make them consider it a bit more realistically, and make them hesitate somewhat before pronouncing wholesale censure.

In France, in 1972, a number of famous Frenchwomen were approached by the French women's liberation movement working for legalized abortion and asked to sign a declaration that stated, "I declare that I have undergone abortion." Three hundred forty-three such women signed. When the declaration was published, the country was rocked. There were Simone de Beauvoir, Jeanne Moreau, Françoise Sagan, Catherine Deneuve, Marguerite Duras, Violette Leduc—to name only a few—declaring in public that they had broken the law, declaring what women in the past had admitted only in private, and only to those closest to them. The declaration read:

> A million women undergo abortion each year in France. They do it under dangerous conditions, because of the clandestinity to which they are condemned, whereas this operation, practiced under medical control, is one of the most simple.
> Silence is kept about these millions of women.
> I declare that I am one of them. I declare that I have undergone abortion.
> Just as we demand free access to anticonceptional methods, we demand freedom of abortion.[3]

The lesbians who drew up the questionnaire used in Chapter Nine of this book suggested that perhaps a similar statement signed by famous in-the-closet American lesbians ("I declare that I am a lesbian") would be possible to obtain. The project failed utterly. For example, one well-known New York lesbian was approached. The woman lives quite openly, is even rather notorious in her way. She said it was a marvelous idea. "We all should sign. However . . . my Aunt Clara is still alive and it would simply kill her." Other women said, Don't be ridiculous, my career, my family, how naïve can you be? Those who would have been willing to sign were lesbian activists who had already declared themselves publicly in some way. The project was dropped.

Hypocrisy rules the day, and caution, fear of libel suits, rules books such as this one. One ends up speaking mostly of the dead. However, there's no doubt that lesbianism, or at least bisexuality, is being declared more openly than ever before. In 1973, within the space of a few months, four young women entertainers publicly admitted that they were bisexual: folksinger Joan Baez, TV comic Lily Tomlin, actress Maria Schneider, and rock star Janis Joplin (posthumously, in a raft of biographies and articles). In addition, since the mid-1960s, a number of serious biographies have been documenting homosexual aspects of the lives of the discreet. Until then, in this country, such open talk in serious print of closet homosexuals was unheard of. Biographers, critics, and obituary writers handled the matter, if it was touched upon at all, with innuendo and euphemism; secretary dash companion was a standard out when mentioning a subject's homosexual lover. Today, however, especially in a raft of biographies about literary figures, the matter is beginning to be met head on, and such openness seems, if one is keeping track of such things, like something close to mania. Were They or Weren't They? is the current literary game.

The newspaper taboo in this country was broken by the 1965 *New York Times* obituary of Somerset Maugham. Toward the end of his life, Somerset Maugham confessed to his nephew Robin that "his greatest mistake had been to persuade himself that he was three-quarters normal and only a quarter queer—'whereas really it was the other way round.' "[4] When Maugham died, the *Times* brought the fact of his homosexuality, long known to the list-keepers, to the attention of its more unaware readers.

One of the first of the literary biographies to treat the subject in detail was Michael Holroyd's 1968 two-volume work, *Lytton Strachey*, in which there, for all to read, was the Bloomsbury crowd in all its gay splendor. Then there was James Woodress's 1971 biography of Willa Cather (!), whose obsession to keep her private life private did not in the end succeed. And, at the time of this writing, we have *Virginia Woolf: A Biography*, by her nephew Quentin Bell, the book that promised to deal with Virginia Woolf's private life minus her husband Leonard's prudish blue pencil.

And, yes, the hints that appeared in Woolf's diary, in some of her novels, and in Leonard Woolf's autobiography, have proved to be true: Vita Sackville-West was in love with Virginia Woolf. But was Virginia in love with Vita? Yes, says Quentin Bell, certainly emotionally, but as for physical love he concludes: "There may have been—on balance I think that there probably was—some caressing, some bedding together. But whatever may have occurred between them of this nature, I doubt very much whether it was of a kind to excite Virginia or to satisfy Vita."[5] It seems likely that this is true. Woolf appears not to have been a very sexual person; by her own admission she found sex with Leonard not very earth-shaking. She left no comments, at least no published comments, about sex with women. But of her love for women there is no doubt. She loved Madge Symonds and Violet Dickinson, and other women were always falling in love with her. The composer Ethel Smyth fell head over heels, as did Jean Thomas, proprietor of a nursing home in which Woolf spent some time. All of this Bell tells us. Sackville-West tells us that Sally Seton in *Mrs. Dalloway* is patterned on Madge Symonds. At one point in the novel Clarissa Dalloway is remembering her youthful crush on Sally:

She [Clarissa] and Sally fell a little behind. Then came the most exquisite moment of her whole life passing a stone urn with flowers in it. Sally stopped; picked a flower; kissed her on the lips. The whole world might have turned upside down! The others disappeared; there she was alone with Sally. And she felt that she had been given a present, wrapped up, and told just to keep it, not to look at it—a diamond, something infinitely precious, wrapped up, which as they walked (up and down, up and down), she uncovered, or the radiance burnt through, the revelation, the religious feeling!—when old Joseph and Peter faced them:
"Star-gazing?" said Peter.

It was like running one's face against a granite wall in the darkness! It was shocking! It was horrible![6]

This picture of an adolescent crush seems little different from the adult Woolf writing to her sister Vanessa Bell in a sort of romantic innocence: "Vita is now arriving to spend 2 nights alone with me & L. is going back. I say no more; as you are bored by Vita, bored by love, bored by me, & everything to do with me. . . . Still, the June nights are long and warm; the roses flowering; and the garden full of lust and bees, mingling on the asparagus beds."

Vita Sackville-West, who was a confirmed lesbian (though married to Harold Nicolson and the mother of two sons),* adored Virginia Woolf. Woolf couldn't bear the gay crowd in which Sackville-West moved, but Vita herself entranced her. She was fascinated, but at the same time it appears she was somewhat awed by Vita's physicality:

I like her and being with her and the splendour—she shines in the grocer's shop in Sevenoaks with a candle lit radiance, stalking on legs like beech trees, pink glowing, grape clustered, pearl hung. . . . There is her maturity and full breastedness; her being so much in full sail on the high tides, where I am coasting down backwaters; her capacity I mean to take the floor in any company, to represent her country, to visit Chatsworth, to control silver, servants, chow dogs; her motherhood (but she is a little cold and off-hand with her boys) her being in short (what I have never been) a real woman. Then there is some voluptuousness about her; the grapes are ripe; and not reflective. . . .

---

* Vita Sackville-West and Harold Nicolson's extraordinary 49-year marriage, asexual after the first few years, is splendidly detailed by their son Nigel Nicolson in *Portrait of a Marriage*. At the center of the book is a poignant memoir by Sackville-West, which chronicles an early lesbian affair. Published too late for inclusion in the above discussion of Sackville-West and Woolf, the book is highly recommended for further reading.

Woolf, being nothing if not reflective, dealt with the relationship through writing and presented to Sackville-West a novel, *Orlando*, her gift of love. The main character of the book, an aristocrat who changes back and forth from a man to a woman, is patterned on Sackville-West; photos appear in the book. If there was one thing that Sackville-West loved more than Virginia Woolf it was Knole, the estate where Vita had been born and brought up and which even though she was her father's only child she could not inherit, because she was a woman. Woolf gave her a fictional Knole in *Orlando*. Needless to say, Sackville-West would much rather have had a real-life Virginia Woolf.

So. Does any of this make Virginia Woolf a lesbian? No, not in the standard definition of the term. A latent lesbian, then? Half a lesbian, since she did love women emotionally? Such questions only attest to the absurdity of our mania for categorization. For the moment and perhaps definitively Virginia Woolf escapes the destiny of being relegated to a lesbian ghetto. Her love for women, however, stands.

There are those who argue, W. H. Auden for one, that such biographic delving is an unfortunate trend, that an author's sexual inclination belongs in the realm of affairs private. Those who disagree, who look to an author's life for illumination of her/his works, feel that a writer's sexual attitude is as important as anything else about her/him. Further, they point out that the love lives of famous heterosexual authors and for that matter famous homosexual authors who lived openly have always been fair game. This present preoccupation of opening closet doors in print does serve to fill in biographical gaps, to unravel puzzling dead ends, to clear away gossip and in the long run to do away with hypocrisy. Whether it serves to enhance the understanding of an author's works depends on what school of literary criticism you follow.

The critics themselves have been very busy. E. M. Forster's

posthumously published early homosexual novel, *Maurice*, has caused some of them to reevaluate the heterosexual relationships in Forster's other novels, thus squeezing him into the male homosexual ghetto. In the case of Willa Cather it is now being pointed out by some that Jim Burden in *My Ántonia* and Niel Herbert in *A Lost Lady* were in actuality a bow to convention; had those novels been written today, some say, Niel and Jim would have been women. Perhaps. It's no secret that many writers have cloaked the sex of their fictional characters. André Gide thought such practice dishonest: "Should poets and novelists pretend to ignore the 'love that dares not tell its name,' when so often it is the only love they know? True art does not live by deception."[7] But Gide was brave, often to the point of tedium. So many other homosexual authors bowed to convention. Proust, for one. Gertrude Stein for another.

Gertrude Stein, unlike Renée Vivien and Radclyffe Hall, never made a public display of her lesbianism. No flamboyant escapades for her, no crazy-quilt soirees of dancing women, no tell-all autobiographical writings—that is, none that she allowed to be published in her lifetime. Just she and Alice B. Toklas living as "companions," as "friends," the exact nature of their thirty-nine years together known only to a few, although guessed at by others, the guessing undoubtedly helped along by Stein's extraordinary haircut. In Paris she lived only minutes from that other salon-keeper Natalie Barney, and although the two knew each other, their meetings were limited to occasional *quartier* promenades with Stein's white poodle Basket, occasional forays into pastry shops—they both had inordinate sweet tooths—and, of course, occasional literary gatherings. Stein was never a member of Barney's circle of international lesbians, a veritable Mafia-like network, and did not participate in their endless game of musical beds.

Gertrude Stein thought Natalie Clifford Barney somewhat corrupt.

Gossip about Stein there always was, in abundance, but not until twenty years after her death and hot on the heels of Toklas's death, the mid-sixties, did documentation of the nature of their friendship begin to appear in print. Today, Stein would be horrified to see, the closet door is wide open and in the process nothing seems to be sacred, not even, alas, her very private uterus.

It happened in *The New York Review of Books*. A reader, a woman, bothered by an article in which the composer Virgil Thomson had discussed lesbian aspects of his good friend Stein's work, and also upset by a new book about Stein's works in which the matter was also lengthily discussed, wrote in a letter to the editor that she found such talk about Stein's "alleged" lesbianism "destructive." This letter writer was no casual reader of Stein, but in fact had acted as editor for a collection of the author's works. Sounding very much like one of Sappho's misguided critics, the letter writer claimed that Stein never was a bona-fide lesbian, that Stein and Alice B. Toklas, with whom Stein lived for thirty-nine years, "made a home for themselves with an emotional attachment as the bond that kept them together. But lesbianism—never." To "prove" that actual things sexual never reared their heads, the letter writer pointed out that just before Stein's death she was operated on and found to have a calcified uterus; this fact prompted the woman, who to all appearances knows as little about medicine as she knows about lesbian relationships, to speculate that "any woman who had experienced any kind of pleasurable genital activity during her adult life, even masturbatory, would [not] develop calcification of the uterus."

Virgil Thomson neatly replied to the letter with a quote from French writer Rémy de Gourmont, good friend of Natalie Barney: "Among all sexual aberrations, chastity remains

the most astonishing." Thomson then continued on his own:
"And crediting this poverty of experience to either Gertrude
Stein or Alice Toklas seems to me no less 'destructive' than
to admit the lesbian practice that has long been known to
have characterized their friendship, also in the case of Miss
Stein, to have achieved innumerable covert references in her
writings."[8]

Most of Gertrude Stein's writings, to say the very least, are
difficult to decipher. Natalie Barney was plainly stumped. In
a very fey introduction to a collection of some of Stein's
writings, Barney confessed that for the most part she couldn't
make head or tail of the writings she was supposed to intro-
duce. She wrote, "I have read steadily through 'Didn't Nelly
and Lilly Love You' [one of the pieces in the collection].
Though I can't make out whether they did or didn't—the
chances being two against one they didn't."[9] She then gave
up and fleshed out her introduction with Steinian anecdotes.

Some of Stein's impenetrability, though by no means all,
can be attributed, as Edmund Wilson once noted, "to a need
imposed by the problem of writing about relationships between women of a kind that the standards of that era would
not have allowed her to describe more explicitly."[10] This is
clearly evidenced in Stein's erotic love poetry, which she began to write when in her forties and which at her own request
was not published during her lifetime. The poems are full of
false names, puns, private language, and difficult erotic imagery. Two examples, the fifty-page love lyric "Lifting Belly"
and the shorter "A Sonatina Followed by Another," read at
first glance like just so much nonsense; without a work like
Richard Bridgman's heavily documented *Gertrude Stein in
Pieces* close at hand, impatience triumphs. Bridgman took
time to read systematically through *all* of Stein, a herculean
task attempted by few critics. Of the erotic love poetry he
says, "Physical passion had been virtually absent from Gertrude Stein's work since *The Making of Americans*, or at

least sufficiently disguised to be invisible. Now, though, as she entered her forties, the demon of noon capered openly through her writing."[11]

It's fairly easy to figure out that "Lifting Belly" is a tribute to Toklas, and to their love. In it Toklas is called Baby, Honey, Pussy (the nicknames we know from Hemingway's 1964 A *Moveable Feast* and Virgil Thomson's 1966 autobiography). "Lifting belly" sometimes refers to Toklas, sometimes to physical lovemaking: "Lifting belly is famous for recipes." "Lifting belly can please me because it is an occupation I enjoy."[12] And so on for fifty pages. At least one Stein enthusiast feels that "lifting belly" may also refer to "lifting the tone of Belley," the French country town in which Stein and Toklas lived, thus making the term a triple private word play.

In "A Sonatina Followed by Another" appear such lines as: "I love you, I know it, how do you know it, I know it by my feeling." "In loving me she of necessity thought first. And so did I. How prettily we swim. Not in water. Not on land. But in love." "How can I thank you enough for holding me on the ladder for allowing me to pick roses, for enjoying my fireside and for recollecting stars. How can I thank you enough for all your kindness to me. How can I thank you enough." All very clear. But there are passages that are very unclear: "Can a cow keep sweet. Yes if it has a blessing. Can a cow keep its retreat. No not if it has a blessing. Can a cow have feet. Yes if it has a blessing. Can a cow be perfect. Yes if it has a blessing. I bless the cow. It is formed, it is pressed, it is large it is crowded. It is out. Cow come out. Cow come out and shout. Have Caesars a duty. Yes their duty is to a cow. Will they do their duty by the cow. Yes now and with pleasure."

And later: "Caesars stay they do not stray. Stretch away not into the distance but close to and successfully separating they permit indeed they insist indeed they cause indeed they aid they do not pause they cause and we register with a smile and a nod that there is no need of a prod indeed we register that satisfaction has been obtained."[13]

Bridgman has pondered the use of the words "cow" and "Caesar" and has quoted from other poems: "Cows are very nice. They are between legs." "Caesars are round a little longer than wide but not oval." Bridgman's modesty prevents him from giving exact meaning to the words "cow" and "Caesar." They "make the most sense as parts of the body, physical acts, and character traits," he says, requiring us to try our own hand. Clearly they make the most sense as symbols for the particular parts of the body involved in the act of cunnilingus. "We have been very wise to enjoy ourselves so much and we hope to enjoy ourselves very much more," says Stein in "A Sonatina Followed by Another." In this poem, "cow" also would seem to mean orgasm: "Now let us say pussy. When did I say pussy. You are so full of a cow factory. You manufacture cows by vows. The cows produce reduce reduce they reduce the produce. Cows are necessary after feeding. We are needing what we have after feeding. After feeding we find cows out. How are cows multiplied. By proper treatment."

Stein's erotic love poetry is a mixture of fun and her famous juggling of words. It is also sometimes just plain coy and silly, but then the private language of lovers, any lovers, does not fall comfortably on foreign ears, nor does it translate well into print, even if accompanied by a scholarly glossary.

There is only one of Stein's books with a lesbian theme that needs no glossary. No obscure symbolism here, just a realistically told story of a lesbian triangle love affair in which, according to her letters and notebooks, Stein herself participated. This book, her first, is *Q.E.D.*, written in 1903 when she was twenty-nine. Stein forbade its publication in her lifetime. Four years after her death it was brought out, in 1950, under a new title, *Things As They Are*, in a limited edition of 516 copies, which hardly anyone read. Even someone acting as an editor for a collection of her works—the letter-to-the-editor writer mentioned earlier—apparently didn't know of its existence; Stein herself had refused to include it in the definitive *Yale Catalogue* of her work. Recently, however, the book has come to life again, reissued under its original title for wider distribution in the collection *Fernhurst, Q.E.D. and Other Early Writings.*

Q.E.D. (which means *quod erat demonstrandum*, the classical signature to a geometric proof) is a detailed account of Stein's discovery of her lesbianism and her coming out, an episode that started sometime around 1900 during her medical-school days at Johns Hopkins and continued through three tumultuous years of a love affair, her first. Stein's coming out was by no means a snap. It was a struggle.

The plot of *Q.E.D.* is patently autobiographical. Adele (Stein in real life) is a terribly bourgeois young woman who subscribes wholeheartedly to society's rules of decency. When she falls in love with another young woman, Helen (in real life May Bookstaver, a Baltimore friend), she is confronted with the fact that her feelings do not fall under things society considers decent. As a young intellectual, she tries to resolve the dilemma in her head. When Helen first kisses her, Adele's response is silence. Helen says, "Well!" Adele says, "Oh, I was just thinking." Helen: "Haven't you ever stopped thinking long enough to feel?" Later, alone, Adele thinks, "I am afraid it's too big for me." She decides to stop thinking. Then, suddenly, it comes to her: "Why, it's like a bit of mathematics. Suddenly it does itself and you begin to see. I am afraid Helen wouldn't think much of that if it's only seeing. However I never thought I saw before and I really do think I begin to see. Yes it's very strange but surely I do begin to see."[14]

Helen, a free spirit, does not help Adele through her puzzlement. Instead she chides her: "Let us go and see Jane

Fairfield. You don't know her of course but that makes no difference. She is queer and will interest you and you are queer and will interest her. Oh! I don't want to listen to your protests, you are queer and interesting even if you don't know it and you like queer and interesting people even if you think you don't and you are not a bit bashful in spite of your convictions to the contrary, so come along." Helen, unknown to Adele, is also having an affair with another woman, Mabel (in real life the liberated Mabel Haynes from Bryn Mawr), a wealthy woman who pays Helen's bills and takes her to Europe.

When Adele does yield physically to Helen she remains troubled. Helen says, "You realize that there ought to be shame somewhere between us and as I have none, you generously undertake it all." Later, Adele finally accepts her own feelings, is ready to take the plunge, to love wholeheartedly. But Helen, still involved with Mabel, asks Adele to please be patient until things work out. Adele spends three years being patient, as Helen shuffles between her and Mabel, in America and abroad. Helen will not give Mabel up, she is tied to her financially. Adele, in love, will not agree to half an affair. In the end Adele recognizes the deadlock when Helen rejects her final plea to please see things as they are.

Q.E.D. is interesting, fascinating really, on a number of levels; for our purposes here it is the lesbian subject matter that is relevant. This was the first and last time Stein was explicit in her writings about lesbian relationships. Critic Leon Katz writes in his introduction to Q.E.D. that the love affair "is used as the paradigm for love" in Stein's short story "Melanctha," which was included in her first innovative book, Three Lives. Katz says, "Ostensibly the story of a mulatto girl and a Negro doctor in Baltimore, 'Melanctha' is in fact the story of Q.E.D. in disguise, with May Bookstaver as Melanctha and Stein as the tormented doctor"— certainly one possible interpretation. After that book all became cows and Caesars.

Q.E.D. is an anomaly in the annals of lesbian fiction. Most of the better-known works with lesbian themes resolved themselves in anguish and despair. No matter the tale told, the ending was assured: a harrowing bloodbath (Balzac's *The Girl With the Golden Eyes*); a heartrending parting (Radclyffe Hall's *The Well of Loneliness*); a fatal accident (D. H. Lawrence's *The Fox*); a suicide (Lillian Hellman's *The Children's Hour*). And so on. If death itself didn't triumph, certainly death of the soul did. In Q.E.D. it is not societal condemnation of lesbianism that turns the plot, but rather the characters of the three women. The novel presents three educated women involved in a slice of human living and loving. It's a classic triangle: Helen, a woman at peace with her lesbianism, juggles two very different lovers; Mabel, one of the lovers, gets the better part of this juggling; Adele, the other lover, does not. A classic triangle, one of literature's lasting themes: someone has to lose. But in Q.E.D. nobody commits suicide, nobody goes insane, and nobody bows to societal pressure. The lover-loser simply loses, a bit of refreshing honesty in lesbian literature. The author, by hiding this book for so many years, was not so honest. Ironically, if she had been more honest, she would have been spared the fact of her posthumous uterus being dragged through the literary mill.

Honesty in lesbian fiction is a rarity. Even Violette Leduc, the French writer who was so open about her lesbianism, admits that in *Thérèse et Isabelle* she failed:

> It was love itself I wanted to describe. . . . I wrote [the book] at a steady three hours a day, with Isabelle's river tresses in my mouth, in my throat. . . . There was more to be said, and I was unable to say it. I failed; there is no doubt in my mind about that. I don't regret my labors. It was an attempt. Other women will go on from there, others will succeed where I failed.[15]

It has been suggested that Stein first hid Q.E.D. because

she never would have found a publisher in the early 1900s.
This is surely true. It has also been suggested that many
years later, in 1941, she refused to include it in the *Yale Catalogue* because she thought of it as merely an apprentice work.
This is possibly true. But no one has mentioned that Stein
probably hid the book because of its autobiographical subject
matter. Actually, it is the autobiographical aspect of the
book that is most intriguing. Not only do we now know that
it took Stein a long time to accept her lesbianism, but from
her notebooks we have learned that it took her an equally
long time to recover from the pain of this first unsuccessful
affair. As we've mentioned, Stein was not a flitting-type
woman, able to jump into any bed and life that crossed her
path. She sat down to write *Q.E.D.* immediately after the
Bookstaver affair. We know that after the deadlock of that
affair and after she had written the book about that affair,
she permanently decided against society's standards of decency and expatriated herself to Paris, where after meeting
Toklas she lived out her discovery for the rest of her years.
She had decided, as she wrote in *The Making of Americans*,
"I like loving. I like mostly all the ways any one can have of
having loving feeling in them. Slowly it has come to be in
me that any way of being a loving one is interesting and not
unpleasant to me."[16]

It is not clear when the word "gay" came to be used to de-
note things homosexual. *The Oxford English Dictionary*
cites no homosexual use of the word. Eric Partridge's *A Dictionary of Slang and Unconventional English*, seventh edition, lists no derivation, merely says that the homosexual
meaning of the term came into use c. 1930, perhaps earlier.
It is interesting to speculate that perhaps it did come into
use earlier, even as early as 1908, when Gertrude Stein wrote
the short story "Miss Furr and Miss Skeene." In this story
Stein seems to juggle the various meanings of "gay," including, one suspects, primarily its homosexual meaning:

Helen Furr and Georgine Skeene were regularly living where very many were living and cultivating in themselves something. Helen Furr and Georgine Skeene were living very regularly then, being very regular then in being gay then. They did then learn many ways to be gay and they were then being gay being quite regular in being gay, being gay and they were learning little things, little things in ways of being gay. . . .[17]

Stein based the two women in her story on two real-life women, Ms. Squire and her friend Ms. Mars, visitors to Stein's rue de Fleurus salon. In 1933 Ms. Squire (the fictional Miss Furr), who was living in Vence, in the south of France, with her friend Ms. Mars, dropped a note to Stein and Toklas:

If you ever come down this way do come & see us. We think Vence a beautiful place, & we have a villa here. I don't believe you liked Vence much—I believe you said it gave the impression of always walking up hill—but we like the scenery and being near Nice & the shore—which is gay & sophisticated. You see Miss Furr still likes gay things & being gay & wanting everybody & everything else to be gay. With lots of love to you both.

She signs the letter "Miss Furr and Miss Skeene."[18] When this letter was written, 1933, Partridge says the word "gay" to mean homosexual was definitely in use.

Stein wrote *A Long Gay Book* during the same general period in which she wrote "Miss Furr and Miss Skeene," 1909–1912. In *A Long Gay Book* Stein states that there are "many kinds of men and women and many millions made of each kind of them." And:

Every one of the kinds of them has a fundamental nature common to each one of the many millions of that kind of them a fundamental nature that has with it a certain way of thinking, a way of loving, a way of having or not having pride inside them, a way of suffering, a way of eating, a way of drinking, a way of learning, a way of working, a way of beginning, a way of ending. . . . Sometimes it takes long to know it in them which kind of fundamental nature is inside them. Sometimes it takes long to know it in them, always there is mixed up with them other kinds of nature with the kind of fundamental nature of them, giving a flavor to them sometimes giving many flavors to them, sometimes giving many contradictions to them, sometimes keeping a confusion in them and some of them never make it come right inside them.[19]

Throughout *A Long Gay Book* Stein argues, in her repetitive and bare-bones fashion, for self-searching and acceptance of what one finds, whatever it may be. Considering what we know of her word-juggling, it seems possible she is using the word "gay" in the title, which never appears in the text (as it does constantly in "Miss Furr and Miss Skeene"), not only to mean the happiness that results from self-knowledge, but also to mean that homosexuality (gayness) is self-knowledge for some of the many millions of different kinds of people.

Among the new facts tumbling out about Stein's personal life, one of the most astonishing concerns her famous break in friendship with Ernest Hemingway. Until recently hardly anyone knew why these two close friends had argued; most assumed it had had something to do with literature, the writing of it or the publishing of it. Not so. Hemingway himself wrote, "I always wanted to fuck her and she knew it."[20] It is probable that Stein was not entirely unwilling. But Toklas put her foot down. "You know," Toklas told good friend Donald Sutherland shortly before her death, "I made Gertrude get rid of [Hemingway]."[21]

It boggles the mind to think what it would have been like if those two extraordinary souls actually had come together.

Neither of them ever wrote explicitly about this attraction, but both did pussyfoot around it. Stein was always quick to list Hemingway's faults, but she invariably ended by saying, Ah, well, "I have a weakness for Hemingway."[22] Hemingway was not so gentle in print. In A Moveable Feast he wrote about their final break: "There is not much future in men being friends with great women although it can be pleasant enough before it gets better or worse, and there is usually even less future with truly ambitious women writers." He then went on to describe a visit to Stein's house, where he overheard an argument she was having with an unnamed "companion" (Toklas, of course): "I heard someone speaking to Miss Stein as I had never heard one person speak to another; never, anywhere, ever. Then Miss Stein's voice came pleading and begging, saying, 'Don't, pussy. Don't. Don't, please don't. I'll do anything, pussy, but please don't do it. Please don't. Please don't, pussy.' "

Don't do what?

Hemingway did not elaborate. "That was the way it finished for me, stupidly enough . . . She got to look like a Roman emperor and that was fine if you liked your women to look like Roman emperors."[23] By the time he wrote this in A Moveable Feast, Hemingway had probably convinced himself that he broke with Stein merely because she was a woman who no longer suited him, a point on which mutual friends (and Hemingway's unpublished letters) cast doubt.

W. G. Rogers, who, with his wife, was a long-time friend of Toklas and Stein, found nothing embarrassing in the women having pet names for each other: "Alone by themselves, Miss Toklas was 'Pussy' and Miss Stein 'Lovey' and a deep attachment united them for almost half a century."[24]

But what of Toklas's admission that she made Stein get rid of Hemingway? Toklas also told Sutherland that she made Stein get rid of someone else: Mabel Dodge.

Those who knew that Stein and Toklas were lesbians regarded Toklas, perhaps modern history's most famous secretary dash companion, as merely the meek appendage of the forceful-looking Stein, someone relegated to sitting in corners talking hats and recipes with the wives and mistresses of the male geniuses who visited the rue de Fleurus salon. It seemed a stereotypic relationship, Toklas playing femme to Stein's butch. But, as Stein herself never tired of saying, things as they seem are not things as they are. Femmes—i.e., appendages—do not say no to the likes of Hemingway and Mabel Dodge, and their butches do not go along with such wishes. In addition, Stein's poetry shows Toklas every bit the equal of her lover. Further, since their deaths we have learned that Toklas not only typed Stein's manuscripts but did a lot of heavy editing, suggesting, arguing, even actual writing. What the public saw and heard about, sturdy square-shaped Stein center stage and her thin companion in the wings busy typing, cooking, and handling servants, was only the public side of the story. Any resemblance between Toklas's relationship with Stein and a butch–femme relationship is pure myth, Stein's masculine haircut notwithstanding. Toklas was one strong dyke.

The recent tell-all literary biographies too often are read simply for their titillation value, and nothing more. Who really cares, except a handful of Stein enthusiasts, that she resorted to subterfuge in her love poems? But we are curious about her sex life. We have an extraordinary curiosity about what people do in bed; for several years now, among the only books that publishers are certain will approach the best-seller lists are books that deal with sex.

For women who live together who are *not* lesbian, open talk in print of lesbianism as a common practice is disquieting; such women become more and more "suspect" and society's disapproval comes unwarranted. For women who live together but for family or professional reasons decide not to make known the lesbian aspect of their relationship, such open talk is frightening. At a New York dinner party, a fifty-three-year-old woman, a lesbian, who holds down one of the few top-echelon establishment jobs that are held by women, reprimanded me for writing this book. "Don't do it," she said, "don't rock the boat." This woman has been in the closet for thirty years. Publicly her boat sails a steady course. It is unthinkable to her to live openly at this point in her life. She has spent thirty years creating her double identity. She refused an invitation to be interviewed about her life, even anonymously. She said it was "too late" for her, she had set her course, she's been successful at it and she did not welcome entrance of what she termed "the leering public" into her life. Any effort by women who do not hide their lesbianism to convince this woman otherwise, to point out that, from their point of view, things could be better, should be better, would fall on deaf ears. This homosexual woman's attitude is little different from the attitude of anti-women's-liberationist Midge Decter in her book *The New Chastity*, which states, never explicitly, of course, that the author has made it in a man's world, what her challengers would call a sexist world, that she has structured her life within society's curbs and has been successful at it. In effect, she too says, Don't rock the boat. One can safely say that both women, one a lesbian, one not, fear a backlash. From the viewpoint of those who want to rock the boat—and, they would say, ultimately bring it into a better port—the fear itself is a telling comment on the two women's lives.

It would seem that at the moment the titillation factor in delving into the lives of famous closet homosexuals overwhelms whatever merit is to be had from such endeavors. And it would seem that until and if an entirely new attitude toward sexuality, a reversal in what has been called our sex-obsessed but anti-Eros time, comes about, the titillation factor will prevail—and the fragile psyches of women like Virginia Woolf along with the private parts of women like Gertrude Stein will be cause only for gawking.

Part III

CONTEMPORARY VOICES

The doctrines which best repay critical examination
are those which for the longest period
have remained unquestioned.

—ALFRED NORTH WHITEHEAD

CHAPTER NINE

Some Questions and Answers

IN THE last few years in this country there has been a tremendous media breakthrough in the covering of the phenomenon that has come to be called the gay liberation movement. Homosexuals who participate openly in liberation actions belong to various autonomous groups whose philosophies and politics differ widely but whose goal is identical: an end to legal, religious, economic and social discrimination. The movement can also be described as a minority group, rejected by society, that is banding together to raise the consciousness of all homosexuals, to declare that the hiding of one's homosexuality inflicts personal psychic damage and that "coming out," admitting one's homosexuality, instills pride and self-esteem.

The movement that is active today is usually dated from a June evening in 1969 when New York City policemen raided a Greenwich Village gay bar and homosexuals, for the first time, fought back, precipitating a riot that lasted three nights. Nothing has been the same since. It is little realized, however, that certain groups of homosexuals have been fighting openly for their rights for some twenty-five years.

This older movement, once called the homophile movement, operated quietly and politely, the groups often working through "safe" organizations, such as sympathetic church groups. The first time an early gay rights group picketed the White House, women members were instructed to wear dresses, high heels, and stockings; the men wore white shirts, neckties, and jackets. This phase of the movement started after World War II and gained impetus from the publication, in 1948, of the first Kinsey Report, which, as has been noted, shocked the American public into the realization that homosexuality was so widely practiced in this country as to be a fairly common occurrence—not merely the bizarre practice of a handful of misfits who could be dismissed as faggots and dykes. Although the more militant of today's gay activists look back on the early agitators as too conservative and fairly ineffectual, it should be pointed out that these early activists survived the McCarthy witch-hunting days, when the silence of the fifties made any sort of protest unusual, if not dangerous.

The earliest lesbian organization of this sort was the Daughters of Bilitis (which took its name from the Pierre Louÿs book).* DOB, as it is called, was organized on the West Coast in 1955 as a social group, an alternative to women meeting in gay bars. The group slowly evolved into working for legal reform, into gathering research and disseminating information about lesbianism. Most of the women in the chapters throughout the United States joined under false names, and the organization's magazine, *The Ladder*, was sent to subscribers in a plain brown envelope. *The Ladder*, founded in 1956, was at first a rather amateurish chitchat sheet; in 1972, when it folded for lack of funds after sixteen continuous years of publication, it was a solid professional sounding board of articles and fiction of concern

---

* See page 166.

to the lesbian community. *The Ladder* had severed its affiliation with DOB in 1970.

Like the early movement, the early Daughters of Bilitis was a conservative organization. With the coming of the seventies (true to the maxim that one of the characteristics of oppressed peoples is that they fight among themselves) various chapters of DOB broke off into militant action groups. For a firsthand account of the early days, see *Lesbian/ Woman*, by Del Martin and Phyllis Lyon, the women who founded DOB and have worked for over twenty years for gay rights.

Although there are conservative gay rights groups working today, most of today's movement is a far cry from those early quiet days. Today's activists are noisy, militant, publicly proud. They don't hide behind high heels and neckties. Their protests occur wherever and whenever discrimination is in evidence. Most lesbians have nothing to do with the movement, choosing to remain in the closet. Others have worked within the movement but have abandoned it, charging that it is basically a male movement, that sexism is as rampant in the gay movement as it is in society in general; these women have formed all-women groups of their own or they are working primarily in the women's liberation movement. Other lesbians work side by side with gay men.

In an effort to find out how some lesbians feel about the gay rights movement (and about other matters), a questionnaire was constructed by three women who are lesbians; they were as curious about the lives of other lesbians as the public in general is curious about the lives of all lesbians. The questionnaire and the responses are not presented as scientifically or statistically valid; but from a humanistic point of view they are of value. The opinions expressed in the responses, like the opinions of the women interviewed at the beginning of this book, say nothing definitive about lesbians or lesbianism. The responses are simply the thoughts and experiences of individual

witnesses and serve to emphasize the heterogeneous nature of
this minority group. The women who responded to the
questionnaire range in age from their early twenties to their
early seventies. They live in all parts of the country, although
few responses came from the South. Their occupations are
various; they are clerks, college professors, printers, students,
editors, and so on. They either hide their lesbianism, are publicly active in gay rights activities, or live life styles somewhere
between the two. Some have had heterosexual experience;
some are married; some are divorced; some are separated; some
are raising children. All consider themselves lesbian. The responses in this chapter are a sampling of the answers to several of the questions asked. The complete questionnaire and
one complete set of responses (from a seventy-five-year-old
woman) will be found in the next chapter.

The question *"What are your feelings about the gay liberation movement?"* elicited the following sampling of responses:

- I got into the movement, worked for several years,
  made progress personally regarding my homosexuality,
  butted my head against a brick wall concerning the almost completely male chauvinistic movement, lost interest in doing their thing, and have decided to do my
  thing for a while.
- Like all movements, the gay lib movement has some
  good things to say and some crazy things. But my feeling is that things, the situation of leading a gay life, can
  only get better. So if gay lib moves one step backward
  for each one forward, I'll settle for it. Personally, I am
  more concerned with women's move to change their
  status as a sex-oppressed majority. I see the problems
  that exist between these two groups, which have some
  things in common but are having a difficult time join-
  ing forces. I do not belong to a gay or women's lib

group as such. I attend no meetings or rallies, yet I write congressmen and public officials, and offer support in living as I see fit as a woman first, a lesbian second.

- I'm all for it.
- It stinks.
- Viva!
- It's irrelevant to lesbians.
- On the whole I think it's a good thing—but I tend to be more conservative than most of the active people in the movement. I pray we don't have a backlash of the sort caused when the black movement began to take more violent steps. I realize we have to be seen and heard to ever make any strides forward, but at times, reading and hearing of some of the ways in which movement people are getting to be seen and heard, I long for a little more dignity in our approach.
- I think we gain ground faster by unpublicized "living propaganda"—i.e., living as a lesbian with no apologies and no trumpeting of superiority.
- I'm afraid I'm for it only abstractly. Group efforts of any sort make me uncomfortable. I'm an elitist at heart.
- I am positive that at this stage, I could not participate, but for the most part I am glad that someone is taking action along this line. I do feel that sometimes they do more harm than good.
- It is wonderful for male homosexuals. It has no bearing on lesbians.
- I've been involved with Mattachine–Daughters of Bilitis type things a long time. A more radical movement took a long time in coming. Hate the maleness of Gay Liberation Front but also am not a "revolutionary" as most of the active woman's lib types seem to be. Right now I can't identify with any specific movement.

- I think it's good. It has gotten people's attention. That's how the blacks have gotten where they are today, that's the *only* way we'll ever get any rights. We have to take them, they'll never be handed to us. But I don't believe in the use of violence unless violence is used against us first.
- I am not entirely·familiar with it, although I applaud any person/group who works for gay understanding via *sensible* means.
- May we keep the strength and determination to go on.
- The more that is said about homosexuality in the media, the more people who personally tell their friends and family, the quicker lesbianism will be known to be a common thing and then we can stop using up our time worrying and marching and get on with our lives.

Individual opinions aside, has the movement in general been effective? It is still too early to judge the final effect of the gay movement; only in historical perspective can the pros and cons be fairly weighed. Here is a miscellaneous list of various gay liberation actions and some of the results:

At the 1972 Democratic National Convention a minority platform plank that would guarantee rights for homosexuals was proposed. A lesbian and a male homosexual, who said they were speaking for twenty million homosexuals, addressed the convention (and, via TV coverage, the nation) in support of the proposal. The proposal was defeated, but its very existence was an unheard-of occurrence. It is interesting to note that before the Democratic convention certain members of the Republican "dirty tricks" organization circulated phony letters that claimed that one Democratic presidential hopeful had been arrested for homosexual offenses. There was also a plan to hire people who would "dress up" as homosexuals to demonstrate in support of the Democratic presidential nominee, the hope being that the public would be turned off, frightened of the influence homosexuals would have if the nominee were elected.

Throughout the country homosexuals have run openly for public office.

State and city legislative bodies are being picketed, lobbied, flooded with literature, all in an effort to influence change in discriminatory laws.

The Pentagon has been invaded by groups of homosexuals protesting policies that bar homosexuals from the armed forces and from jobs in the Department of Defense.

Sit-ins have occurred at employment agencies that use special codes for applications from homosexuals (as they do for blacks). Boards of education and other bodies that discriminate against the hiring of homosexuals have been attacked.

Gay librarians have formed a task force within the American Library Association. They have protested discriminatory hiring practices; they have battled anti-homosexual prejudice that is reflected in library card catalogues; they have drawn up a bibliography of sound books on homosexuality; they have established an annual Gay Book Award.

Gay churches run by gay ministers have been formed.

On college campuses gay rights organizations have formed and have demanded the recognition of gay social activities; university courses on homosexuality are offered on dozens of campuses; homosexuals are running openly for campus offices.

Protest groups have appeared in force at major psychiatric conventions; a recent group gathered together a solid body of research against the "sickness theory" and presented it to the American Psychiatric Association in an effort to get the organization to revise their "Diagnostic & Statistical Manual of Mental Disorders" that lists homosexuality as one of the mental disorders.* Counseling centers, staffed by sympathetic

* Their efforts have been successful. See footnote in Chapter Four, page 92.

professionals, have been established in various cities to aid
those homosexuals and their families who seek such aid.

The media, archenemies to many militants, have been
attacked in a myriad of ways. In turn, homosexuals are using
the media, as never before, to get across their message; they
are appearing on talk shows, giving interviews, publishing
their own newspapers and magazines and hosting their own
radio shows. They are also lecturing everywhere, from college campuses to women's garden clubs. And they are writing books.

Lesbian mothers have formed groups to deal with their
special problems and have granted media exposure of their
life styles.

Marches, dances, Gay Pride Weeks, film festivals, poetry
readings, and so on attest to a new feeling of self-esteem.

Certainly a large proportion of the public questions these
activities. When activists point out, for example, that legal
discrimination exists, this segment of the public counters
with, Well, lesbianism is against the law, isn't it? A strong
enough statement, certainly, but for the most part these people don't really know what the law says and have no idea
that various legal bodies have been taking a hard look at
these laws in an effort to adjust them. What are the facts?

There are laws against lesbian sexual acts in most U.S.
states (all but nine). However, lesbians are seldom arrested
and almost never convicted. These laws, like those that pro-
hibit oral–genital sex among heterosexuals, are seldom en-
forced—mostly because they are unenforceable. Lesbian acts
generally take place between consenting adults in the privacy of their homes. Those male homosexuals who commit
public sex acts (in washrooms, in parks), or who cruise a
cop, bear the brunt of the laws. This is not to say that lesbians are never arrested. They are, but usually in connection

with other illegal activities. Harassment, however, does occur, as does blackmail.

A number of legal organizations have come to the conclusion that homosexual acts in private between consenting adults should not be prohibited by law. These include the American Law Institute in its Model Penal Code and the Ninth International Congress on Criminal Law. They have based their judgments on the fact that such acts do no damage to others or to the property of others, and they do not threaten the security of the total group. Only when such acts offend "public decency" or when they involve force against minors do the legal bodies feel they should be legally prohibited. The National Institute of Mental Health Task Force on Homosexuality concurs:

> the majority of this Task Force considers that it would be remiss if it did not express its serious misgivings about certain policy measures currently employed with respect to homosexual behavior. We believe that most professionals working in this area—on the basis of their collective research and clinical experience and the present overall knowledge of the subject—are strongly convinced that the extreme opprobrium that our society has attached to homosexual behavior, by way of criminal statutes and restrictive employment practices, has done more social harm than good and goes beyond what is necessary for the maintenance of public order and human decency."[1]

In England, lesbianism has never been illegal. When the Criminal Law Amendment was passed, in 1885, making homosexual acts between adults punishable, lesbians had been included, but Queen Victoria refused to sign the act until all references to women were stricken out. Victoria said that to her knowledge lesbianism did not exist. The references were duly removed. In 1921, with Victoria dead, an attempt was made in Parliament to penalize lesbianism, but it did not succeed. In 1967, male homosexual acts between consenting adults in private were legalized.

In answer to the question *"Have you ever been harassed or treated unfairly because of your lesbianism?"* here are some sample replies:

- I've been called names—lousy butch, etc. And I've been physically threatened once but generally am amazed that most people don't see me as a lesbian and so I have had little trouble.
- Yes, I have been fired from a top state administrative position in the public library system and I have been unable to continue in my chosen field because I will never be recommended by this state agency.
- Never, but I know of some who have, mostly they have been WACs. The ones who followed Frank Kameny's* slogan "Say nothing, sign nothing" came out at worst being transferred away from their lovers. Those who admitted had a rough time and I know several who have gotten dishonorables.
- A little bit on picket lines and in marches. One minor incident with some teenagers laughing at "the dykes." Otherwise no.
- Yes, our landlord didn't like us. He constantly harassed us and even called us "lesbian pigs." We called the police once to make an assault complaint against him because he had pushed his way into our apartment. He took the police into his apartment to talk to them and I think he perhaps told them we were lesbians because when they came out they were sarcastic and threatened to "run us in" if we didn't quit "mouthing off."
- Only community harassment such as name calling.

---

* Kameny was head of the Mattachine Society, a gay rights organization.

Lesbians in this country are barred from military service and from "sensitive" government work; there are lesbians in both fields, of course; they pretend to be heterosexual, so they keep their jobs. Only if their private lives become known are they drummed out. The reasoning behind this seems to be irrational. It is supposed that a woman in "sensitive" government work or in the armed forces who is lesbian could be sexually seduced and then blackmailed into giving away government secrets or committing military sabotage. Treason, a frightenening possibility, rears its ugly head; the fact that the only treasonous acts committed by women that we hear of are committed by Mata Hari–type heterosexual female spies is overlooked. But even more serious is the fact that women like the librarian who responded to the questionnaire have been deprived of their economic rights because of their private sex lives. Since the bugaboo of national security does not pertain in this woman's case, the only fear the state agency can possibly have had is that she would have seduced someone in the stacks. The fact that heterosexual males are the seducers and rapists in our society, and not lesbian librarians, is overlooked. Do heterosexuals ever get drummed out of their livelihoods because of their sex lives? After the fact, yes, sometimes, but *before*, as a preventive measure, as in the case of lesbians in certain professions?

Granted, most lesbians do not lose their jobs. They hide. But what of life on a day-to-day basis that is lived against the background of illegality? Well, for example, two lesbians who live together do not constitute a couple, and if they are raising children they do not constitute a family. They are looked upon as two individual citizens. If one partner dies, the survivor cannot receive benefits that a widow can—Social Security, pension plans for wives, veteran and union benefits. Mortgages for single women are notoriously difficult to obtain; the incomes of a lesbian couple do not constitute joint incomes, they constitute two individual incomes. All sorts of other mundane things, like reduced family-plan airline tickets, are not available. In addition, it is difficult to adopt children into a lesbian household. And in the case of a divorced lesbian who has borne children, there is always the possibility, if the ex-husband brings charges, that the mother will be declared unfit and her children taken from her.

As for inheritance, it is possible through an airtight will drawn up by a competent lawyer to ensure inheritance to the partner. However, families of the deceased can contest the will, or at least delve for minute irregularities. Take the case of Gertrude Stein and Alice B. Toklas.

When Stein died, in 1946, she left hanging on the walls of the Paris apartment she shared with Toklas her famous and valuable collection of paintings and drawings. Stein willed the entire collection to Toklas. Nineteen years later, with the collection valued at more than a million dollars, Toklas was penniless, living in a nursing home without money enough to buy, she sarcastically complained, a bottle of toilet water. The story behind this, as related by the couple's friend Janet Flanner, is not a pretty one.[2]

In her will Stein had stipulated that the paintings could be sold for only two purposes: to publish her unprinted manuscripts and to provide for Toklas's proper maintenance. In both cases Toklas, as heir, was required to ask the Baltimore courts, through which the will had been processed, for permission to sell. For seven years after Stein's death, the collection was untouched. Then, in 1953, Toklas sold some Picasso drawings in order to publish the last of Stein's manuscripts. And in 1961 she sold one Picasso drawing, presumably to provide for her proper maintenance.

The 1961 sale came to the attention of one of Stein's in-laws, Mrs. Allan Stein, wife of Stein's nephew; after Toklas, Allan had been first in line of inheritance. At the time of the discovery of the 1961 sale Allan was dead, and it was his children who now stood second in line. Mrs. Allan Stein, mother of the inheritors, demanded an inventory of the collection. It was learned that in addition to the 1961 sale, other Picasso drawings were missing (the ones Toklas had sold in 1953). It was also learned that Toklas, now eighty-four, had gone on holiday to Rome to escape the cold Paris winter; Mrs. Stein was appalled that Toklas had left all that money hanging on the walls of her apartment. She put some legal machinery into operation and it was discovered that Toklas had neglected the technicality of asking the Baltimore courts for permission to sell—on both occasions. The paintings were removed from the rue Christine apartment and stuck into a bank vault.

Five years later, Toklas was penniless. Thanks to friends like Janet Flanner, Joe Barry, and Donald Sutherland, a Toilet Water Fund was established to see her through her last days.

Legally, Toklas had erred in the paintings episode. Mrs. Stein argued that she was concerned because the apartment had been left unoccupied, easy prey to thieves. (During World War II, when Stein and Toklas had to flee to the French countryside, they had left the paintings in the apartment unattended for five years. Everything survived, intact.) It would seem that anyone with even a bare minimum of compassion would have seen that Toklas's error was a minor one. And that now, when she was old and ill, and because it had been Stein's written and notarized request, she would be looked after in her final days. But Gertrude Stein and Toklas had never really gotten along with the Stein family. When Gertrude Stein was dying and her nephew and his family had just left the hospital room she turned to Toklas and said, "We don't have to see them again."[3] Ununderstanding families are frequent reminders of a lesbian's outsider social status. Toklas was not "family" in general societal terms, but one can't help wondering what thirty-nine years of life with someone makes one.

Aside from legal discrimination, there is, of course, religious discrimination. This, perhaps more than any one thing, has made of the homosexual's life a plight. Detractors say, Well, the Bible says lesbianism is a sin, doesn't it? Tough words to deal with. To answer, So what? immediately brands one. Even though most Americans are only nominally religious, they seldom admit it in such stark terms. What *does* the Bible say?

There is one reference to lesbianism in the Bible, in the New Testament, in Saint Paul's Epistle to the Romans, 1:26, in which women who "did change the natural use into that which is against nature" are said to harbor "vile affections." Judeo-Christian strictures against male homosexuality are much more severe.

Early Jewish religious codes did not mention female homosexuality and condemned male homosexuality only if it took place between fathers and sons. Indeed, male homosexuality was practiced in certain religious rites of the early Jews, Hittites and Chaldeans. General condemnation of male homosexuality in Jewish religious codes appears later, in the seventh century B.C., upon the return of the Jews from Babylonian exile. A wave of nationalism swept these people; they were warned to avoid the way of the Chaldean—i.e., the way of the pagan. In the Old Testament, in Leviticus xx:13, male homosexuality is severely condemned: "If a man also lie with mankind as he lieth with a woman, both of them have committed an abomination; they shall surely be put to death; their blood shall be upon them." The Talmud considers lesbianism a "mere obscenity" and bans the practitioners from marrying priests. Maimonides suggested lesbians should be flogged; male homosexuals, he suggested, should be put to death. Saint Paul, raised a Jew, brought these Jewish sex codes into Christian sex codes. Catholic sex codes condemn lesbianism on an equal footing with male homosexuality.

Throughout medieval Europe moral questions were decided by ecclesiastic law. These laws in turn acted as foundation for English common law, which in turn acted as foundation for the laws of individual U.S. states.

Religious condemnation of homosexuality takes for granted that man's and woman's sexual nature should be governed by divine law. Judeo-Christian sex codes take for granted that procreation is the sole function of sexual acts; a waste of semen and a lack of motherliness is frowned on. It is believed by some that homosexuality would lead to the breakup of the family, the home, and eventually to the extinction of the species. Naturally, biologists don't see it that way. Kinsey comments that such an argument

> ignores the fact that the existent mammalian species have managed to survive in spite of their widespread homosexual activity, and that sexual relations between males seem to be widespread in certain cultures (for instance, Moslem and Buddhist cultures) which are more seriously concerned with problems of overpopulation than they are with any threat of underpopulation. Interestingly enough these are also cultures in which the institution of the family is very strong.[4]

A group of San Francisco ministers, concerned that the civil and human rights of homosexuals were being violated, formed an investigative organization, the Council on Religion and the Homosexual. They have drawn up a "Brief of Injustices" that documents how many basic rights are denied the homosexual. The ministers close their brief with these words: "Fear will never set man free, and fear itself is perhaps the greatest obstacle which man must overcome. In our efforts to become free men we must be guided by the central ethical command of our Judeo-Christian tradition: 'You shall love the Lord your God with all your heart, and with all your soul, and with all your mind, and your neighbor as yourself.' "[5]

Liberal ministers aside, there seems to be no way in which one side can convince the other. If one buys the story of Adam and Eve, lesbianism is an unnatural phenomenon. If one buys the story of evolution, lesbianism is a natural possibility. Although many have tried to reconcile these opposing views, it would seem that reconciliation is quite impossible.

Another common manner in which the uninformed put down lesbianism is to say that the whole world condemns homosexuality, and certainly the whole world could not be wrong. This kind of misguided thinking comes about because we tend to think that what our society disapproves of is universally disapproved of by other societies. The facts do not support this assumption. The most authoritative work in the field of anthropology concerning homosexuality is Clellan S. Ford and Frank A. Beach's *Patterns of Sexual Behavior*. The book, *not* a mass-marketed popular one, is based on a detailed analysis and comparison of the sexual patterns of 190 contemporary societies. By surveying anthropological literature the authors found that in forty-nine (sixty-four percent) of the seventy-six societies about which information on homosexuality was available, homosexuality was considered normal and acceptable in some form. However, since anthropological investigation of female sexual practices that do not include males—lesbianism and masturbation—has seldom been undertaken, of the forty-nine societies that considered homosexuality normal and acceptable in some form, there existed data on female homosexuals in only seventeen. In summing up, Ford and Beach stated: "Our own society disapproves of any form of homosexual behavior for males and females of all ages. In this it differs from the majority of human societies."[6]

Lesbians active in gay liberation urge their sisters who are hiding their lesbianism to "come out," to declare themselves. The women in hiding claim that coming out may be instant

euphoria, but then, how does one deal with day-to-day societal disapproval? One can deal with legal and religious discrimination, but social censure is another thing. Social censure is in fact an almost daily encumbrance. It seems that the
greatest stumbling block to coming out is a fear of how one's
family will react and a fear of possibly ruining one's career.
It is this fear that lesbian activists want to eliminate. Most
lesbians who are in the closet are not at all content with the
situation. Here are some responses to the questions *"Are you
generally in or out of the closet?"* and *"If you are leading a
double life are you content about doing so?":*

- Generally in. For ten years I was completely in. It has
  been only within the last six months that I have really
  opened the door. I have begun telling my close friends
  who are straight (the reactions have been favorable so
  far), as well as making myself known to lesbian acquaintances (who knew anyway). But I don't think I
  am quite ready for the streets. Does that sound about
  halfway out of the closet? I hope eventually to be open
  with everyone who matters to me. This decision was
  prompted by an affair with an older woman who is so
  uptight about being a lesbian that she is miserable. I
  just couldn't face the possibility of being that unhappy
  with myself twenty years from now.
- Totally out. There seemed to be no compelling reason
  not to, since I had nothing—no job, no status, no position to maintain. I had nothing to lose.
- Out, except with my family, and that only because we
  have never openly discussed it; I make no pretenses,
  but they never push the point. When I became very ill
  about seven years ago I realized that could have been
  the game, it doesn't go on forever. I decided to live the
  rest of my life for me as I am and I have never before
  known such happiness and freedom.

- In and out, and the in I'm not content with. It's very hard being schizoid.
- Totally in. I wish I had the courage to be honest.
- I live and work in the art world, where it is accepted fairly generally.
- Totally in. I hate it, but I've learned to live with it.
- Totally in. It is both ridiculous and self-denigrating to deceive others, but I feel society has deceived me all my life by telling me that lesbianism is wrong and bad.
- I did lead a double life for a few years and I was nearly wrecked in the process. A year ago I allowed my full name, age, and city of residence to be printed in a big-city newspaper in an article covering the first church service for homosexuals in this area in which I participated. That is the most open I have been so far.
- In and out, especially with my family. I think my family is aware I'm gay, but I've never really discussed the situation with them—partly because it's not relevant but mostly, I suppose, because I'm scared to. No one in my family has ever discussed sex (I learned everything except about menstruation from books) and it would be a very difficult thing for any of us to talk about among ourselves. I wish I could tell my family I'm gay and I'm happy and content, but I guess I'm still afraid of them. Also, I can't think of a way to say it. I'm not too worried about my job—but just in case, I avoid saying anything definite. Actually, I'm not so concerned about my employers, I can fight them legally. I used to think I was out of the closet, and back then, when gay lib hadn't progressed so much, I guess I was. But times have changed, and the old up-front position has become farther back because of the passage of events. But I do get involved in local gay organizations, all using my own real name.
- Fairly much out; still in with my love's family though.

We know they know, but they can't face it within themselves, so they could never confront us with questions. We do often wish we could be open with them, but they are quite old and our love and respect for them demands silence. My entire family knows. I told my grandmother (she's seventy-eight), and considering the public attitude toward homosexuality in her generation, this is a mighty big step for her. My grandmother loves my mate and I think Gran is actually relieved that I am "married," even though she still can't understand the entire situation. At least she knows I am not alone, 1,300 miles away from her, possibly sick with no one to take care of me—all of those things mothers worry about.

No lesbian likes to be called a "dyke" (except perhaps by other lesbians, much as male homosexuals and blacks use disparaging terms among themselves without attendant onus). The power of the word itself is so strong that many heterosexual women's liberationists have been cowed into silence when anti forces used it against them, dismissing them as a bunch of bull dykes. Where does the word come from? It's not certain, but The Oxford English Dictionary lists as one meaning for it "a louper," from the Scotch, meaning "a person or animal (e.g. an ox or sheep) that leaps over fences; figuratively, a transgressor of the laws of morality." Eric Partridge's A Dictionary of Slang and Unconventional English, seventh edition, lists no derivation of the term but claims that its use as a meaning for "lesbian" started c. 1935. "Dyke" usually connotes a lesbian whose mannerisms are what society calls masculine—the old image of the tough-talking woman who smoked big black cigars and ran around in men's suits. Wherever the word came from, the use of it as applied to heterosexual women's liberationists has scared the hell out of many of them. Which brings up the terribly complicated situation that developed in the women's movement when it was being dismissed as nothing more than a lesbian plot. There are lesbians in the current women's movement, as there have been during any period when women were struggling for their rights. But it is by no means a lesbian dominated movement. In fact, many older lesbians tend to look upon today's movement with a weary eye. We've been there before, they say, now it's the heterosexual woman's turn. Feminists are rejecting the traditional role of woman as an impotent, insecure and inferior being, who lives vicariously through a man. Lesbians have come to this conclusion without benefit of a movement. What lesbians reject is their *femininity*, in the sense that feminist Germaine Greer defines it, as meaning "without libido, and therefore incomplete, subhuman"[7]—their passivity, a result of deeply engrained enculturation, a condition that makes of women female eunuchs. Lesbians do not reject their *femaleness*, far from it; they do in effect claim it, as heterosexual feminists are now doing. In so doing, both groups of women suffer extreme disapproval for not adopting the role of *femininity*, the only female role society deems worthy of reward. Some people still dismiss lesbians by insisting that they are not "real" women. In Simone de Beauvoir's view, this so-called mannishness has nothing to do with their sex lives: "What gives homosexual women a masculine cast is not their erotic life, which, on the contrary, confines them to a feminine universe; it is rather the whole group of responsibilities they are forced to assume because they dispense with men."[8]

So anxious are certain segments of society to deny and wreck the women's movement that when feminist Kate Millett publicly declared her bisexuality they reacted in total glee and negated her book *Sexual Politics*. Since the media had elevated this book—the first of the new wave of feminist writings—to the position of a feminist Bible, denigrating its value on the basis that it was not written by a "real" woman did in effect destroy some of the public's interest in the movement itself. Some feminist groups (by no means all, but some of the more vocal) were quick to purge the lesbians in their midst. Afraid that the onus of lesbianism would negate their efforts, these feminists were quick to destroy some of the women they had called their sisters. There developed within the movement itself terrific backbiting. For a detailed inside look at the question from the point of view of two feminist lesbian activists, see *Sappho Was a Right-On Woman*, by Sidney Abbott and Barbara Love. Millett's personal tailspin, from which she *has* recovered, is detailed in her autobiographical book *Flying*.

In our questionnaire to lesbians we asked, "*What are your feelings about the women's liberation movement, especially in relation to lesbianism?*" Here are some responses:

- It is the *only* movement. Women must unite or the world is doomed to destruction.
- It's worthy of support, but I do nothing to support them except give lip service (no pun intended).
- I feel lesbians can teach straight women a thing or two about surviving without male aid. Once women's lib gets used to the idea of having lesbians among their number they should benefit nicely.
- I feel they are courting us for our bodies and when their cause is won they will turn from us.
- My one encounter with a women's movement group made me feel as though we had nothing in common except job discrimination. The situation may have changed since.
- It's a valid and important movement, but at the moment *so* fragmented. The levels of consciousness of women are *so* various. It's difficult for me to participate actively since so many feminists are uncomfortable with lesbians in their midst. These particular feminists

are terribly afraid of being put down for associating
with lesbians; it seems that in many cases they are not
secure enough in their sexuality to take the chance of
being called a dyke. This is a shame.

- Personally, I'd rather devote any possible energies
  strictly to the lesbian movement.
- It's great. It's especially good for lesbians because we
  generally have to go and work in the "man's world."
  We need all the help we can get for equal pay and job
  opportunities. Also, I think we're glad to see straight
  women wise up to the fact that they can be independent and not just a man's slave and baby-maker.
- I wonder if (1) total equality or (2) mutual appreciation can ever exist between men and women.

And here are some of the other questions that elicited
more than run-of-the-mill responses:

What are your general feelings about heterosexual men?
- They're okay. Women's liberation will eventually
  straighten them all out. Then we can all get on with
  the business of living.
- It depends on the person. Generally speaking, I have
  found that communication is difficult.
- I do not hate men. Some I like very much. I do think
  that they are generally chauvinistic, but that they cannot be blamed for this so much individually as society
  should be for making them this way.
- I hate them. I find them pompous, foolish, unquestion-
  ing in terms of their roles—and far less intelligent than
  most women I have met.
- The rare non-sexist male is a beautiful human being,
  of which there are so few—of either genital sex.
- I like them. I just don't want to sleep with them.
- Some of them are O.K. A few (mostly family) I am
  quite fond of. But the general heterosexual male atti-

tude of big-almighty-prick-rules-the-world irks me no
end.

- Pricks! A few I like, but very few.
- They're pigs.
- I think you're probably looking for answers filled with
  hate and disgust for heterosexual men. I must be in the
  minority of lesbians who think heterosexual men
  should be judged on individual merit. The rage I may
  feel at the double standard/sexual discrimination is not
  directed to a particular man. Most men are conditioned
  to believe this double standard. Some are intelligent
  enough to see its folly. These are the heterosexual men
  whom I want to know.
- The nice ones are nice; the not-nice ones are not nice.

*Discuss your thoughts on role playing in lesbian relationships
—i.e., butch–femme, mother–child, teacher–pupil. Does it
exist? Is it common?*

- It exists among unevolved women. With evolved
  women the roles (society's roles) are shared. Exactly
  the same thing holds true for heterosexual couples.
- I think in most relationships there is a butch–femme
  and a mother–child role. I have observed this in nearly
  all my lesbian couple acquaintances. I think butch–
  femme roles are necessary. This is not, however, as important sexually. I think both can be aggressive and
  passive sexually—I've heard that the butch–femme
  thing is on the way out. This may be so as "unisex" becomes more the thing, but personally I can't see it as
  workable.
- Most of the relationships I have observed, and the one
  I am in, seem to me to be equalitarian relationships of
  adults relating to one another's needs.
- Yes, role playing exists—unfortunately. I've seen each

aspect mentioned above. It is disturbing in its confinement of any personality.

- Role playing is probably the most harmful single aspect of marriages of any kind, straight or gay. It is also the most difficult to understand in oneself and to correct. Every day I am guilty of role playing, especially adopting the "master" or male role at home but using the "servant" or female role at work.

- I'm sure it exists and it may be common especially in the cities, but I've never considered any of my friends or my mate in a certain role. My mate and I simply complete one another.

- My partner and I have a sort of butch–femme relationship in the sense that I like to do the heavy labor around the house, whereas she likes the other things— i.e., cooking, etc. But, since we both work, I sometimes do the cooking, etc. I really feel that the butch–femme thing is a label imposed by our society, because they feel the need to carry over the ridiculous role differences that exist in heterosexual relationships.

- It definitely exists, but I feel it exists less and less with the younger lesbians than it did in years past. Personally, I could never last in a fifty-fifty relationship—I am femme and I need someone butch—but I don't consider that roles should carry through completely even into the bedroom. To the younger gay group we probably look to be the stereotype of role players—but we do not consider ourselves as playing roles. The very term implies one of the partners "playing" a part not quite natural to her. We are both being ourselves and we feel that if we were to try to avoid the butch–femme appearance, then we would be playing roles.

- Lesbians are born into the heterosexual world of sex stereotypes just as are heterosexuals. As they mature and gradually surmount the first big hurdle, that of acknowledging and accepting their nature, they are, for the most part, quite without lesbian models on the one hand, while imbued with heterosexual stereotyping on the other. Some lesbians fall in with that stereotyping easily and thoughtlessly. Those lesbians who persist in denying any meaning to butch–femme are simply those who either have no experience of this attraction or who are denying it in their fear of being accused of copying heterosexuals. I cannot say that all lesbians fall into these two categories, nor is the answer to this of much importance.

If you have ever sought psychiatric help in hopes of being "cured" of lesbianism, please describe why you sought such help and also what happened.

- I have had analysts' help but not to be "cured," only to cope.
- What's to be cured?
- I saw a psychologist about five times to try to get some things straight in my own mind. Basically, I had no one with whom I could talk. He acted as a sounding board for my ideas. He did not try to change me. He was a help. He could look at my situation objectively. I was lucky to find a psychologist who was not "sick" or hung up about lesbians.
- I never have, but once my parents sent me for counseling to "cure" me, but the therapist was a lesbian.
- I went once when I was eighteen and asked to be cured. In the first meeting the psychologist said it was unlikely that I would change. I never went back.
- I sought psychiatric help when I was twenty-five because I had gone through two marriages and was an unhappy person. I decided I wasn't getting better (after a six-month, three-times-a-week stint) and quit.
- I have never considered it.

What myth about lesbianism would you most like to see destroyed?

- That we're sick.
- That all we need is a good screw.
- That lesbianism is an extension of adolescence.
- That we're ugly, hate men, seduce straights, are desperately unhappy.
- That it's an abnormality.
- The butch–femme myth.
- That we are tough or indeed different from other people.
- The myth that homosexual women can never be happy because they really want a man. That kills me!
- That all a lesbian needs is a good fuck to turn her into a docile, sex-hungry heterosexual pussycat.
- The idea that all lesbians hate men. That lesbians are lesbians because they have been rejected by men.
- Hate most the idea that we're sex pots, as even this questionnaire exhibits. Love is the central fact of lesbianism.
- That we are all sexually promiscuous. My father had the idea that any time two women realized they were both gay, they hopped right into bed. I asked him if he hopped right into bed (Mother had died) with every straight woman he knew. He was offended. Also the stereotype butch idea (all lesbians wear short hair and stomp); the idea that we seduce straight women and try to recruit them to our ranks; the idea that we molest children (I used to teach—can just imagine some fourth-grader's parent worried sick that I might make advances to her snotty-nosed brat). And on and on.

Why do you think you are a lesbian?

- Because when I fell in love it was with a woman.

- Chance.
- Because growing up I saw that men had the best of it. I didn't care to imitate my mother. I identified with my brothers and father. For as far back as I can recall, this male I.D. also meant I was vis-à-vis interested in females sexually. My earliest sex fantasies were toward women. I've *always* felt this way. And after marriage and a number of heterosexual affairs I decided it would always be this way, so relax and enjoy it. Now that I'm "well into fade" (old age) I'm really enjoying it.
- Because I couldn't relate mentally to a man in any way.
- Because (a) because; (b) why not; (c) it's fun; (d) I was born this way; (e) who knows. Actually, this is a ridiculous query.
- I think there are many things in my life which have influenced my behavior along this line. My mother is an intelligent and capable woman who has subjected herself to my father, who is her inferior in every way. . . . I spent ten long years being sad and trying to figure out why this has happened to me. I have stopped that now and I intend to spend the next fifty or sixty years being happy and considering myself lucky that my mother's fate will never befall me.
- I can't imagine why you put this question at the end, or why you even bothered to ask it at all.
- I feel that I was born a lesbian—no other explanation.
- I definitely reject the genetic theories—feel that homosexuality is a creation of our early environments and that the mold is probably set before we are even old enough to know there is a difference in little boys and little girls. The environmental influences are probably mostly parental in most cases, in mine I feel sure.
- Somebody up there likes me.
- I don't know.
- I've never been able to accept what the female role in

our society calls for; even as a kid, when I knew nothing
of sexuality, I was not content being a mere reflection
of another human being. Then when sex came along I
found that with men it was always just blah, even with
the rare lover who was able to get out of his narrowly
confined role (which society structured for him too) to
see the joys to be had from an androgynous mix of
activity and passivity. With women, sex is something
in which all our energies get full airing. Not to mention
the incredible tenderness of rhythms and psyches in
tune. And aside from sex, which really is only a small
part of loving, there's that marvelous feeling of day-to-
day independences that reach full expression growing
old together.

A male homosexual friend of mine sent me one of
Rilke's letters to a young poet the other day in which
Rilke talks about love. In it he predicts the day when
the male–female love experience, "which is so full of
error," will alter drastically, after women have "stripped
off the conventions of mere femininity." Someday, he
says, "there will be girls and women whose name will
no longer signify merely an opposite of the masculine,
but something in itself, something that makes one
think, not of any complement and limit, but only of
life and existence: the feminine human being . . ."
What will result, he predicts, is a more human love.
"And this more human love (that will fulfill itself, infinitely considerate and gentle, and kind and clear in
binding and releasing) will resemble that which we are
preparing with struggle and toil, the love that consists
in this, that two solitudes protect and border and salute
each other."

Something very much like lesbian love, I think.

Being a homosexual in today's world is certainly a lot

easier than ever before (at least since the time of ancient Greece). The legacy of negativism under which homosexuals have had to operate is being chipped away, however slowly and painfully. Dissent from the sin/crime/sickness pronouncements is terribly vocal and is coming not only from outside the establishment institutions, especially from gay rights groups, but from within the institutions themselves— from certain bio-scientists, clergy, lawyers, and psychiatrists, who are looking at the matter in new perspective. *However,* the greater part of the general public continues to condemn. Even in the minds of those who consider themselves evolved on the matter, there remains a lingering malaise that there is something not quite right, not quite acceptable, about homosexuality. During a university class on homosexuality, a New York film critic who had been attacked by gay rights activists for his anti-homosexual reviews said that he could accept that homosexuality was not sinful, not criminal, and not a disease. He then shook his head, his eyes mournful and uncomprehending, and said, "But the children—what would we tell our children?" A minister in the classroom seconded the critic's anxiety.

What we tell our children now is that sex between members of the same sex is unnatural. They learn, in Freud's terms, "shame, loathing, and morality." They are not born with these feelings. If we didn't tell them it was unnatural they would simply accept that it was natural—i.e., something that exists in nature. This does not necessarily mean that more children would grow up to be homosexual; it could possibly mean that more children who grow into adults with homosexual feelings would express those feelings in an open, acceptable manner and thus avoid the guilt, depression, and anxiety that accompany repression. Hemingway once said that as a young man on the road in the United States he had to carry a knife to ward off homosexual advances—"you had to be prepared to kill . . ."[9] And Caprio in *Female Homo-*

sexuality made this extraordinary statement in speaking of
latent homosexuals: "Nature protects them against giving
way to their homosexual desires by developing strong prejudices and attitudes against homosexuals. This phenomenon
explains why a man will sometimes assault or even kill a man
who makes improper advances to him."[10] It is, of course, not
nature that develops strong prejudices, but custom. That
aside, the really serious question is this: Should children
grow into adults so fearful of their own possible impulses
that they are "prepared to kill" other human beings? Yes?
No? It depends? The question is very much worth ponder-
ing.

CHAPTER TEN

Words from an Elder Stateswoman

ALTHOUGH no final word on the subject of lesbianism is possible, we yield the final words of this particular book to a woman who was born in the latter days of Krafft-Ebing, who lived through the early Freudian theories, who was in her early fifties when Kinsey published his report on the sexual behavior of American women, and who today, at the age of seventy-five, is witnessing the gay rights movement with some perspective. Save for two or three lines that could possibly pinpoint her identity (the respondents to the questionnaire were guaranteed anonymity), here are her opinions as she wrote them:

BACKGROUND

How old were you when you had your first sexual experience with a woman?
  Eighteen.
Was it also your partner's first such experience?
  No.
Was she younger, older, same age?

About ten years older or slightly less. She was a sophisticated, cultivated woman, musically gifted.

*Had you had sex with a man (men) before this first lesbian
experience?*

No.

How do you define a lesbian?

A spiritual descendant of Sappho of Lesbos: open to the
passionate love of women; accepting "womanness" as a
totally, beautifully creative complex of qualities. Not necessarily rejecting erotic appreciation of and experience
with male beings. An attitude of strong self-acceptance of
being a woman and of the being of other women. I do not
feel that it includes in any way imitating maleness.

How do you define bisexuality?

My observations of self and others lead me to feel that we
are all potentially omnisexual—at that level. Everyone I
have ever known well or intimately seems to me to have
embodied qualities usually defined as belonging both to
the male or the female. Different cultures or upbringing
repress or encourage degree of surfacing.

*Where do you fall on Kinsey's Heterosexual-Homosexual
Rating Scale:*

0: entirely heterosexual?

*1: largely heterosexual, but with incidental homosexual his-
tory?*

2: largely heterosexual, but with distinct homosexual history?

3: equally heterosexual and homosexual?

4: largely homosexual, but with distinct heterosexual history?

*5: largely homosexual, but with incidental heterosexual
history?*

6: entirely homosexual?

[She checked number 5.]

Do you presently consider yourself bisexual?

I consider myself an erotic being.

Stating that one is bisexual is considered by some lesbians a cop-out to societal pressure. What are your feelings on this matter?

I feel, generally, they are trying to be honest concerning their feelings. Some may be "copping out," as you say; I would not know.

Have you ever filled out a questionnaire pertaining to lesbianism? For what purpose?

No; I don't care for them or for such external, sociological attempts to understand and delineate the mysteries of personality, ways of loving, being, relating. Am answering this one because so much nonsense is written about these matters.

LIFE STYLE

Do you presently live with a female lover? For how long? How many other female lovers have you lived with? How long in each case?

I've had four long-term relationships with women: thirteen years (to death of partner); six years; ten years; four years to now. Some loving but casual erotic relationships between commitments to one friend.

Do you live alone and have occasional affairs?

I don't have occasional affairs at present, but don't rule it out.

Are one-night stands a way of life for you? Have they ever been?

No, never have been; but live and let live.

Is the gay bar an integral part of your life either for sexual contacts, for socializing, or for both?

No; visited them only a few times in my life. Do not like their dark, noisy, smoky atmosphere. Would like to see better meeting places.

With how many women have you had sexual experience?

Haven't kept count.

Discuss your thoughts on role playing in lesbian relationships —i.e., butch–femme; mother–child; teacher–pupil. Does it exist? Is it common?

None of above; except perhaps once, in role of mentor, experience-opener, to younger friend. I define my relationships as "friend and lover: equals"—no role playing; no imitation of heterosexual ways.

Do prepubescent girls turn you on? If so, have you ever acted on this feeling?

NO. I often see them as lovely, but they do not attract erotically.

Have you ever deliberately tried to seduce or succeeded in seducing a woman with no homosexual experience? Has such a woman ever tried to seduce or succeeded in seducing you?

NO. Some have shown willingness to be approached; but I am not attracted to the thoroughly heterosexual-seeming women; like some sexual ambiguity.

What is your general feeling about bringing out such women?

I would never seduce anyone from their chosen way of life; but if it happens in the relationships of other individuals, other couples, that is their affair. Anyone who could really be "brought out" (whatever that really means) would be latently inclined.

What are your thoughts on lesbian marriage ceremonies now offered in some churches?

No objection, for those who feel the need of this affirmation by society and religious authority. I do not care for it. Marriage is a social institution for the care and nurture of children, their economic protection, in this society.

What are your feelings regarding a transsexual (sex change) operation?

I can't see its necessity; but for those who want it, I wouldn't make it illegal. As I feel, the spirit, the heart, the feelings, shape the body: why cut it up? What is inwardly gained?

Are you generally in or out of the closet?

I've never felt myself "in" or "out." I live as I please, let others assume what they will.

Are you specifically in or out of the closet: with your family, with your colleagues, with straight friends?

All my family and close friends know my way of life; I make no solemn declarations; I live as I am, hide nothing, wear no placards. People take me or leave me. I am not "obvious."

If you are leading a double life, are you content with it?

I have never lived a double life. But regardless of what my erotic preferences are or were, I would have my reserves. Frank with intimates, "straight" or otherwise. The rest may think what they will.

If you are leading a totally open life as a lesbian, can you pinpoint what prompted your decision to do so?

I feel that I—anyone—has a right to be who they are, to express and realize their being, but not to infringe on others' similar rights. This I declare when pertinent.

Are most of your close friends gay?

No; far from it. I choose or attract friends on the basis of a wide range of interests.

What are your feelings about the gay liberation movement?

It's undoubtedly healthy, liberating for those who are in it; I do not care for too much aggressiveness. Do believe it is good and brave to struggle for any denied rights (work rights, economic nondiscrimination, acceptance on all levels as simply human, another sort of self-expression). I have supported various activities; but am not a "demonstrator" or joiner, fundamentally.

Have you ever been harassed or treated unfairly because of your lesbianism, in your work, while trying to find housing, by the police, by the community, or in other instances? Please give examples and explain.

No.

WOMEN

What are your feelings about the women's liberation movement, especially in relation to lesbianism?

It has done a lot of good, generally. Too bad it's needed; but injustices must be brought into the open, it seems, before they can be seen for what they are. All women have been oppressed for too long; it's bad for them and unhealthy for oppressors.

Do you know what a "political lesbian" is? Define and discuss.

I don't know how to answer this. People must act according to their situation and lights. Cannot place much faith in politics. We need radical changes: but they begin in our lives.

Do you feel superior or inferior to heterosexual women? Why?

Neither. Wouldn't that be rather silly? I like my way, or wouldn't follow it; assume they like theirs.

MEN

Are you presently married? Is it a sexual relationship? Are you divorced, separated, widowed?

No.

How many men have you slept with (if any)?

Three, two very casually; experimental.

Since realizing that you are a lesbian, how many men have you slept with?

As above.

Have your sexual relationships with men (if any) differed from those with women? In what way?

No strong emotional involvement with the men; with women, strong and passionate emotional involvement.

Have never tended to fall in love with men at all; but life-long have enjoyed good friendships with men.

What are your general feelings about heterosexual men?

How can one generalize? Some are obnoxious; some neutral; some delightful companions.

What are your general feelings about homosexual men?

Pretty much as above. Depends on the individuals. Have had lifelong friendships with several, on a good friendship-companionship level.

Have you ever been raped?

No.

CHILDREN

Have you ever given birth? How many children? Grandchildren? Do you presently feel you'd like to give birth? Have you ever felt so? Do you have adopted children? If they were adopted while you were living in a lesbian relationship, will you please elaborate on the experience?

No to all the above.

Do you presently feel you'd like to adopt a child?

Definitely not. Had all the mothering I needed helping younger sisters.

Have you ever had an abortion?

No.

SEX

How would you describe your lesbian lovemaking: Assertive? Yielding? Combination of both? Does it vary with different partners?

Of course it varies—subtly—with different partners; but the main approach would always be mutuality. We are both women, made the same, have the same erotic needs.

Does your lesbian lovemaking include (clinical terms from Kinsey): simple kissing; deep kissing; generalized body caresses; manual stimulation of breast; manual stimulation of genitalia; oral stimulation of breast; oral stimulation of genitalia; genital apposition (tribadism); use of dildo; other?

All of the above would enter in. One does what comes naturally, whenever, wherever. I have not tried the dildo; hands are good lovers.

What are your thoughts on the vaginal versus clitoral orgasm?

Both are involved deeply; vaginal stimulation or exercise communicates with clitoris, and vice versa: we are totally erotic beings. The orgasm is felt all over, toes to teeth, if you will, toenails to hair of head. Leave nothing out. Love the entirety.

Have your sexual affairs with women always been accompanied by emotional involvement?

Lasting affairs, certainly. Some casual ones just delightfully erotic. If one makes love fully, how help loving, if only for a week?

Do you ever long to have or have fantasies about having a penis?

Never.

It's fairly commonly supposed that dildoes or other penis substitutes are frequently used in lesbian relationships. What do you think?

I would not know; have never seen a dildo; but believe most lesbians probably use fingers, which are warm, soft, part of the human lover.

SHRINKS

Just one question: If you have ever sought psychiatric help in hopes of being "cured" of lesbianism, please describe why you sought such help and also what happened.

Am probably one of the few individuals of any sexual orientation who has never gone to a psychiatrist or other confessional adviser. Have never desired to be other than I am, but to grow to my full stature and potential as I am.

Anyone who feels he or she is badly off as a homosexual should, I feel, try to decide if they feel that deep down or are projecting society's condemnation.

WRAP-UP

What myth about lesbianism would you most like to see destroyed?

Any myths that exist, of course. We differ in few respects other than that we love others of our own sex. Generally do not seduce others; are not trying to be imitation males. Young people are safe with us.

Do you feel that a woman's sexuality has anything to do with her creativity?

How could it not? Everything we are affects our creativity (if you mean creativity in arts, enterprises, whatever work we engage in). Obviously, energies and time not going into child-bearing and rearing leave more for other commitments, so lesbians may seem to accomplish more in the "world."

Why do you think you are a lesbian?

It's one of the mysteries. Probably born with the strong predisposition; good experiences in that way of life reinforce it. Maybe we are one of Nature's ways of population control. I never had any urge toward motherhood (I'm eldest of family of seven). A profound study of other forms of life, sea, land, animal, plant, does not suggest that male–female reproduction is the exclusively favored way of being. With homo-erotic individuals, maybe Nature is trying an experiment. Why should we put it down as "unnatural" since it occurs to us naturally? Maybe society *needs* more than two sexes. (Why have religious sects denied the sexual expression of their monks, priests, nuns, putting priests in frocks, etc.?) It's good to have a few mysteries.

Notes

PRELUDE (pages 9–16)

1. Sarah Whitworth, "Lesbian and Feminist Images in Greek Art and Mythology," in *The Ladder*, February–March 1972.
2. Simone de Beauvoir, *The Second Sex*, trans. H. M. Parshley (New York: Knopf, 1953), p. 424.
3. "Final Report of the Task Force on Homosexuality," National Institute of Mental Health, Health Services and Mental Health Administration, U.S. Dept. of Health, Education and Welfare, Washington, D.C., Oct. 10, 1969, p. 3.

INTERVIEW 1 (pages 19–37)

1. "Final Report of the Task Force on Homosexuality," National Institute of Mental Health, Health Services and Mental Health Administration, U.S. Dept. of Health, Education and Welfare, Washington, D.C., Oct. 10, 1969, p. 4.
2. George Steiner, "Night Words," in *Language and Silence* (New York: Atheneum, 1967), p. 76.
3. Jess Stearn, *The Grapevine* (New York: Doubleday, 1964). Stearn calls lesbians members of the "fourth sex" and deals in the main with those women who are members of lesbian organizations and those who move in lesbian bar circles.

CHAPTER ONE (pages 38–54)

1. Natalie Clifford Barney, *Pensées d'une amazone* (Paris: Émile-Paul, 1920), p. 205.
2. William Carlos Williams, *The Autobiography* (New York: Random House, 1951), p. 229.
3. Richard von Krafft-Ebing, *Psychopathia Sexualis*, adapted from the 12th German ed. by F. J. Rebman (New York: Rebman, 1906), p. 79.
4. Sigmund Freud, "The Sexual Life of Man," in *A General Introduction to Psycho-Analysis*, trans. Joan Riviere (New York: Clarion, 1969), p. 266.
5. Alfred C. Kinsey et al., *Sexual Behavior in the Human Female* (Philadelphia: Saunders, 1953), p. 448.
6. Wardell B. Pomeroy, *Dr. Kinsey and the Institute for Sex Research* (New York: Harper & Row, 1972), *passim*.
7. Edmund Bergler, "The Myth of a New National Disease: Homosexuality and the Kinsey Report," in *Psychiatry Quarterly*, Vol. XXII (1948).
8. David Reuben, *Everything You Always Wanted to Know About Sex* (New York: McKay, 1969).
9. *Ibid.*, p. 217.
10. Norman Mailer, of course, at "A Dialogue on Women's Liberation," sponsored by the Theatre for Ideas, at New York City's Town Hall, April 30, 1971.
11. Kinsey, *op. cit.*, p. 584.
12. The phrase "the myth of the vaginal orgasm" was coined in an early women's liberation pamphlet so entitled—Anne Koedt, "The Myth of the Vaginal Orgasm" (Boston: New England Free Press, n.d.).
13. Colette, *The Pure and the Impure*, trans. Herma Briffault (New York: Farrar, Straus & Giroux, 1967), p. 104.
14. Kinsey, *op. cit.*, p. 468.
15. Simone de Beauvoir, *The Second Sex*, trans. H. M. Parshley (New York: Knopf, 1953), p. 416.
16. Mailer, *loc. cit.*
17. William H. Masters and Virginia E. Johnson, *Human Sexual Response* (Boston: Little, Brown, 1966), p. 134.

18. Colette, *The Ripening Seed*, trans. Roger Senhouse (London: Secker & Warburg, 1955).

19. Krafft-Ebing, *op. cit.*, p. 400.

20. Kinsey, *op. cit.*, p. 467.

21. Edmund Bergler and William S. Kroger, *Kinsey's Myth of Female Sexuality* (New York: Grune & Stratton, 1954).

22. Anonymous, "Introducing: The Lesbian Experience," *Cosmopolitan*, June 1971, p. 174.

23. Phyllis and Eberhard Kronhausen, *Erotic Fantasies: A Study of the Sexual Imagination* (New York: Grove Press, 1969), pp. 127–138.

24. Frank A. Beach, "Comments on the Second Dialogue in *Corydon*," in André Gide, *Corydon* (New York: Farrar, Straus, 1950), p. 185.

25. Pomeroy, *op. cit.*, p. 183.

26. Beach, *op. cit.*, p. 179.

27. Harry F. Harlow, "Sexual Behavior in the Rhesus Monkey," in *Sex and Behavior*, ed. Frank A. Beach (New York: Wiley, 1965), p. 252.

28. Beach, *op. cit.*, p. 187.

29. Sigmund Freud, *Three Essays on the Theory of Sexuality*, trans. James Strachey (New York: Basic Books, 1962), p. 57.

CHAPTER TWO (pages 55–67)

1. Richard von Krafft-Ebing, *Psychopathia Sexualis*, adapted from the 12th German ed. by F. J. Rebman (New York: Rebman, 1906), p. vi. All subsequent quotations in this chapter attributed to Krafft-Ebing are from this book.

2. Edward M. Brecher, *The Sex Researchers* (Boston: Little, Brown, 1969), p. 58.

3. Radclyffe Hall, *The Well of Loneliness* (New York: Covici-Friede, 1928), p. 223.

CHAPTER THREE (pages 68–87)

1. Sigmund Freud, "The Psychogenesis of a Case of Homosexuality in a Woman" (1920), in *Collected Papers*, Vol. II, trans. Joan Riviere (New York: Basic Books, 1959), p. 206.

2. *Ibid.*, p. 229.

3. Sigmund Freud, "The Sexual Life of Man," in A *General Intro-duction to Psycho-Analysis*, trans. Joan Riviere (New York: Clarion, 1969), p. 267.

4. This paraphrase of Freud's theory of female sexuality is taken from Sigmund Freud, "The Psychology of Women," in *New Introductory Lectures on Psycho-Analysis*, trans. W. J. H. Sprott (New York: Norton, 1933), pp. 153–185, and Sigmund Freud, *Three Essays on the Theory of Sexuality*, trans. James Strachey (New York: Basic Books, 1962).

5. Freud, "The Psychogenesis of a Case of Homosexuality in a Woman," p. 230.

6. All the quotes used to detail this case history are taken from *ibid.*

7. H.D., *Tribute to Freud* (New York: Pantheon, 1956). All sub-sequent quotes in this chapter attributed to H.D. or to Freud, ex-cept where otherwise noted, are from this book.

8. All the quotes attributed to Bryher are from Bryher, *The Heart to Artemis* (New York: Harcourt, Brace & World, 1962).

9. Freud, "The Psychology of Women," p. 171.

10. As quoted in Helen Walker Puner, *Freud, His Life and His Mind* (New York: Dell, 1959), p. 133.

11. Helene Deutsch, "On Female Homosexuality," in *The Inter-national Journal of Psychoanalysis*, Vol. XIV (1933). All subse-quent quotes attributed to Deutsch are taken from this article.

CHAPTER FOUR (pages 88–110)

1. Thomas Szasz, *The Manufacture of Madness* (New York: Harper & Row, 1970), pp. 242, 259.

2. Frank S. Caprio, *Female Homosexuality* (New York: Evergreen Black Cat, 1962), pp. 304, viii, 40.

3. As quoted in Louis Crompton, *Homosexuality and the Sickness Theory* (London: Albany Trust, 1969), p. 8.

4. As quoted in "When Women Love Other Women: A Frank Discussion of Female Homosexuality," *Redbook*, November 1971.

5. Sigmund Freud, "The Sexual Life of Man," in *A General Introduction to Psycho-Analysis*, trans. Joan Riviere (New York: Clarion, 1969), p. 266.

6. *The New York Times*, March 4, 1971, p. 32.

7. *Ibid.*, Feb. 28, 1971, p. 1.

8. Crompton, *op. cit.*, p. 6.

9. Edmund Bergler and William S. Kroger, *Kinsey's Myth of Female Sexuality* (New York: Grune & Stratton, 1954), pp. 142–153.

10. Harvey E. Kaye, "Lesbian Relationships," in *Sexual Behavior*, Vol. I, No. 1 (April 1971), p. 80.

11. David Susskind Show, New York, Oct. 10, 1971.

12. Wardell B. Pomeroy, *Dr. Kinsey and the Institute for Sex Research* (New York: Harper & Row, 1972), p. 70.

13. Caprio, *op. cit.*, pp. 118, 119. All subsequent quotes attributed to Caprio are from this book.

14. Ernest van den Haag, "Notes on Homosexuality and Its Cultural Setting," in *The Problem of Homosexuality in Modern Society*, ed. H. M. Ruitenbeek (New York: Dutton, 1963), p. 297.

15. Richard von Krafft-Ebing, *Psychopathia Sexualis*, adapted from the 12th German ed. by F. J. Rebman (New York: Rebman, 1906), p. 402.

16. Evelyn Hooker, "The Adjustment of the Male Overt Homosexual," in *Journal of Projective Techniques*, Vol. XXI (1957).

17. *The New York Times*, Aug. 3, 1971.

18. Remarks made during a university lecture by a former Kinsey team member who prefers to remain anonymous.

19. Havelock Ellis, "Sexual Inversion," in *Studies in the Psychology of Sex*, Vol. I (New York: Random House, 1936), p. 291.

20. "Final Report of the Task Force on Homosexuality," National Institute of Mental Health, Health Services and Mental Health Administration, U.S. Dept. of Health, Education and Welfare, Washington, D.C., Oct. 10, 1969, p. 3.

21. As quoted in Peter and Barbara Wyden, *Growing Up Straight* (New York: Signet Books, 1968), p. 25.

22. John Money and Anke A. Ehrhardt, *Man & Woman Boy & Girl* (Baltimore: Johns Hopkins Univ., 1973), *passim*.

23. M. Sidney Margolese, as quoted in *Newsweek*, April 26, 1971, p. 55.
24. "Final Report of the Task Force on Homosexuality," p. 7.
25. As quoted in Arlo Karlen, *Sexuality and Homosexuality* (New York: Norton, 1971), p. 283.

CHAPTER FIVE (pages 129–160)

1. The translations of Sappho's poems, unless otherwise indicated, are by Mary Barnard, *Sappho: A New Translation* (Berkeley: Univ. of California, 1958).
2. Plato, *Phaedrus*, trans. Harold North Fowler (Cambridge, Mass.: Loeb Classical Library, Harvard Univ., 1966), p. 437.
3. *The Greek Anthology*, trans. W. R. Paton (Cambridge: Loeb Classical Library, Harvard Univ., 1958), Book IX, No. 506.
4. Aristotle, *Rhetoric*, trans. John Henry Freese (New York: Loeb Classical Library, Putnam, 1926), Book II, p. 307.
5. As quoted in H. D. F. Kitto, *The Greeks* (London: Penguin Books, 1957), p. 221.
6. See, for example, Sidney Abbott and Barbara Love, *Sappho Was a Right-On Woman* (New York: Stein & Day, 1972), p. 158.
7. As quoted in Kitto, *loc. cit.*
8. Thomas Burnett Swann, *The Classical World of H.D.* (Lincoln: Univ. of Nebraska, 1962), p. 77.
9. Natalie Clifford Barney, *Pensées d'une amazone* (Paris: Émile-Paul, 1920), p. 15.
10. *Selected Satires of Lucian*, edited and translated by Lionel Casson (New York: Norton, 1962), p. 303.
11. John Addington Symonds, *Studies of the Greek Poets* (New York: Harper, n.d.), Vol. I, p. 309.
12. Moses Hadas, *A History of Greek Literature* (New York: Columbia Univ., 1950), p. 44.
13. Merivale's translation is quoted in *Longinus on the Sublime*, trans. A. O. Prickard (Oxford: Oxford Univ., 1906), p. 85. It is of interest to note that Prickard's translation of Longinus was reprinted "with corrections" in 1930, 1946, 1949, 1954 and 1961. In none of these "corrected" versions of Longinus was

Merivale's wrong use of the pronoun in Sappho's poem corrected.

14. *Ibid.,* p. 22.
15. Barnard, *op. cit.,* from the foreword by Fitts, p. ix.
16. Philips' translation is quoted in Henry Thornton Wharton, *Sappho,* 3rd ed. (London: Lane, 1895), p. 67.
17. Algernon Swinburne, *Selected Poetry and Prose,* ed. John D. Rosenberg (New York: Modern Library, 1968), p. 113.
18. *Ibid.,* pp. 328–329.
19. Hunt is quoted in Leo Deuel, *Testaments of Time* (New York: Knopf, 1965), p. 162.
20. David M. Robinson, *Sappho and Her Influence* (New York: Cooper Square, 1963), p. 44.
21. Denys Page, *Sappho and Alcaeus* (Oxford: Clarendon, 1955), p. 296.
22. Ovid, *Heroides and Amores,* trans. G. Showerman (London: Heinemann, 1921).
23. Charles Seltman, *Women in Antiquity* (London: Thames & Hudson, 1956), p. 92.
24. Symonds, *op. cit.,* p. 307.
25. H.D. (Hilda Doolittle), "She Contrasts Herself with Hippolyta" in *Collected Poems of H.D.* (New York: Boni & Liveright, 1925).

CHAPTER SIX (pages 161–178)

1. Mlle. Souvestre's influence on Eleanor Roosevelt is amply documented in Joseph P. Lash, *Eleanor and Franklin* (New York: Norton, 1971).
2. Natalie Clifford Barney, *Souvenirs indiscrets* (Paris: Flammarion, 1960), p. 80.
3. Colette, *The Pure and the Impure,* trans. Herma Briffault (New York: Farrar, Straus & Giroux, 1967), p. 69. All subsequent quotes attributed to Colette, except where otherwise noted, are taken from this book.
4. The first two are from Natalie Clifford Barney, *Pensées d'une amazone* (Paris: Émile-Paul, 1920), pp. 66, 17. The third is

from Natalie Clifford Barney, *Nouvelles Pensées de l'amazone* (Paris: Mercure de France, 1939), p. 198.

5. As quoted by Mary Blume, "Natalie Barney, Legendary Lady of the Rue Jacob," *Réalités*, February 1966, p. 20.

6. Renée Vivien, "Nocturne," from *Études et préludes* (Paris: Lemerre, 1901), p. 151.

7. Barney, *Souvenirs indiscrets*, p. 52.

8. *Ibid.*, p. 57.

9. Pierre Louÿs, "The Songs of Bilitis," from *The Collected Works of Pierre Louÿs*, trans. Mitchell S. Buck (New York: Liveright, 1932), p. 259.

10. The baroness was born Helen Betty Louise Caroline Rothschild; Vivien dedicated her second volume of poems, *Cendres et poussières* (Paris: Lemerre, 1902), to "H.C.L.B.," undoubtedly mixing up the initials on purpose. The baroness was married to Baron van Zuylen; Roger Peyrefitte, in his gossipy book *L'Exilé de Capri* (Paris: Flammarion, 1959), p. 234, says Vivien was the friend of a certain "Baronne d'Hélène Zuyderzee," intentionally not giving the woman her real name. Colette, in a letter to her friend Léon Hamel, discusses the Baroness van Zuylen: *Earthly Paradise*, ed. Robert Phelps (London: Secker & Warburg, 1966), p. 164.

11. Renée Vivien, "En Débarquant à Mytilène," from *À l'Heure des mains jointes* (Paris: Lemerre, 1906), p. 47.

12. Barney, *Souvenirs indiscrets*, p. 187.

13. As quoted in Colette, "Lettres au petit corsaire," in *Earthly Paradise*, ed. Robert Phelps (London: Secker & Warburg, 1966), p. xxi.

14. Vivien, "Vaincue," from *À l'Heure des mains jointes*, p. 143.

15. As quoted in the publishers' note in Renée Vivien, *Dans un Coin de violettes* (Paris: Sansot, 1910).

16. Mario Praz, *The Romantic Agony*, 2nd ed., trans. from the Italian by Angus Davidson (London: Oxford Univ., 1951), p. 307.

17. Eugène Martin-Mamy, *Les Nouveaux Païens* (Paris: Sansot, n.d.).

18. Charles Maurras, *Le Romantisme féminin* (Paris: À la Cité des Livres, 1926), p. 49.

19. Barney, *Souvenirs indiscrets*, p. 46.
20. Praz, *op. cit.*, p. 374.

CHAPTER SEVEN (pages 179–195)

1. Compton Mackenzie, *Extraordinary Women* (New York: Vanguard, 1928), p. 39.
2. Radclyffe Hall, *The Well of Loneliness* (New York: Covici-Friede, 1928), p. 311.
3. Ernest Hemingway, *A Moveable Feast* (New York: Scribner's, 1964), p. 119.
4. As quoted in Gertrude Stein, *The Autobiography of Alice B. Toklas* (New York: Harcourt, Brace, 1933), p. 304.
5. *The New York Times*, April 14, 1971, p. 52, and April 25, 1971, p. 19.
6. *Ibid.*, April 25, p. 17.
7. The facts of Radclyffe Hall's personal life have been taken, except where otherwise noted, from Una, Lady Troubridge, *The Life and Death of Radclyffe Hall* (London: Hammond Hammond, 1961). Although this biography is a moving tribute by Lady Troubridge to their love, it is at the same time terribly precious and not very well written. Troubridge never speaks openly about lesbianism, nor, curiously enough, is there a detailed account of the obscenity trial.
8. London *Times*, Nov. 17, 1928, p. 5.
9. *Ibid.*
10. C. H. Rolph in his introduction to Vera Brittain, *Radclyffe Hall: A Case of Obscenity?* (London: Femina, 1968), p. 14.
11. London *Sunday Express*, Aug. 19, 1928.
12. As mentioned in Paul S. Boyer, *Purity in Print* (New York: Scribner's, 1968), p. 228.
13. As quoted in H. Montgomery Hyde, *Norman Birkett* (London: Hamilton, 1964), p. 254.
14. *Ibid.*
15. Boyer, *op. cit.*, p. 133.
16. *The New York Times*, Feb. 22, 1929, p. 11.
17. Beresford Egan, *The Sink of Solitude* (London: Hermes Press, 1928).

18. Harold Acton, *Memoirs of an Aesthete* (New York: Viking, 1971), p. 365.
19. London *Times*, Oct. 1, 1963, p. 14.
20. As quoted in H. Montgomery Hyde, *The Other Love* (London: Heinemann, 1970), p. 184.
21. *Times Literary Supplement*, Aug. 2, 1968, p. 566.
22. Egan, *op. cit.*
23. Frank S. Caprio, *Female Homosexuality* (New York: Evergreen Black Cat, 1962), p. 39.

CHAPTER EIGHT (pages 196–215)

1. Noel I. Garde, *Jonathan to Gide: The Homosexual in History* (New York: Vantage, 1964).
2. From Valentino's private journal, June 5, 1924: "A very good-looking boy followed me for a quarter of an hour, and in the end he came up to me outside the Opera. I went back with him to his home and he kissed me with frenzy even on the staircase. . . . I was wildly passionate. We made love like two tigers until the dawn . . ." Quoted in Raymond de Becker, *The Other Face of Love*, trans. Margaret Crosland and Alan Daventry (London: Spearman & Rodney, 1967), caption for illustration.
3. *Le Nouvel Observateur*, April 5, 1971, p. 5.
4. Robin Maugham, *Escape from the Shadows* (New York: McGraw-Hill, 1973), p. ix.
5. Quentin Bell, *Virginia Woolf* (New York: Harcourt Brace Jovanovich, 1972), p. 119. All subsequent quotations regarding Woolf, except where otherwise noted, are from this book.
6. Virginia Woolf, *Mrs. Dalloway* (New York: Harvest, 1953), p. 52.
7. André Gide, "Letter to François Porché," in *Corydon* (New York: Farrar, Straus, 1950), p. 161.
8. *The New York Review of Books*, Oct. 7, 1971, p. 41.
9. Natalie Clifford Barney in her foreword to Gertrude Stein, *As Fine As Melanctha* (New Haven: Yale Univ., 1954), p. xvii.
10. Edmund Wilson, "Gertrude Stein Old and Young," in *The Shores of Light* (New York: Farrar, Straus, 1952), p. 581.

11. Richard Bridgman, *Gertrude Stein in Pieces* (New York: Oxford Univ., 1970), p. 149.
12. Gertrude Stein, "Lifting Belly," from *Bee Time Vine* (New Haven: Yale Univ., 1953), pp. 107, 96.
13. Stein, "A Sonatina Followed by Another," *ibid.*, pp. 5, 12, 10, 9, 29.
14. Gertrude Stein, *Fernhurst, Q.E.D. and Other Early Writings* (New York: Liveright, 1971), pp. 66–67. All subsequent quotations regarding *Q.E.D.* are from this book.
15. Violette Leduc, *Mad in Pursuit*, trans. Derek Coltman (New York: Farrar, Straus & Giroux, 1971), p. 304.
16. Gertrude Stein, *The Making of Americans* (Paris: Contact Editions, 1925), p. 606.
17. Gertrude Stein, "Miss Furr and Miss Skeene," from *Selected Writings of Gertrude Stein*, ed. Carl Van Vechten (New York: Modern Library, 1962), p. 566.
18. Donald Gallup, ed., *Flowers of Friendship: Letters to Gertrude Stein* (New York: Knopf, 1953), p. 268.
19. Gertrude Stein, "A Long Gay Book," in *Matisse, Picasso and Gertrude Stein* (Millerton, N.Y.: Something Else Press, 1972), p. 15.
20. From an unpublished Hemingway letter.
21. As quoted by Donald Sutherland in "Alice and Gertrude and Others," *Prairie Schooner*, Winter 1971–72, p. 297.
22. Gertrude Stein, *The Autobiography of Alice B. Toklas* (New York: Harcourt, Brace, 1933), p. 271.
23. Ernest Hemingway, *A Moveable Feast* (New York: Scribner's, 1964), pp. 117–119.
24. W. G. Rogers, *When This You See Remember Me: Gertrude Stein in Person* (New York: Rinehart, 1948).

CHAPTER NINE (pages 219–248)

1. "Final Report of the Task Force on Homosexuality," National Institute of Mental Health, Health Services and Mental Health Administration, U.S. Dept. of Health, Education and Welfare, Washington, D.C., Oct. 10, 1969, p. 17.

2. Janet Flanner, *Paris Journal* (1944–1965) (New York: Atheneum, 1969), p. 494.

3. As quoted in Virgil Thomson, *Virgil Thomson* (London: Weidenfeld & Nicolson, 1967), p. 377.

4. Alfred C. Kinsey *et al.*, *Sexual Behavior in the Human Female* (Philadelphia: Saunders, 1953), p. 448.

5. "A Brief of Injustices" (San Francisco: Council on Religion and the Homosexual, 1965), p. 12.

6. Clellan S. Ford and Frank A. Beach, *Patterns of Sexual Behavior* (New York: Harper, 1952), p. 125.

7. Germaine Greer, *The Female Eunuch* (New York: McGraw-Hill, 1971), p. 61.

8. Simone de Beauvoir, *The Second Sex*, trans. H. M. Parshley (New York: Knopf, 1953), p. 421.

9. Ernest Hemingway, *A Moveable Feast* (New York: Scribner's, 1964), p. 18.

10. Frank S. Caprio, *Female Homosexuality* (New York: Evergreen Black Cat, 1962), p. 162.

Selected Bibliography

This is not a comprehensive list of books and articles quoted in the text (they are duly referenced in the Notes) but is instead a *selected* list of all works consulted. It is put forth as a suggested reading list.

I. NOVELS, POETRY, PLAYS

Barnes, Djuna, *Ladies Almanack*. New York: Harper & Row, 1972.
———, *Nightwood*. New York: Harcourt, Brace, 1937.
Barney, Natalie Clifford, *Poems-poèmes: autres alliances*. Paris: Émile-Paul, 1920.
Baudelaire, Charles, *Flowers of Evil*, trans. George Dillon and Edna St. Vincent Millay. New York: Harper, 1936.
Bedford, Sybille, *A Compass Error*. New York: Knopf, 1969.
Bowen, Elizabeth, *The Hotel.* New York: Dial, 1928.
Bowles, Jane, *The Collected Works of Jane Bowles*. New York: Farrar, Straus & Giroux, 1966.
Brophy, Brigid, *The Finishing Touch*. London: Secker & Warburg, 1963.
Colette, Sidonie Gabrielle, *Œuvres complètes*. Paris: Fleuron, 1950.
Diderot, Denis, *Memoirs of a Nun*, trans. Francis Birrell. London: Routledge, 1928.

H.D. (Hilda Doolittle), *Collected Poems of H.D.* New York: Boni & Liveright, 1925.

———, *Palimpsest.* Boston: Houghton Mifflin, 1926.

———, *Selected Poems.* New York: Grove, 1957.

Duffy, Maureen, *The Microcosm.* New York: Simon and Schuster, 1966.

Gautier, Théophile, *Mademoiselle de Maupin,* trans. Burton Rascoe. New York: Knopf, 1920.

Hall, Radclyffe, *The Well of Loneliness.* New York: Covici-Friede, 1928.

Hellman, Lillian, *The Children's Hour.* New York: Knopf, 1941.

Lawrence, D. H., *The Fox.* New York: Viking, 1923.

———, *The Rainbow.* New York: Viking, 1967.

Leduc, Violette, *Thérèse et Isabelle.* Paris: Gallimard, 1966.

Louÿs, Pierre, *The Collected Works of Pierre Louys,* trans. Mitchell Buck. New York: Liveright, 1932.

Mackenzie, Compton, *Extraordinary Women.* New York: Vanguard, 1928.

Mallet, Françoise, *The Illusionist,* trans. Herma Briffault. New York: Farrar, Straus & Young, 1952.

Meaker, Marijane, *Shockproof Sydney Skate.* Boston: Little, Brown, 1972.

Miller, Isabel, *Patience and Sarah.* New York: McGraw-Hill, 1972.

Nin, Anaïs, *Ladders to Fire.* New York: Dutton, 1945.

———, *Under a Glass Bell.* New York: Dutton, 1948.

Olivia (Dorothy Strachey Bussy), *Olivia.* London: Hogarth, 1949.

Peyrefitte, Roger, *L'Exilé de Capri.* Paris: Flammarion, 1959.

Renault, Mary, *The Middle Mist.* New York: Morrow, 1945.

Rule, Jane, *The Desert of the Heart.* New York: World, 1965.

Sappho, *Sappho: A New Translation,* trans. Mary Barnard. Berkeley: Univ. of California, 1958.

Sarton, May, *Mrs. Stevens Hears the Mermaids Singing.* New York: Norton, 1965.

Sartre, Jean-Paul, *No Exit.* New York: Knopf, 1947.

Stein, Gertrude, *Bee Time Vine and Other Pieces.* New Haven: Yale, 1953.

———, *Fernhurst, Q.E.D. and Other Early Writings.* New York: Liveright, 1971.

———, *Matisse, Picasso and Gertrude Stein*. Millerton, N.Y.: Something Else Press, 1972.

Strachey, Lytton, *Ermyntrude and Esmeralda*. New York: Stein & Day, 1969.

Tey, Josephine, *Miss Pym Disposes*, in *Three by Tey*. New York: Macmillan, 1954.

Vivien, Renée, *Cendres et poussières*. Paris: Lemerre, 1902.

———, *Études et préludes*. Paris: Lemerre, 1901.

———, *Poésies complètes*. Paris: Lemerre, 1948. (This collection does *not* contain Vivien's complete works.)

———, *La Vénus des aveugles*. Paris: Lemerre, 1904.

Wittig, Monique, *Les Guérillères*, trans. David Le Vay. New York: Viking, 1971.

———, *The Opoponax*, trans. Helen Weaver. New York: Simon and Schuster, 1966.

Woolf, Virginia, *Mrs. Dalloway*. London: Hogarth, 1925.

———, *Orlando*. London: Hogarth, 1928.

II. AUTOBIOGRAPHIES, MEMOIRS, JOURNALS, LETTERS

Acosta, Mercedes de, *Here Lies the Heart*. New York: Reynal, 1960.

Anderson, Margaret, *The Autobiography*. New York: Horizon, 1970.

Barney, Natalie Clifford, *Aventures de l'esprit*. Paris: Émile-Paul, 1929.

———, *Nouvelles Pensées de l'amazone*. Paris: Mercure de France, 1939.

———, *Pensées d'une amazone*. Paris: Émile-Paul, 1920.

———, *Souvenirs indiscrets*. Paris: Flammarion, 1960.

———, *Traits et portraits*. Paris: Mercure de France, 1963.

Beach, Sylvia, *Shakespeare and Company*. New York: Harcourt, Brace, 1959.

Bengis, Ingrid, *Combat in the Erogenous Zone*. New York: Knopf, 1972.

Brooks, Romaine, "No Pleasant Memories," in *Life and Letters Today*, Vol. XVIII, No. 12, and Vol. XIX, No. 15.

Bryher, *The Heart to Artemis*. New York: Harcourt, Brace & World, 1962.

Colette, Sidonie Gabrielle, *Earthly Paradise*, ed. Robert Phelps. London: Secker & Warburg, 1966.

————, *The Pure and the Impure*, trans. Herma Briffault. New York: Farrar, Straus & Giroux, 1967.

H.D. (Hilda Doolittle), *Tribune to Freud*. New York: Pantheon, 1956.

Frederics, Diana, *Diana: A Strange Biography*. New York: Citadel, 1939. (This may be piped, but the experience described rings true.)

Glassco, John, *Memoirs of Montparnasse*. New York: Viking, 1973.

Goncourt, Edmond, and Jules de, *Pages from the Goncourt Journal*, trans. Robert Baldick. London: Oxford, 1962.

Günderode, Fräulein, and Bettine von Arnim, *Correspondence*, trans. Margaret Fuller. Boston: Burnham, 1861.

Hemingway, Ernest, *A Moveable Feast*. New York: Scribner's, 1964.

Jacob, Naomi, *Me—And the Swans*. London: Kimber, 1963.

James, Alice, *The Diary of Alice James*, ed. Leon Edel. New York: Dodd Mead, 1934.

Leduc, Violette, *La Bâtarde*, trans. Derek Coltman. New York: Farrar, Straus & Giroux, 1965.

————, *Mad in Pursuit*, trans. Derek Coltman. New York: Farrar, Straus & Giroux, 1971.

McAlmon, Robert, and Kay Boyle, *Being Geniuses Together*. New York: Doubleday, 1968.

Nin, Anaïs, *The Diary of Anaïs Nin*, Vol. I, *1931–1934*. New York: Harcourt, Brace, 1966.

Stein, Gertrude, *The Autobiography of Alice B. Toklas*. New York: Harcourt, Brace, 1933.

Thomson, Virgil, *Virgil Thomson*. London: Weidenfeld & Nicolson, 1967.

Toklas, Alice B., *What Is Remembered*. New York: Holt, Rinehart & Winston, 1963.

Williams, William Carlos, *The Autobiography of William Carlos Williams*. New York: New Directions, 1967.

Woolf, Virginia, *A Writer's Diary*. London: Hogarth, 1953.

III. BIOGRAPHY, LITERARY CRITICISM

Bell, Quentin, *Virginia Woolf: A Biography*. New York: Harcourt Brace Jovanovich, 1972.

Breeskin, Adelyn D., *Romaine Brooks, Thief of Souls*. Washington, D.C.: Smithsonian, 1971.

Bridgman, Richard, *Gertrude Stein in Pieces*. New York: Oxford, 1970.

Brittain, Vera, *Radclyffe Hall: A Case of Obscenity?* London: Femina, 1968.

Crosland, Margaret, *Colette: The Difficulty of Loving*. New York: Bobbs-Merrill, 1973.

Freeman, Gillian, *The Undergrowth of Literature*. London: Nelson, 1967.

Green, David, *Queen Anne*. New York: Scribner's, 1970.

Hadas, Moses, *A History of Greek Literature*. New York: Columbia Univ., 1950.

Masson, Georgina, *Queen Christina*. New York: Farrar, Straus & Giroux, 1968.

Mavor, Elizabeth, *The Ladies of Llangollen*. London: Joseph, 1971.

Nicolson, Nigel, *Portrait of a Marriage*. New York: Atheneum, 1973.

Page, Denys, *Sappho and Alcaeus*. Oxford: Clarendon, 1955.

Patrick, Mary Mills, *Sappho and the Island of Lesbos*. London: Methuen, 1912.

Pomeroy, Wardell B., *Dr. Kinsey and the Institute for Sex Research*. New York: Harper & Row, 1972.

Praz, Mario, *The Romantic Agony*, trans. Angus Davidson. London: Oxford, 1951.

Rogers, W. G., *Ladies Bountiful*. New York: Harcourt, Brace & World, 1968.

————, *When This You See Remember Me: Gertrude Stein in Person*. New York: Rinehart, 1948.

Swann, Thomas Burnett, *The Classical World of H.D.* Lincoln: Univ. of Nebraska, 1962.

Symonds, John Addington, *Studies of the Greek Poets*, Vols. I and II. New York: Harper, n.d.

Troubridge, Lady Una, *The Life and Death of Radclyffe Hall*. London: Hammond Hammond, 1961.

Wharton, Henry Thornton, *Sappho*. London: Lane, 1895.

Woodress, James, *Willa Cather*. New York: Pegasus, 1970.

IV. HOMOSEXUALITY, SEXUAL BEHAVIOR, PSYCHOLOGY

Bailey, Derrick Sherwin, *Homosexuality and the Western Christian Tradition*. London: Longmans, 1955.

Beach, Frank A., ed., *Sex and Behavior*. New York: Wiley, 1965.

Becker, Raymond de, *The Other Face of Love*, trans. Margaret Crosland and Alan Daventry. London: Spearman & Rodney, 1967.

Brecher, Edward M., *The Sex Researchers*. Boston: Little, Brown, 1969.

Davis, Katherine B., *Factors in the Sex Life of Twenty-two Hundred Women*. New York: Harper, 1929.

Deutsch, Helene, *The Psychology of Women*, Vol. I. New York: Grune & Stratton, 1944.

Ellis, Havelock, *Studies in the Psychology of Sex*, Vols. I and II. New York: Random House, 1936.

"Final Report of the Task Force on Homosexuality," National Institute of Mental Health, Health Services and Mental Health Administration, U.S. Dept. of Health, Education and Welfare, Washington, D.C., Oct. 10, 1969.

Ford, Clellan S., and Frank A. Beach, *Patterns of Sexual Behavior*. New York: Harper, 1951.

Freud, Sigmund, *A General Introduction to Psycho-Analysis*, trans. Joan Riviere. New York: Clarion, 1969.

———, *New Introductory Lectures on Psycho-Analysis*, trans. W. J. H. Sprott. New York: Norton, 1933.

———, *Three Essays on the Theory of Sexuality*, trans. James Strachey. New York: Basic Books, 1962.

Gagnon, John, and William Simon, eds., *Sexual Deviance*. New York: Harper & Row, 1967.

Gide, André, *Corydon*. New York: Farrar, Straus, 1950.

Guyon, René, *The Ethics of Sexual Acts*. New York: Knopf, 1934.

Hirschfeld, Magnus, *Sexual Pathology*. New York: Emerson, 1940.

Hoch, P. H., and F. Zubin, eds., *Psychosexual Development in Health and Disease*. New York: Grune & Stratton, 1949.

Hyde, H. Montgomery, *The Other Love*. London: Heinemann, 1970.

Kinsey, Alfred C., *et al.*, *Sexual Behavior in the Human Female*. Philadelphia: Saunders, 1953.

Krafft-Ebing, Richard von, *Psychopathia Sexualis*, adapted from the

12th German edition by F. J. Rebman. New York: Rebman, 1906.

Kronhausen, Phyllis and Eberhard, *Erotic Fantasies: A Study of the Sexual Imagination.* New York: Grove, 1969.

Licht, Hans, *Sexual Life in Ancient Greece.* London: Routledge, 1932.

Marmor, Judd, ed., *Sexual Inversion.* New York: Basic Books, 1965.

Masters, W. H., and V. E. Johnson, *Human Sexual Response.* Boston: Little, Brown, 1966.

Money, John, and Anke A. Ehrhardt, *Man & Woman Boy & Girl.* Baltimore: Johns Hopkins Univ., 1973.

"Report of the Committee on Homosexual Offences and Prostitution" (the Wolfenden Report). London: Her Majesty's Stationery Office, 1957.

Ropp, Robert S. de, *Sex Energy.* New York: Dell, 1969.

Ruitenbeek, Hendrik M., ed., *The Problem of Homosexuality in Modern Society.* New York: Dutton, 1963.

Szasz, Thomas S., *The Manufacture of Madness.* New York: Harper & Row, 1970.

Taylor, G. Rattray, *Sex in History.* New York: Vanguard, 1954.

West, D. J., *Homosexuality.* London: Pelican, 1968.

Wolff, Charlotte, *Love Between Women.* New York: St. Martin's, 1971.

V. GAY AND WOMEN'S LIBERATION

Abbott, Sidney, and Barbara Love, *Sappho Was a Right-On Woman.* New York: Stein & Day, 1972.

Altman, Dennis, *Homosexual Oppression and Liberation.* New York: Outerbridge & Lazard, 1971.

Beauvoir, Simone de, *The Second Sex,* trans. H. M. Parshley, New York: Knopf, 1953.

Cooke, Joanne, and Charlotte Bunch-Weeks, eds., *The New Women.* New York: Bobbs-Merrill, 1970.

Gornick, Vivian, and Barbara K. Moran, *Woman in Sexist Society.* New York: Basic Books, 1971.

Greer, Germaine, *The Female Eunuch.* New York: McGraw-Hill, 1971.

Johnston, Jill, *Lesbian Nation*. New York: Simon and Schuster, 1973.

Martin, Del, and Phyllis Lyon, *Lesbian/Woman*. San Francisco: Glide, 1972.

Millett, Kate, *Sexual Politics*. New York: Doubleday, 1970.

Morgan, Robin, ed., *Sisterhood Is Powerful*. New York: Random House, 1970.

Roszak, Theodore, and Betty Roszak, eds., *Masculine/Feminine*. New York: Harper & Row, 1969.

Teal, Donn, *The Gay Militants*. New York: Stein & Day, 1971.

VI. OTHER

Abbott, Berenice, *Photographs*. New York: Horizon, 1970.

Bowra, C. M., *The Greek Experience*. New York: World, 1957.

Damon, Gene, and Lee Stuart, *The Lesbian in Literature: A Bibliography*. Reno: *The Ladder*, 1967.

Foster, Jeannette H., *Sex Variant Women in Literature*. New York: Vantage, 1956.

Hamilton, Edith, *The Great Age of Greek Literature*. New York: Norton, 1942.

Kitto, H. D. F., *The Greeks*. London: Penguin, 1957.

The Ladder, San Francisco and Reno, 1956–72.

Lorenz, Konrad, *King Solomon's Ring*. New York: Crowell, 1952.

Mahaffy, J. P., *The Social Life of the Greeks*, Vol. I. London: Macmillan, 1902.

Marcuse, Herbert, *Eros and Civilization*. Boston: Beacon, 1956.

Robinson, Paul, *The Freudian Left*. New York: Harper & Row, 1969.

Roszak, Theodore, *The Making of a Counter Culture*. New York: Doubleday, 1969.

Seltman, Charles, *Women in Antiquity*. London: Thames & Hudson, 1956.

Index

[Note: *Opinions* expressed by interviewees and by respondents to the circulated questionnaires are not indexed. These opinions, which are comments on a good deal of the subject matter indexed below, will be found on pages 19–37, 49–50, 111–25, and 219–57 *passim*.]

A few of the publications of
THE NAIAD PRESS, INC.
P.O. Box 10543 ● Tallahassee, Florida 32302
Phone (904) 539-5965
Mail orders welcome. Please include 15% postage.

WOMAN PLUS WOMAN by Dolores Klaich. 300 pp. Supurb
Lesbian overview. ISBN 0-941483-28-2 $9.95

SLOW DANCING AT MISS POLLY'S by Sheila Ortiz Taylor.
96 pp. Lesbian Poetry ISBN 0-941483-30-4 $7.95

DOUBLE DAUGHTER by Vicki P. McConnell. 216 pp. A Nyla
Wade Mystery, third in the series. ISBN 0-941483-26-6 $8.95

HEAVY GILT by Delores Klaich. 192 pp. Lesbian detective/
disappearing homophobes/upper class gay society.
ISBN 0-941483-25-8 8.95

THE FINER GRAIN by Denise Ohio. 216 pp. Brilliant young
college lesbian novel. ISBN 0-941483-11-8 8.95

THE AMAZON TRAIL by Lee Lynch. 216 pp. Life, travel & lore
of famous lesbian author. ISBN 0-941483-27-4 8.95

HIGH CONTRAST by Jessie Lattimore. 264 pp. Women of the
Crystal Palace. ISBN 0-941483-17-7 8.95

OCTOBER OBSESSION by Meredith More. Josie's rich, secret
Lesbian life. ISBN 0-941483-18-5 8.95

LESBIAN CROSSROADS by Ruth Baetz. 276 pp. Contemporary
Lesbian lives. ISBN 0-941483-21-5 9.95

BEFORE STONEWALL: THE MAKING OF A GAY AND
LESBIAN COMMUNITY by Andrea Weiss & Greta Schiller.
96 pp., 25 illus. ISBN 0-941483-20-7 7.95

WE WALK THE BACK OF THE TIGER by Patricia A. Murphy.
192 pp. Romantic Lesbian novel/beginning women's movement.
ISBN 0-941483-13-4 8.95

SUNDAY'S CHILD by Joyce Bright. 216 pp. Lesbian athletics, at
last the novel about sports. ISBN 0-941483-12-6 8.95

OSTEN'S BAY by Zenobia N. Vole. 204 pp. Sizzling adventure
romance set on Bonaire. ISBN 0-941483-15-0 8.95

LESSONS IN MURDER by Claire McNab. 216 pp. 1st in a stylish
mystery series. ISBN 0-941483-14-2 8.95

YELLOWTHROAT by Penny Hayes. 240 pp. Margarita, bandit,
kidnaps Julia. ISBN 0-941483-10-X 8.95

SAPPHISTRY: THE BOOK OF LESBIAN SEXUALITY by
Pat Califia. 3d edition, revised. 208 pp. ISBN 0-941483-24-X 8.95

CHERISHED LOVE by Evelyn Kennedy. 192 pp. Erotic
Lesbian love story. ISBN 0-941483-08-8   8.95

LAST SEPTEMBER by Helen R. Hull. 208 pp. Six stories & a
glorious novella. ISBN 0-941483-09-6   8.95

THE SECRET IN THE BIRD by Camarin Grae. 312 pp. Striking,
psychological suspense novel. ISBN 0-941483-05-3   8.95

TO THE LIGHTNING by Catherine Ennis. 208 pp. Romantic
Lesbian 'Robinson Crusoe' adventure. ISBN 0-941483-06-1   8.95

THE OTHER SIDE OF VENUS by Shirley Verel. 224 pp.
Luminous, romantic love story. ISBN 0-941483-07-X   8.95

DREAMS AND SWORDS by Katherine V. Forrest. 192 pp.
Romantic, erotic, imaginative stories. ISBN 0-941483-03-7   8.95

MEMORY BOARD by Jane Rule. 336 pp. Memorable novel
about an aging Lesbian couple. ISBN 0-941483-02-9   8.95

THE ALWAYS ANONYMOUS BEAST by Lauren Wright
Douglas. 224 pp. A Caitlin Reese mystery. First in a series.
ISBN 0-941483-04-5   8.95

SEARCHING FOR SPRING by Patricia A. Murphy. 224 pp.
Novel about the recovery of love. ISBN 0-941483-00-2   8.95

DUSTY'S QUEEN OF HEARTS DINER by Lee Lynch. 240 pp.
Romantic blue-collar novel. ISBN 0-941483-01-0   8.95

PARENTS MATTER by Ann Muller. 240 pp. Parents'
relationships with Lesbian daughters and gay sons.
ISBN 0-930044-91-6   9.95

THE PEARLS by Shelley Smith. 176 pp. Passion and fun in
the Caribbean sun. ISBN 0-930044-93-2   7.95

MAGDALENA by Sarah Aldridge. 352 pp. Epic Lesbian novel
set on three continents. ISBN 0-930044-99-1   8.95

THE BLACK AND WHITE OF IT by Ann Allen Shockley.
144 pp. Short stories. ISBN 0-930044-96-7   7.95

SAY JESUS AND COME TO ME by Ann Allen Shockley. 288
pp. Contemporary romance. ISBN 0-930044-98-3   8.95

LOVING HER by Ann Allen Shockley. 192 pp. Romantic love
story. ISBN 0-930044-97-5   7.95

MURDER AT THE NIGHTWOOD BAR by Katherine V.
Forrest. 240 pp. A Kate Delafield mystery. Second in a series.
ISBN 0-930044-92-4   8.95

ZOE'S BOOK by Gail Pass. 224 pp. Passionate, obsessive love
story. ISBN 0-930044-95-9   7.95

WINGED DANCER by Camarin Grae. 228 pp. Erotic Lesbian
adventure story. ISBN 0-930044-88-6   8.95

PAZ by Camarin Grae. 336 pp. Romantic Lesbian adventurer
with the power to change the world. ISBN 0-930044-89-4   8.95

A HOT-EYED MODERATE by Jane Rule. 252 pp. Hard-hitting essays on gay life; writing; art. ISBN 0-930044-57-6   7.95

INLAND PASSAGE AND OTHER STORIES by Jane Rule. 288 pp. Wide-ranging new collection. ISBN 0-930044-56-8   7.95

WE TOO ARE DRIFTING by Gale Wilhelm. 128 pp. Timeless Lesbian novel, a masterpiece. ISBN 0-930044-61-4   6.95

AMATEUR CITY by Katherine V. Forrest. 224 pp. A Kate Delafield mystery. First in a series. ISBN 0-930044-55-X   7.95

THE SOPHIE HOROWITZ STORY by Sarah Schulman. 176 pp. Engaging novel of madcap intrigue. ISBN 0-930044-54-1   7.95

THE BURNTON WIDOWS by Vickie P. McConnell. 272 pp. A Nyla Wade mystery, second in the series. ISBN 0-930044-52-5   7.95

OLD DYKE TALES by Lee Lynch. 224 pp. Extraordinary stories of our diverse Lesbian lives. ISBN 0-930044-51-7   8.95

DAUGHTERS OF A CORAL DAWN by Katherine V. Forrest. 240 pp. Novel set in a Lesbian new world. ISBN 0-930044-50-9   7.95

THE PRICE OF SALT by Claire Morgan. 288 pp. A milestone novel, a beloved classic. ISBN 0-930044-49-5   8.95

AGAINST THE SEASON by Jane Rule. 224 pp. Luminous, complex novel of interrelationships. ISBN 0-930044-48-7   8.95

LOVERS IN THE PRESENT AFTERNOON by Kathleen Fleming. 288 pp. A novel about recovery and growth. ISBN 0-930044-46-0   8.95

TOOTHPICK HOUSE by Lee Lynch. 264 pp. Love between two Lesbians of different classes. ISBN 0-930044-45-2   7.95

MADAME AURORA by Sarah Aldridge. 256 pp. Historical novel featuring a charismatic "seer." ISBN 0-930044-44-4   7.95

CURIOUS WINE by Katherine V. Forrest. 176 pp. Passionate Lesbian love story, a best-seller. ISBN 0-930044-43-6   8.95

BLACK LESBIAN IN WHITE AMERICA by Anita Cornwell. 141 pp. Stories, essays, autobiography. ISBN 0-930044-41-X   7.50

CONTRACT WITH THE WORLD by Jane Rule. 340 pp. Powerful, panoramic novel of gay life. ISBN 0-930044-28-2   7.95

YANTRAS OF WOMANLOVE by Tee A. Corinne. 64 pp. Photos by noted Lesbian photographer. ISBN 0-930044-30-4   6.95

MRS. PORTER'S LETTER by Vicki P. McConnell. 224 pp. The first Nyla Wade mystery. ISBN 0-930044-29-0   7.95

TO THE CLEVELAND STATION by Carol Anne Douglas. 192 pp. Interracial Lesbian love story. ISBN 0-930044-27-4   6.95

THE NESTING PLACE by Sarah Aldridge. 224 pp. A three-woman triangle—love conquers all! ISBN 0-930044-26-6   7.95